369 0213361

DATE DUE

Hospitals and the Nursing Profession: Lessons from Franco-Japanese Comparisons

Paths to Modernization

Hospitals and the Nursing Profession: Lessons from Franco-Japanese Comparisons

Paths to Modernization

Philippe Mossé, Tetsu Harayama,
Maryse Boulongne-Garcin, Toshiko Ibe, Hiromi Oku,
Vaughan Rogers

Translation from the French: Jessica Blanc

This publication was funded by:
the "Japan Foundation Support Program
for Translation and Publication on Japan", 2010
and the "Mire-Drees" (French Ministry of Health)

Acknowledgements

The authors wish to thank David Marsden; Adam Oliver; Martine Bellanger, Seli Arslan; Claude Dubar; Sylvie Cheroutre; François-Xavier Léger; M.-A. Guéraud and B. Lucet at Assistance Publique – Hôpitaux de Paris; all the members of the managerial and nursing staff at the Bichat-Claude-Bernard and Henri-Mondor Hospitals. They also thank all the participants in the 1987-1989 and 2007-2008 surveys, the results of which are presented in this book.

ISBN: 978-2-7420-0796-7

Éditions John Libbey Eurotext
127, avenue de la République
92120 Montrouge, France
Tél.: 01 46 73 06 60
E-mail: contact@jle.com
Site Internet: http://www.jle.com

Editor: Maud Thévenin

John Libbey Eurotext
42-46 High Street
Esher, Surrey
KT10 9KY
United Kingdom

Contents

Contributors

Philippe Mossé
Health Economist, Research Director at the LEST, CNRS & Aix-Marseille University; visiting Professor at Keio University (spring 1998) and at the University of Tokyo (November 2009). His research and teaching focus on Health Policy, Hospital and Labour Market Economics in international comparative perspective.

Tetsu Harayama
Visiting scholar at the École Normale Supérieure de Paris 1987-1989; visiting scholar at the LEST, Aix-en-Provence 2007-2008; professor of sociology, Toyo University. His research interests involve comparisons of nurses' social worlds in Paris and Tokyo; principal researcher of the project "Youths' world of work in Japan" by Japan Society for the Promotion of Science 2007-2011.

Maryse Boulongne-Garcin
Master of nursing administration (Université de Paris, Dauphine); former director of the Nursing Department, l'Assistance Publique de Paris (Hôpital Bichat, Hôpital Pompidou); researcher for the project "Social recognition in work" by Japan Society for the Promotion of Science 2009-2012.

Toshiko Ibe
RN (registered nurse), doctor of nursing science; vice-president of the Japanese Nursing Association; professor and president of St. Luke's College of Nursing, Tokyo.

Hiromi Oku
RN (registered nurse), master of nursing science; assistant-professor of St. Luke's College of Nursing 2006-2010; researcher in nursing administration, St. Luke's College of Nursing, Graduate School of Nursing, Tokyo.

Vaughan Rogers
Senior Lecturer in European Languages and Cultures at the University of Edinburgh, Scotland. The focus of his current research is on the implementation, in comparative perspective, of healthcare reform in France, particularly at the sub-national level.

Introduction:
A View from the Bridge

The aim of this book is to analyze and compare the relationships between the nursing profession and hospital institutions in France and Japan. The nursing profession will be studied via the modes of occupational recognition and identification adopted in these two countries, nurses' careers and their relations with other healthcare workers, and the positions held by the members of this profession both inside an outside the hospital walls.

At a time when these professions are undergoing some far-reaching changes and the institutions involved are being constantly reformed, international comparisons of this kind seemed likely to shed interesting light on the subject. Although lively debate has recently focused in both France and Japan on the organization of healthcare the few references made to hospital practices in other countries have been mostly restricted to rough indicators (hospital expenditure as a proportion of the gross domestic product (the GDP), the density of the supply, the life expectancy of the population, etc.). These indicators have sometimes been used to draw up schemes of classification or hit-parades, and very few attempts have been made to compare the situation in various countries.

Examples of other countries' practices have all too often been presented in terms of the authors' own national traditions, which rules out the possibility of using this information for explanatory purposes. For example, the fact that healthcare expenditure in Japan amounts to only 8% of the GDP (as compared with almost 11% in France) (OECD, 2010) can be seen in either a positive or negative light (bringing expenditure under control or neglecting the quality of healthcare). For lack of a more general analytical framework, quantitative statistics of this kind can only serve as slogans.

The idea underlying this project was therefore to take advantage of the change of viewpoint and the objectivity which can be gained by making international comparisons, with a view to "denaturalizing" the problems defined and the solutions proposed. The authors felt that this was not only a necessary task but also an urgent one. The many attempts being made these days to erase national specificities for functional purposes and harmonize modes de regulation for political reasons are combining to form a smooth, homogeneous global picture of the world resulting from a process of convergence.

By describing the links between occupations and institutions, it is hoped to discover the national logics at work and thus to understand the situation in each country more clearly.

However, at the same time, the objective here is to suggest paths of change which are neither imported nor imposed, contrary to what is often being held up as the inevitable course of events in public circles.

Hospital systems in all the industrialized countries are certainly being subjected these days to a common network of constraints, which tends to look alarmingly various and dense. The long list of purportedly decisive parameters at work includes ageing populations, technological progress, the demands of increasingly well-informed patients, the need to limit public spending, the trend towards greater staff specialization and the lack of suitable incentives, to mention but a few examples.

The authors of many analyses have actually claimed that these constraints are not only inevitable, but that there is only one possible way of meeting all these various requirements. The approach they have recommended consists in looking for means of balancing the economic requirements with the increasingly large healthcare needs. On these lines, the compromises which are expected to be most effective and sustainable are those which rely more heavily than at present on competitive mechanisms on the side of healthcare supply as well as that of health insurance providers. Not only international organizations, but also an increasingly large number of national governments are tending to adopt this enlightened market approach.

After the turn of the 19th century, which marked the emergence of modern medicine, the end of the 20th century was swamped by a wave of managerial rationalization. In terms of this change, which is becoming a concrete historical fact, it might seem tempting to qualify the differences observed between various countries as "progressive" or "backward" tendencies.

However, we must not forget that apparently identical technical reforms can be adopted in response to different needs from one country to another, and that these changes can elicit attitudes (of support, opposition, avoidance, etc.) which are rooted in previous practices. The outcome of these reforms will therefore differ considerably, depending on the national healthcare system to which they are applied.

This shows how shaky ideas about the "transferability" of a particular reform from one country to another tend to be, although they are often brandied about for political benchmarking purposes (Busse & Schlette, 2003). It has been stressed that many things are not transferable, in which case, the "functionalists" are obliged to recognize the limitations of their own philosophy. Focusing on transferability has led to overlooking the fact that it is essential to take the implementation phase into account right from the start when reforms are being defined, rather than waiting until it is time to put them into practice.

This statement is particularly true in the case of hospital nurses: it may look at first sight like a purely rhetorical question, but as we will see in the light of the concrete facts, it is extremely relevant.

In these occupational spheres, two developments are often presented as being inevitable. On the one hand, the status of hospital nurses has sometimes been said to be too closely protected, which is no longer consistent with modern occupational and productive standards, which call for flexibility, multitasking skills and mobility. Likewise, it has been objected that the present quality standards are no longer in keeping with/on a par with nurses' status, which is tending to resemble that of civil servants, even in non-profit institutions.

On the other hand, the increasing technological hold over the world of healthcare has given rise to a quasi Taylorist organisation of work. It has been frequently claimed by the authorities that these two complementary developments will have emancipating effects, since they will set healthcare professionals in all the industrialized countries on a pathway leading to the acquisition of new technical skills. Their social and occupational status is thus said to have improved while meeting the needs of the hospitals who employ them and those of the patients for whom they care. Although this process is undeniably under way, the analyses presented in this book show that the pattern of events involved is extremely varied, reflecting the great diversity of the national contexts.

In order to illuminate more fully the issues involved in developments in Japan and France for the Anglophone reader, elements of comparison with changes in the hospital service and the nursing profession in the United Kingdom (UK) will be highlighted and explored at different strategic points in the analysis. Of particular concern in this regard will be the question of gender and the impact of work-life adjustment factors on career patterns within the nursing profession in the United Kingdom. In a predominantly female profession, the obstacles militating against the successful pursuit of long, regular careers appear to stand out as particularly significant among British nurses. The dynamics of relative empowerment or disempowerment over time, as reflected in the relationships between the nursing profession, doctors and managers in the UK, represent a further, closely associated question to which attention will be devoted.

Another major point of comparison is constituted by the different trajectories followed by processes of "modernization" between different states. A key stage in such changes in the UK is represented by the transformation of hospitals into Trusts during the 1990s, as an attempt to move towards the development of the internal market, in line with the neo-liberal principles which underpinned many of the policy initiatives undertaken by the Thatcher administration. Despite the rhetoric of New Labour, both before and immediately after coming into office in 1997, many features of the internal market have prevailed in England under both the Blair and the Brown administrations. However, in a further significant point of comparison with France and Japan, divergent health policies are now pursued in England, Scotland, Wales and Northern Ireland, due to the devolution of power in this sphere since 1997. In consequence, approaches to challenges such as cost containment, quality assurance and cohesion, as well as their outcomes, may not only differ from one state to another, but in the case of the UK, may also vary considerably between different parts of the same state.

Given the contextual approach adopted in this book, it was obviously necessary to use a method in which the historical background and the logics and specificities of each country were taken into account in order to be able to do justice to these complex issues. This book also presents the results of a multidisciplinary research project focusing on the interplay between individual and collective actors on the field. Our approach to these international comparisons involved searching for national patterns of cohesion and analysing these patterns. They are taken to be permanently ongoing constructs rather than forming a set of predetermined cultural features liable to escape socioeconomic analysis.

This approach was initiated and applied to the issues of employment and pay by the proponents of *societal analysis* (Maurice *et al.*, 1982). Subsequent research on these lines has shown the importance of the links ("nexus") existing between social relations of the following three kinds:

• The first link is that between vocational training, qualifications and companies; it has been called the "'educational' or 'occupational' nexus". It can be used to analyze the structure of qualifications and their interactions with the modes of vocational training.

• The second link is that between the type of monitoring exerted and the type of work organization. This has been called the "organisational nexus": it involves the balance between autonomy and hierarchical control;

• The third link, which is known as the "industrial nexus" focuses on the social management of workers, *i.e.*, on the collective management of conflicts about classification issues raising questions about the organization of work and systems of promotion.

The specific way in which these three aspects are assembled in a given country gives a coherent picture of an economy and a society which cannot be accounted for simply in terms of labour market differentials. It can help to explain phenomena which cannot be grasped using classical methods of economic analysis.

The authors of the present work will frequently refer to the above approach, which makes it possible to draw a cohesive analytical picture based on a combination of historical, sociological and economic descriptors. It is not intended to apply this theory to the case of hospital nurses in France and Japan, but to use it rather as a guideline. This will make it possible to draw theoretical conclusions from comparative studies in which qualitative data were collected on the nursing profession in France and Japan using strictly scientific methods, while at the same time presenting analyses of statistical information about hospitals and the ongoing reforms in the countries in question.

The following example precises what can be expected from this method.

If one compares the hospitals in France and Japan on the basis of the data published by the Organization for Economic Cooperation and Development (OECD), one cannot fail to notice the striking quantitative difference in terms of the mean length of patients' hospital stays: 35 days in Japan *versus* approximately 5 days in France. The difference is so great that one is bound to wonder how this technical variable was defined and calculated. It turns out that the Japanese system of hospital classification is quite different from that pertaining in most of the other OECD member countries. Short-stay and medium-stay hospitals are pooled together by the Japanese Ministry of Health, whereas the statistics are recorded separately in all the other countries. Once this point has been elucidated, statisticians are somewhat at a loss. What can be done other than calling this anomaly a statistical artefact and asking the Japanese authorities to correct it? In actual fact, to be eligible to feature in the international nomenclatures, the Japanese Ministry of Health is revising its system of hospital classification and has proposed to make the distinction between the various kinds of hospital establishments. The need to harmonize international nomenclatures has thus led to reducing the apparent differences between countries, and thereby to supporting the ideology of convergence. This vicious circle ends up by masking the very sources of the information on which contextual analyses are based.

In this process of healthcare policy globalization, the differences between reform expectations and achievements might be described metaphorically in terms of a graft which either "takes" or otherwise. As a result, assessing a policy tends to amount to assessing the impact of the resulting change on the whole battery of common indicators used by all the developed countries in the world.

On the contrary, pointing out the existence of these differences will be the starting point of our analysis, and not the final objective. Since the aim is to bring to light the logics underlying hospital systems, differences in performances are relevant indexes which will have to be combined and analysed (Maurice, 2003).

As regards the length of hospital stays, looking at the links between occupations and institutions should show the existence of quantitative differences between France and Japan in terms of practices and the organization of work. Far from being a mystery, these differences should prove keys to understanding the systems under investigation. They may not be artefacts, but may reflect specific ideas about what hospital interventions involve, and what skills can be expected to be available at French and Japanese hospitals.

The differences observed between the situation of nurses in France and Japan seem to be mainly attributable to differences in the prevailing occupational principles. In Japan, the nursing profession upholds principles other than those based on medical technology and managerial criteria. In France, where there is a fast rate of patient turnover and short stays are thought to epitomize medical efficiency, the principles of industrial efficiency predominate to the point of constituting the basis of nurses' professional identity.

The main aspects which will be taken into account here include the role of hospitals in the national healthcare system, the approach to health insurance coverage, and the division of labour between medical and paramedical professions in each country. Hospital institutions' historical background and the sociological aspects of the healthcare professions can then be introduced and related to public and organisational economics in order to obtain a comprehensive overall picture.

The emphasis has therefore been placed in this book on describing the changing relationships between nurses and the institutions at which they are employed, and the logics which have predominated at each stage in the process. It is worth noting that in recent times, two fairly simultaneous phases occurred in both countries.

As the result of the processes occurring during the first of these phases, which are described in Chapter 1, nursing developed into a proper profession. This profession can be defined and presented in relation to a hospital system on the road to modernization. This phase, which began in the 19th century and ended in the mid-20th century, was characterized by changes in the relationships between the hospital nursing and medical professions. In both Japan and France, the space occupied by the budding nursing profession was determined by that which the physicians had succeeded in carving out for themselves. As these two spaces were not identical in both countries, the historical conditions under which the nursing profession emerge differed considerably between France and Japan. Here we will examine how the historical factors weighed differently in these two countries on nurses' professional identity and their relationships with hospital institutions.

During the second phase, which extended from the 1960s up to the present day, the nursing profession was set up as the result of collective efforts. The usual factors on which studies on occupational relations have classically focused (the struggle for recognition, the stakes involved in vocational training, etc.) came into play here. In this case, however, the specificities of the situation in France and Japan also played an important part. These specificities will be described in Chapter 2 in terms of the gender differentials involved in the process of nurses' professionalization and how they have been challenged.

The main key to understanding how nurses' occupational identity developed on completely different lines in France and Japan focuses on the extent to which a compromise has been reached between domestic and professional conventions.

The second part of this book will deal with the "social world" of French nurses and that of Japanese nurses. The term social world is used here to denote the relationships between working spheres and extra-working spheres. It is also proposed to study the representations, images, roles, etc. of nurses in France and Japan using the latest methods of discourse analysis: this part of our research will involve working back a long way into history, looking for the events which shaped the latest social changes (gender relations, technological change, the rationalization of occupational practices, etc.). The second part of this book will be devoted to analysing the data collected in two surveys conducted 20 years apart in Paris and Tokyo (in 1987-1989 and 2007-2008).

In order to describe these changes, the theory of Economics of Worth (*Économie de la grandeur*) (Boltanski & Thévenot, 2006) seemed to provide a useful tool. According to this theory, people set up conventions before starting to coordinate their efforts. The latter authors defined six "worlds" based on different conventions, between which compromises are possible. In the light of this theory, the nursing profession in France up to the mid-20th century was governed by a compromise between the "inspired" and "domestic" worlds. Nurses, who were females and usually also nuns, had a very lowly status and enjoyed little real autonomy. With the advent of modern medicine and new gender relations, this convention and the corresponding values were replaced by a "civic" model, which was strongly promoted by the trend towards a lay society. However, the gender relations imposed by the previous domestic model were not completely abolished. This process only started to occur quite recently, when the "civic" model began to decline in favour of the "industrial" model. The latter model, which started to gain ground after the events of 1988, is based on the idea that efficiency requires specialization and greater division of labour between the members of healthcare teams.

The 1988 protest movement known as "coordination" can be said to have reflected the fundamental criticisms aimed at the previously predominant modes of thought: those of the "inspired" and "domestic" worlds. These criticisms were aptly expressed in the slogan *"ni bonnes, ni connes, ni nonnes"* (neither servants, idiots or nuns) which was highly popular at that time. However, this method of strategic positioning by default left the way wide open to the industrialization of the nursing profession, in line with what was going on in the rest of the healthcare system.

As we will see throughout this book, the series of successive conventions described above owed much to the occupational, social and economic changes occurring concomitantly at the time. This can also be said of the most recent period. It is perfectly obvious that the changes undergone by public hospitals under the banner of "new governance" have been setting the foundations for a market model. As the results of the 2007-2008 survey showed, however, this model cannot become fully entrenched unless a compromise is reached with the industrial model which currently obtains.

The history of events in Japan can be interpreted on similar lines, but the shift from one world to another and their order of succession have been slightly different. Before the Japan of the Meiji period was modernized in the late 19th century, healthcare was dispensed by women in their homes. The domestic model therefore consecrated the picture of devoted Japanese wives confined to their homes. The Western model was then introduced by enforcing voluntaristic State measures, which led to a compromise between the previous domestic convention and a form of market convention.

After the Second World War, the status of the Japanese nursing profession was again challenged by the move to defend patients' interests. More "civic" arguments were then put forward to justify the gradual changes undergone by the nursing profession and the improvement of their working conditions. However, as in France when the shift occurred from the "inspired" to "civic" model, gender relations and the domestic aspects of nurses' work remained much the same. During the nurses' protest movements which occurred in the 1980s in Japan, none of the demands made focused on gender issues. It is true that these movements were weaker than in France. They were led by organizations known as "paramedical trade unions", which were not very strong because the only powerful unions in Japan were the company workers' unions (Sohyo & Rengo).

A compromise therefore took place between the principles inherited from the domestic world and those of the industrial world. The persistence of the domestic convention in Japan is attributable to the fact that the medical profession in this country is mainly organized around many small clinics at which the nurses are obliged to perform many different tasks under rather difficult working conditions. Since Japanese nurses are not encouraged to undergo vocational training or become specialized, they do not tend to invest in continuing vocational training, which French nurses regard as the path to autonomy. Any vocational training they undergo usually takes place outside their hours of work, at their own personal expense. The results of the 2007-2008 survey show that although the nursing profession is now fairly well recognized and organized in Japan, there is little scope for acquiring qualifications and benefiting from mobility in this context.

In the third part of this book, recent policies and reforms affecting the hospital institutions in both countries will be studied with a view to analyzing the interactions between these organizations and professions more closely.

Special emphasis will be placed here on the emerging managerial tendencies. Although technically speaking, the methods adopted are similar in both countries, it has been established that since the socioeconomic contexts are quite different, their real content is not the same, because different interactions with pre-existing processes are occurring. As we will see later on, the concepts of contracts and assessments correspond to quite different realities in France and Japan, for instance (Oliver, 2003).

As far as the content of nurses' activities is concerned, the distinction traditionally made between dispensing real healthcare and merely providing for patients' comfort (Pouchelle, 2003) is relevant to present-day contexts and organisational constraints. Nurses in France have had to adopt a rather ambiguous position towards this distinction, which is basic to their professional identity: they are torn between working to acquire technical skills for the sake of efficiency and the need for their patients' gratitude. In Japan, the risk inherent to this distinction is masked by the ambivalent general image of the nursing profession: all the protagonists, including the managers, are convinced that efficiency includes performing tasks which are simply pleasing to the patients but do not contribute to curing them (*ibid.*, p. 160).

In the latest configuration, the modes of nursing practice differ between these two countries because they have social roots, but in both cases, they are paving the road towards nurses' emancipation.

The validity of the comparative approach adopted here thus becomes obvious: the fact that we start off by taking a critical look at past relationships between the nursing profession and hospital institutions will make it possible to detect and interpret the ongoing changes occurring in both countries.

REFERENCES

• Boltanski L, Thévenot L. *On justification; Economics of Worth*. Princeton University Press, 2006.

• Busse R, Schlette S. Health policy developments. *International Trends Analysis* 2003.

• Eymard-Duvernay F. Conventionalist approaches to enterprise. Chapter 2 in: Favereau O, Lazega E (eds). *Conventions and structures in economic organization: Markets, networks and hierarchies*. Cheltenham: Edwar Elgar, 2002: 60-78.

• Maurice M. À propos de comparaisons internationales et d'interdisciplinarité : questions théoriques et méthodologiques. *Sociologie du Travail* 2003; vol. 45: 267-84.

• Maurice M, Sellier F, Silvestre JJ. *Politique d'éducation et organisation industrielle en France et en Allemagne. Essai d'analyse sociétale*. Paris: PUF, coll. « Sociologie », 1982.

• Oliver A. Health economic evaluation in Japan. *Health Policy* 2003; vol. 63, n° 2: 197-204.

• OECD, Health data 2010.

• Pouchelle MC. *L'Hôpital corps et âme. Essais d'anthropologie hospitalière*. Paris: Seli Arslan, 2003.

• Storper M, Salais R. *Worlds of Production. The Action Frameworks of the Economy*. Cambridge MA: Harvard University Press, 1997.

Part I
The Nursing Profession:
From its emergence
to the present-day picture

In both France and Japan, the nursing profession emerged during the second half of the 19th century and began to take shape during the first half of the 20th century. Although the timing was similar in both countries, the modes and dynamics involved were quite different. The history of these two roads to professionalization will be described and compared in the first chapter. Chapter 2 will be devoted to the second half of the 20th century, when nurses' professional identity developed in various ways and gender issues began to come to the fore.

1. Two paths to professionalization

The course of development of the nursing profession into a "civil professional activity" can be compared between France and Japan in terms of the two models which J. Saliba (1993) has described as follows:

– in the model developed in the English-speaking world in the footsteps of the Florence Nightingale, the process evolved from the inside, starting with the world of nurses themselves;
– whereas the Republican model is characterized by voluntaristic interventions imposed from the outside by the administrative and medical powers that be: the developments initiated in France by Dr. Désiré Bourneville in the late 19th century provide an example of this model.

A VIEW FROM UNITED KINGDOM

While this Republican model will be analysed in greater detail below, it is appropriate at this point, in order to clarify the comparative parameters concerned, to provide some amplification with regard to the substance and dynamics of the Anglo-Saxon model, including the tensions to which it gave rise, thereby establishing parallels with the broader themes of this study. In contrast with the Republican model, the Anglo-Saxon mode of nursing reform which began to emerge in the 19th century was not driven by initiatives emanating from the central state, but from non-state actors or private individuals, in the context of the limited form of liberal interventionism practised by the governments of the day. In this regard, much emphasis has been placed on the role played by the iconic figure of Florence Nightingale, who is often presented as "the founder of modern nursing".

The Nightingale "story"

Nightingale was a highly-educated, affluent, well-connected woman, for whom the "mission" to transform nursing may be seen in part as stemming from a personal need for self-liberation from the stifling constraints suffered by upper-class English women of the time. From an early age, she sought to escape from the tedium and absence of opportunities for self-fulfilment imposed by Victorian mores, according to which women should work only when compelled for financial reasons to do so, in order to support themselves and their families. Despite, or because of, fierce opposition from her own family, Nightingale went to gain practical hospital nursing experience in Kaiserswerth, Germany, after which she embarked from 1854 to 1856 upon the work for which she initially became renowned, tending soldiers wounded during the Crimean War at the military hospital in Scutari. During this time, observing that the major cause of patient mortality was poor sanitation and infection, she reorganised nursing care for the military personnel, introducing procedures to improve standards of hygiene and diet, which led to the reduction of the death rate at Scutari from 42% to 2% within a period of six months (Smith, 1981).

On her return to England, Nightingale set out to bring her experience and commitment to organised training in appropriate standards of care to bear upon nursing at home. Through her personal charisma, her powers of effective advocacy and her access to powerful establishment figures including aristocrats and government ministers, Nightingale was able to secure financial support from philanthropic members of the social élite, adding a contribution from her own personal wealth in order to drive the reform movement forward. By such means, it became possible to establish the Nightingale Fund, through which financial resources were made available to support nursing reform initiatives, most notably, the setting up of the Nightingale School of Nursing, the first establishment dedicated specifically to this purpose, at St. Thomas's Hospital, London, in 1860. Despite this link to St. Thomas's, the School was nevertheless an independent educational establishment, which may be seen as the embodiment of Nightingale's objective to establish both a curriculum and a philosophy for nursing education, rooted in the need for organised, practical and scientific training. The fundamentals of this curriculum and philosophy were published in her famous text of 1860, *Notes on Nursing*.

The Nightingale School of Nursing opened at St. Thomas's Hospital, London, with the declared objective of producing not only properly trained, but also morally respectable nurses, in contrast with the frequently expressed view of the old-fashioned nurse as an ignorant, decadent drunkard, as represented by Charles Dickens through the fictional character of Sairey Gamp in the novel Martin Chuzzlewit, published in 1844. Thus, much importance was attributed in the Nightingale model of nursing care reform to "reforming" the working-class women who had traditionally provided it (Sarkis & Connors, 1986). Strict rules of sobriety and honesty were imposed, involving English boarding-school style discipline, with severe restrictions on social activities outside the School. At the same time, trainee nurses were provided with technical training in the use and cleaning of equipment, as well as receiving instruction in the importance of keeping accurate, written records of a patient's condition, treatment and progress. Whilst undergoing such training, nurses were deemed to be "probationers", without qualified status until they had demonstrated their ability to acquire the skills taught by the School and apply them under the guidance of a senior, Nightingale-trained, hospital-based nurse, or sister, to the satisfaction of still more senior Nightingale-trained nurse, the hospital matron.

Indeed, one of the most significant consequences of the Nightingale reforms was the development of the role of matrons in hospitals, thereby contributing to major improvements in the management of nursing care, along with other aspects of hospital organisation (Black, 2005). By the end of the 19th century, many hospitals had begun to appoint experienced nurses trained in the Nightingale School as matrons, with a recognised role as head of nursing provision, along with responsibility for training, as well as cleaning, catering and laundry services. Thus, a new mode of nursing management developed, which involved the construction of a sphere of authority for women, establishing a key position for matrons in a female hierarchy. The ultimate logic of these changes, as Wildman and Hewison (2009) have observed, was to remove responsibility for nursing practice from doctors and to place it under the control of women in such senior nursing positions. Great emphasis was also placed by Nightingale in her *Notes on Nursing* upon overall conditions of sanitation in hospitals, with particular regard to ventilation, the benefits of natural light and the use of space. As a result, a contributory role began to be carved out for senior nurses in the planning and design of hospital buildings. In their interaction with doctors, nurses were expected to obey the directions of physicians or surgeons, but this was to be an "intelligent obedience", to some extent conditional upon discretion and the principles stemming from "the silent power of a consistent life" (Bradhaw, 1999). However, this somewhat ambiguous position raised as many questions as it answered and, as will be illustrated below, certain elements of ambivalence may be identified within the Nightingale system, resulting in significant divergences of interpretation.

A "golden age" of British nursing?

Without seeking to deny the major contribution made by Nightingale and her followers, it is important to qualify the somewhat idealised, but prevalent view of Nightingale as being almost single-handedly responsible for UK nursing reform, breaking radically with the past and bringing about a "golden age of British nursing", to which nostalgic commentators in more recent years have repeatedly advocated a return. Firstly, her pioneering role notwithstanding, numerous initiatives tending in the direction of nursing management reform were undertaken prior to the emergence of the Nightingale system. One of the most notable examples of this is represented by the contribution of the religious sisterhoods in the 1840s and 1850s, which introduced management structures comparable to those instituted by Nightingale, organised around the strategic function of a senior, female head of nursing (Wildman & Hewison, 2009). Thus contextualised, the Nightingale reforms should be seen as a major stage in a process of change, rather than as an unprecedented departure from previous practice.

Furthermore, the introduction of changes inspired by Nightingale was by no means universally accepted, encountering serious obstacles in the form of adverse reaction and major conflict in a number of cases, the most widely publicised of which occurred at Guy's Hospital, London, in 1879. Although coverage in professional publications such as the British Medical Journal, as well as the more popular press, tended to focus on the dispute at Guy's, the controversy spread to other parts of the country. It became clear that significant sections of the medical profession and a minority of nurses had severe reservations with regard to the Nightingale system. While few contested the need for nurses to be properly trained, a powerful current of opinion was opposed to what it considered to be the relative detachment of the new system from the control and authority of hospital doctors, many of whom came from a less privileged social background than that of the "new" nurses whom they perceived to be undermining their professional status. Proper treatment of patients, it was insisted, could only be carried out under the direction of the doctors, rather than the matron. This hostility from the male-dominated medical profession also stemmed partly from their lack of experience in working with highly-trained, self-confident women, reinforcing fears that their authority was being threatened. More specifically, the Nightingale system of rotation, whereby nurses were deployed in different parts of the hospital on a regular basis, in order to provide them with comprehensive training and experience, was viewed as disruptive to smooth-running teamwork and detrimental to effective supervision by doctors. The risk of confusion between roles, implicit in Nightingale's own ambiguous formulation of nursing philosophy, thus appeared to have materialised in the form of inextricably intertwined disagreements relating to professional status, gender and power relations. Furthermore, the new system was presented as a threat to cohesion within the nursing occupation as a whole, through the claim that many of those nurses who belonged to the "old" system, who bore no resemblance to the "ignorant, drunken" stereotype disseminated by the Nightingale school of thought, had been driven out of Guy's as a result of the hostility directed towards them by Nightingale's followers. While this kind of resistance is to some extent inevitable in any process of change, a further objection contended that the increased nursing expertise entailed by the reforms tended to remove well-qualified personnel from their primary function, the provision of care at the bedside, leading to suggestions that nurses with the level of training provided through the Nightingale system should be employed only in highly specialised areas of activity, thereby leaving the bulk of routine care in the hands of competent, but less qualified (and therefore more malleable) personnel. This kind of concern continues to be expressed, albeit in more sophisticated terms, over a century later (Cook & Webb, 2002).

The unquestionable element of empowerment represented by the "new model" has led to a widespread assumption that the acquisition by matrons of autonomous control over nurses and nursing management had become the general norm by around the end of the 19th century, but in reality, the application of the logic of the Nightingale system proved to be incomplete. Conflicts of the type outlined here led Nightingale nurses, frequently supported by the lay social elites who controlled the Boards of Governors of the hospitals concerned, to engage in power struggles with members of the medical profession and other nurses. As a result, even for senior nurses, the processes of professionalization and empowerment took place according to a pattern of unequal development, depending to a large extent upon local circumstances and the variable capacity of individual matrons to stamp their managerial mark on the organisation of nursing care within their own particular hospital. Furthermore, despite its undeniably innovative dimension, an underlying feature of the Nightingale system was its social conservatism, which tended to perpetuate and reinforce the social hierarchy of Victorian England, along with its moral prejudices with regard to the lower classes. The Nightingale system divided nurses into two distinct categories: a small number of "ladies" were recruited and educated for leadership roles as matrons, whereas a larger group of working class probationers received less training and were provided with fewer opportunities for advancement. It could therefore be argued that, while the Nightingale system represented genuine empowerment for a select few, "genteel" ladies, destined for positions of responsibility in the hospital system, it also entailed a process of increasingly institutionalised and legitimised subordination for a considerably larger group of women.

However, it must be emphasised that Nightingale and her followers, despite their influence on the development of nurse training and the emergence of hierarchical structures within the profession, did not have a monopoly over such training, nor by any means did they exercise control over nurse recruitment and promotion procedures within hospitals as a whole. Consequently, although the number of senior nurses and especially matrons of upper class origin did increase significantly in the latter part of the 19th century, the expansion in the nursing labour market at this time, accompanied by an intensifying competition between hospitals for high-quality recruits, also offered opportunities for social advancement to those from a more modest background. Thus, at St. George's Hospital in London, by the late 1890s 30% of head nurses (sisters) and over 35% of staff nurses, their immediate subordinates, were of working class origin, promoted internally on the basis of their professional expertise. Despite the existence of social segmentation, especially within the upper strata of the professional hierarchy, where it was exceptional (but not impossible), for working class women to accede to the position of matron, elements of a meritocratic labour market were generated with regard to positions of middle-ranking responsibility by the socioeconomic evolution of the profession (Hawkins, 2010).

With regard to the professional identity of nurses, clear differences of emphasis may be discerned between two main tendencies within the reform movement *(ibid.)*. On the one hand, Nightingale and her supporters viewed nursing primarily as a moral activity, a vocation, giving pride of place to strength of character, dedication and discipline. Despite the independent, secular status of the Nightingale School of Nursing, the importance of Christian (Protestant) ethics is evident in its principles and its organisation. Figures such as Ethel Fenwick, on the other hand, without repudiating all the vocational connotations of the Nightingale model, sought to promote the development of nursing as a fully-fledged profession, deriving its legitimacy from specialist training and a system of registration or licensing, through which a nationally approved set of standards and skills could be recognised. Nightingale, however, consistently opposed such proposals, maintaining that nothing could replace the individual judgement of the experienced senior figure in charge of the training of nurses in her schools and that certification could lead to complacency, a lack of dedication and commitment to learning on a permanent basis. In this way, Nightingale hindered the accession of nurses as an occupational group to the status of a fully-recognised profession and the advent of certification was not complete until the 1920s, a decade beyond her lifetime. Indeed, despite such advances, and for many years after the establishment of the UK National Health Service following World War Two, a deeply embedded tradition continued to consider rank-and-file nurses as fulfilling the function of "handmaidens" to senior hospital doctors, with deference to the consultant remaining an integral part of the nursing socialisation process (G. Currie & O. Suhomlinova, 2006). The Anglo-Saxon model should thus be seen as a curious mix of embryonic feminism and social conservatism, of "bottom-up" reform driven by "top-down" influences, leading to tensions which the model illuminates, but does not resolve.

In France, the administrative and medical powers-that-be were certainly prime movers when the hospital physicians and administrators decided to enrol and train lay members of staff and supervise their competences. At this stage, the role of nurses was something of a compromise between the above two models:

> "The compromise reached in France between these two logics originated in the efforts made by the Protestant Anna Hamilton and especially the Catholic pioneer Léonie Chaptal, who attempted to reconcile nurses' professional autonomy with their religious traditions and their recognition by the State and the other members of the medical profession." (Saliba, 1993, p. 39-40) [1]

This idea of a combined socio-historical model can also be applied to the Japanese setting. Contrary to what occurred in France, however, the interventionist model in which the control was in the hands of the administrative and medical powers-that-be prevailed in Japan as far as the emergence of the nursing profession was concerned, since this profession was set up at the initiative of the Japanese physicians at the end of the 19th century.

The difference between the two countries actually resulted from the different patterns of development shown by the two hospital systems during the second half of the 20th century. When the French physicians gained entry to hospitals at the end of the 19th century, the hospital system did not become "monocratic", since the members of the medical profession and the administration formed a "dual system of authority" (Smith, 1955). The French hospital system, which was reputed to be a *système de profession libérale* up to the 1940s, was therefore characterized by the development of a system of hospital medicine in which an open structure was preserved within an increasingly bureaucratic system of administration (Steudler, 1974, p. 40).

The structure of the Japanese hospital system, on the contrary, was highly "monocratic", since the physicians kept the administrative prerogatives entirely to themselves. A strong tradition of administrative and medical power has existed in Japan since the Meiji state set up a hospital system focusing on the training of physicians, in order to introduce the Western approach to hospital organization. In the Japanese system, the physicians were the sole authorities, since they were entirely responsible for running the hospitals, and the hospital directors were therefore always doctors (Vianden, 1994, p. 90; Sugaya, 1981, p. 38-41). The Japanese hospital system can therefore be said to be a "hyper-professionalising" system since it has always been assumed that hospitals should be managed by people with specific knowledge of medical matters, *i.e.*, by the doctors themselves (Steudler, 1974, p. 216).

THE EMERGENCE OF THE NURSING PROFESSION

In his study on the history of nursing, G. Charles mentioned that nursing did not exist as such before the advent of Christianity. In ancient societies, no difference was made between the role of nurses and that of doctors:

---

1. Passages from works published in French have been translated for the purpose of this book.

> "During the early and archaic periods in the history of medicine – whether we are talking about Egypt, Mesopotamia, Greece or Rome – it was not possible to distinguish between nurses and doctors, since their roles were inextricably intertwined." (Charles, 1979, p. 13)

In the days of Hippocrates, healthcare was dispensed by the doctors' assistants, "who cannot be said to be the equivalent of our own nurses", but could rather be classified as doctors themselves (*ibid.*, p. 15).

In ancient societies, women cared for patients who were members of the household, but did not dispense medical care outside their own homes:

> "It is highly significant that despite the prestige of Hygeia and the admiration expressed by Homer for the fair-haired Agamedea, who was "skilled in recognizing all the medicinal plants which the wide world contains", Greek women do not seem to have ever carried out the occupation of physicians or nurses. At least up to the 4th century, they led a secluded, sedentary existence, which was not compatible with performing a social function." (*ibid.*, p. 15-16)

As G. Charles has pointed out, the fact that the nursing profession was firmly established in the Western world in the old days (since the advent of Christianity) contrasts with the fact that this profession was strikingly absent on the Eastern hemisphere right up to the premodern period, which started 19 centuries later (*ibid.*, p. 11-32). In France, as in the rest of Europe, nursing activities involving care dispensed beyond the family circle began to develop under the influence of Christianity back in the 4th century. As explained by A. Petitat, Western practices as far as sickness and health were concerned were characterized up to the 19th century by a sort of "symbiosis" between traditional learned medicine which never stopped readjusting it physiological bases, and charitable religious and public interventions, which mainly targeted the poor and needy (Petitat, 1989, p. 27). It was only at the end of the 19th century that the nursing profession really began to take shape in Europe.

In Japan, on the contrary, the nursing profession developed at a much later date: up to the end of the 19th century, when modern medicine was imported from the West by the Meiji State, healthcare was a purely family affair. However, the Buddhist tradition of charity for the poor *(hiden)* dates back to the 8th century and continued up to the Kamakura period, which occurred during the Middle Ages. At that time, Buddhist priests themselves performed some medical interventions. No evidence has been found about the division of labour between doctors and carers (care was dispensed either by apprentice physicians or mutually between the patients themselves) (Kameyama, 1993, p. 19-21 and p. 37-40). However, this tradition of charity does not seem to have had much impact on the process of professionalization of the nursing profession which occurred during the modernization of Japan (Kameyama, 1984, III, p. 198-209).

Healthcare therefore used to be a family matter in Japan. The moral principle of caring for the other members of the family, which was closely linked to other principles focusing on the home *(i.e.)*, was typical of the policy adopted by the Tokugawa shogunate *(bakuhu)* and the seignory *(han)*, when the task of caring for patients was removed from the hands of public servants and imposed on women in their homes (Sugano, 1993, p. 395-403). Healthcare as a moral obligation imposed on women was justified and supported by the Confucian precept of "piety", which set up hierarchical relations between men and women in their homes (*cf.* Weber, 1989, p. 225-227 and p. 321-323). This tradition constituted a real obstacle to the development of the nursing profession in Japan, even during the 20th century.

The incomplete intervention
of administrative and medical authorities on French nurses

In the 16th century, during the Reform and the subsequent dispersal of Christianity, the religious communities were expelled from French hospitals and the state and municipal authorities introduced new measures, as described by Petitat. Three kinds of healthcare workers existed in those days: poorly paid lay workers, Catholic sisters who did not belong to any formal religious community but led austere lives devoted entirely to performing their charitable tasks, and Protestant sisters belonging to some kind of religious associations, who also dedicated their whole lives to caring for the sick (Petitat, 1989, p. 43).

When the first attempts were made to transform hospitals into lay institutions during the 16th and 17th centuries, the female orders played a leading role in the field of healthcare practice, whereas the first hospital orders which developed during the 11th and 12th centuries included both male and female "branches" (Charles, 1979, p. 27-39). G. Charles has stressed how important it was for hospital workers such as the sisters belonging to hospital orders to be able to perform multiple tasks: their approach to care was based on a complex overall picture of the patient as a "sick person":

> "They were constantly in contact with their patients from their admission to hospital onwards, and attended to their nourishment, their hygiene, their medical consultations and care, supporting them during their sickness and preparing them for death, in keeping with the wishes of Saint Vincent de Paul." (*ibid.*, p. 48)

To respond to the "social issues" generated in the 19th century by increasing urban development and the industrial revolution, the Catholic Church set up "Christian care congregations" and developed a whole network by channelling all "charitable, teaching, and proselytic initiatives", while refusing all State-controlled initiatives (Petitat, 1989, p. 49). This congregationalist movement, which was initiated in France during the Restoration and the Second Empire, spread to all the other Catholic countries where the Industrial Revolution was taking place.

According to G. Charles, the "vocational calling" model developed not only in hospital congregations, but also in Protestant organizations at the time when the Catholic religion was undergoing a period of restoration and Protestantism was being regenerated (Charles, 1979, p. 65-68). This author describes how the "vocational calling" model influenced the genesis of an occupational convention:

> "Despite all attempts to transform hospitals and their workers into lay institutions, the idea remained firmly rooted in people's minds that people who do not belong to some religious group or have not taken perpetual or temporary vows cannot be good carers." (*ibid.*, p. 69)

In most of these hospital congregations, training was acquired on the job:

> "Training healthcare workers was never a major concern for either public opinion, legislators, or physicians. [...] Hospital work was never thought of as a possible choice of profession which men and women were free to carry out in exchange for payment." (*ibid.*, p. 69)

The hospital congregations' activities were brought to an end under the 3rd Republic, which began to transform French schools and hospitals into lay institutions. It was in this socio-historic context pertaining at the end of the 19th century that the strongly interventionist efforts of the administrative and medical authorities led to the work of nurses becoming a proper professional activity (Saliba, 1993, p. 39). The resulting model for the nursing profession, which J. Saliba calls "the Bourneville system", was characterized by strongly directive State and hospital administration action supported by a fringe group consisting of members of the medical profession (*ibid.*, p. 59).

The "collective bureaucratic" process involved in training the new lay hospital nurses was staunchly defended at the end of the 19th century by Dr. D. Bourneville, "a doctor, a civil servant and a militant":

> "This highly reputed hospital physician who was also Deputy of the Department of the Seine and a member of the Paris Municipal Council, took an interest in the nursing profession only insofar as it enabled him to further the progressive, lay, strongly anticlerical Republican ideals he was promoting" (*ibid.*, p. 50-51)

Dr D. Bourneville's interventionist methods consisted in involving the new nursing staff in the hierarchic organization of their institutions via administrative and medical directives:

> "His aim was not to open the nursing profession to young ladies from the upper ranks of society, but to give the lowest hospital workers opportunities for social promotion. His idea was not just to give nurses proper qualifications, but to motivate them by presenting them with career prospects; in this way, he hoped to attach them to the establishments at which they were employed." (*ibid.*, p. 52)

The skills required in this walk of life can be seen to have corresponded to those of hospital auxiliaries:

> "Their *merits* in performing the task of caring for patients will be measured in terms of their ability to act as diligent auxiliaries to the medical and administrative staff." (*ibid.*, p. 59)

It is worth noting here that gender differentials subtended the fact that the members of the nursing staff were classified at the start as mere "auxiliaries". Their administrative and medical superiors decided that these jobs should preferentially go to women; nursing therefore developed into a women's occupation. As Y. Knibiehler *et al.* have put it:

> "Physicians and republican ministers began to draw the portrait of hospital workers of a new kind, who were imbued with the principles of hygiene, extremely submissive to physicians (because they were aware of the limitations of their role), as well as to the administration which employed them, which offered in exchange some non-negligible advantages and chances of social promotion. These people who were laymen, Republicans, of lowly origin, and last but not least females who, although they had been divested of the nuns' robes, had all the qualities of gentleness and devotion associated with their sex." (Knibiehler *et al.*, 1984, p. 45)

The decision to recruit women as "auxiliary" hospital nursing staff involves the assumption that women naturally acquire essentially feminine qualities, although nurses must have suitable skills for pursuing hospitals' mainly therapeutic mission:

> "For this purpose, hospitals needed to recruit more competent members of staff, whose domestic skills could be adapted to the needs of hospital hygiene. This new training was termed *technical instruction*. It was intended mainly for women. The medical profession needs to be surrounded by preferably female auxiliaries, who are trained to assist physicians with their therapeutic activities without ever presuming to question their authority. Municipal training courses were launched in 1878 to provide auxiliaries corresponding to this description." (*ibid.*, p. 47-48)

In the "Bourneville system", however, the initiative for the vocational training dispensed in France was taken by the physicians and not the nurses, and the content of this training did not always match the needs. As a result, French nurses had difficulty at that time in putting the knowledge transmitted by the physicians into practice:

> "Unfortunately, these efforts came to nothing. Instead of teaching nurses practical skills, making them familiar with the names of instruments and machines as they were supposed to and giving them professional competences, the physicians who ran these courses focused on the principles of anatomy, physiology and pathology. Most of the pupils were incapable of assimilating the information they were given: they turned out to have so little elementary education that they had to first catch up on their primary schooling. The attitude of the administration towards these educational efforts was somewhat ambiguous: nurses were never required to attend these courses regularly, and no promises were ever made that only trained employees, *i.e.*, those with the requisite occupational skills, would be promoted to the rank of healthcare unit supervisors". (Charles, 1979, p. 76-77)

It was during the last third of the 19th century that the revolution launched by Pasteur took place and the modern approach to medicine began to develop. However, as described by M. Poisson, during the 1870s, while the system of hospital administration (*l'Assistance Publique de Paris*) was being set up in Paris, the doctors had not yet gained full power at hospitals, although they enjoyed a legal monopoly to the provision of medical care:

> "Care and auxiliary tasks were still subject to the approval of nuns under the authority of their mother superior, who was entitled to oppose the hospital administration. Physicians had no powers at the hospitals, apart from the right to practice their art. However, they were represented by three of their number on the board of supervisors, where they could express opinions on an equal footing with the other board members. Their prescriptions and advice were not put into practice without the assent of the nuns and their mother superior. In addition, the presence of one or more almoners at each hospital reinforced this parallel autonomous ecclesiastical system of control." (Poisson, 1998, p. 36)

As described by M. Poisson, a rift occurred during this period of evolution towards a lay system of hospital administration. This rift was between the nuns who tended to play the role of supervisors and the lay members of staff, who dealt with the domestic cleaning jobs:

> "Nuns with no medical knowledge at all were preferably chosen [as supervisors], and the physicians actually approved of their independence, as they intended to keep their continuously updated knowledge to themselves, which gave them the energy required to conquer their monopoly. In addition, this situation confirmed that supervisory work was not a caring function which did not involve dispensing treatment but was a completely separate activity, whereas

treating patients was the physicians' prerogative, or so they thought. Male and female nurses constituted an lowly category of domestic staff, for whom the idea of career prospects was quite out of the question." (*ibid.*, p. 52)

Bourneville's project therefore consisted in attempting to create direct links between supervisors and hospital carers by replacing the nuns by women originating from civil society (*ibid.*, p. 53). Bourneville's system had difficulty in being adopted because of the apathy with which the hospital administration reacted to this project:

> "But the motives were not the same on both sides, and although the administration included some sympathisers, it may not have realized as clearly as Bourneville did how urgent it was to train the nurses and incite them to comply by proposing salary incentives. The administration made do with having simple employees, whereas what Bourneville wanted was professionals." (*ibid.*, p. 89).

Nor did the medical profession show a very positive attitude towards implementing Bourneville's project. Many of its members argued in favour of keeping nuns at hospitals because of their great devotion to their work; this attitude has been explained by M. Poisson as being due to the underlying fear that if nurses were more highly trained, the doctors' prerogatives might be undermined:

> "Basking in the increasing prestige they had been acquiring towards the end of the century, the physicians hardly deigned to envisage what Bourneville was proclaiming so loudly, namely that completely mastering the whole picture of hospital work depended on sharing out medical knowledge to a reasonable extent, or in a carefully distilled form. On this point, the medical profession continued to bar the road to Bourneville's heady course, although the latter was less suicidal than perspicacious, since he was showing how to keep the power which the physicians were in the process of gaining. Despite all his precautions and the efforts he made not to go against the interests of his colleagues, his initiatives were strongly criticized up to the end of the century in medical circles because the path on which he had set out from the start looked too risky." (*ibid.*, p. 92-93)

The one point on which Dr D. Bourneville and his colleagues did agree, however, was that the role of nurses must be kept to that of assisting physicians. This picture of nurses' activities, which took no account of the relationship between nurses and their patients, focused purely on the usefulness of nurses from the physicians' point of view:

> "Nurses were explicitly defined as professionals providing services to physicians rather than to their patients. In fact, they were regarded as nothing more than a tool which could be used by physicians when making diagnoses (helping to assess the patients' condition) and prescribing treatment (delivering the drugs exactly as prescribed)." (*ibid.*, p. 98)

At the end of the 19th century, although the doctors in France had acquired a monopoly over medical activities, they had still not gained full powers at the hospitals. In other words, their presence at hospitals did not lead immediately to a strong partnership between the administrative and medical corps: this situation was tellingly reflected in the apathy shown by the administration towards Dr. D. Bourneville's interventionist projects and the objections it raised in medical circles.

This rather weak arrangement between the administrative and medical hospital authorities can be said to have left the door wide open to the model for the professionalization of nurses adopted in the English-speaking world in the early 20th century.

Foreign modes of professionalization were only transiently imposed on Japanese nurses

When the Japanese form of Buddhism was expanding during the Kamakura period (in the 13th century), the Buddhist priests developed charitable practices for the sick and the poor (Kameyama, 1993, p. 37-42). However, during the Tokugawa period (from the 17th to 19th century), the Confucianist doctors were the main medical practitioners, although Western medical practices were being imported from Holland. Under the influence of Confucianism, which was the main moral doctrine adopted the Samurai warriors, patients were usually cared for by members of their own family. The socio-sexual division of labour resulting from the Confucian principle of piety in the home forbade women (apart from female servants) to dispense medical care to men outside the family circle (Kameyama, 1984c, p. 199-208).

Several historical reports show that the nursing profession still did not exist during pre-modern times. In 1722, during the Tokugawa period, a Japanese doctor named S. Ogawa created a small hospital for the poor (Koishikawa yojosho) in Edo (the former name for Tokyo) with the help of the shogun lords. Although the hospital staff included both male and female servants, there were no employees specialized in nursing care (Kameyama, 1993, p. 74-75).

In 1881, at the end of the Tokugawa era, a Belgian doctor named J.-L. Pompe Meerdervoort was invited to Nagasaki by the Shogun to set up a Western-style hospital (Nagasaki yojosho) and train the Japanese doctors. Based on the hospital rules edicted at that time, the staff responsible for caring for patients can be said to have consisted mainly of members of the patients' families and apprentice physicians. This confirms that medical care was rarely dispensed outside the family circle (Kameyama, 1984d, p. 25).

At the military hospital in Yokohama *(Yokohama gunjin byoin)*, which was set up on a temporary basis in 1868 during the Boshin civil war (the Meiji Revolution), two English doctors, W. Willis and J.B. Siddal, started to dispense medical care. J.B. Siddal reported that some auxiliaries were also working at this hospital, and that there was usually one auxiliary per patient. They were all middle-aged women and none of them had any medical training. A Japanese doctor named T. Ishiguro spoke rather dismissively about these auxiliaries, calling them no-goods and whores *(bakuren)* (Kameyama, 1984b, p. 14-16). As noted by M. Kameyama, most of them were widows over 40 years of age, which was the minimum age required by Confucian mores:

> "The moral principles prevailing at that time required women to stay at home. It was not the done thing for women to go out to work. If they were obliged to do so, it was often because they were widows." *(ibid.,* p. 85)

Women therefore had to stay at home and were not allowed to care for men who did not belong to their family.

In 1869, the Medical Institute *(Igakusho)*, which had been the seat of Western medicine in Edo (Tokyo) since the mid-19th century, was taken over by the administration of the Meiji Revolution's government and renamed *Daigaku higashi ko* (the Eastern school of medicine). The military hospital in Yokohama was transferred to Tokyo and renamed *Dai-Byoin* (the Great Hospital) and used to partly train the doctors working at the Eastern school of medicine. At the request of the Japanese Government, the Government of Prussia sent two military doctors, L. Müller and T. Hoffman to train Japanese doctors to work at the Great Hospital (Vianden, 1994, p. 90). Dr L. Müller reported that all the inpatients at this hospital were accompanied by members of their family for lack of professional caregivers (Kameyama, 1984d, p. 43-44):

> "Inpatients were always accompanied by relatives because the services provided by the hospital were very poor. The relatives installed their own bedding in the patient's bedroom. They even cooked the patient's food on a *brasero*, which made the air smell extremely unpleasant." *(ibid.,* p. 91)

The Meiji state was beginning at that time to modernize Japanese society starting at the top, by introducing some of the Western ways of life. The State attempted to apply the Western medical teaching system at the hospitals, as we have seen above: the Great Hospital and the Eastern medical school, which merged in 1877, became the Medical Faculty of the University of Tokyo. This hospital system had a "monocratic" structure, whereby the power was entirely in the hands of the doctors, in line with German military hospital practices. The decision made by the Japanese government to replace traditional Chinese medical practices by Western methods, especially those used in Germany, also resulted in the publication of a set of medical regulations *(isei)* in 1874 *(ibid.,* p. 33-83).

On the other hand, the Catholic and Protestant missionaries originating from the United States attempted to apply their national nursing practices at Japanese hospitals without any regard for Japanese State policy. Their plans for converting Japan were suspended, however, by a decree issued by the Tokugawa shogunate, until it was resumed in 1873 as the result of the Meiji revolution. Sisters from the Catholic congregation of the Franciscan Missionaries of Mary were sent over to set up a hospital in Kumamoto in 1889 and another one in Sapporo in 1908. It was the Presbyterian Church of America, however, which eventually proposed to install its system of vocational training for nurses in Japan at the end of the 19th century.

At the beginning of the Meiji era, some high schools *(jo-gakko)* were created for girls leaving compulsory primary education. In 1887, M.T. True, an American Presbyterian lady missionary, started to take an interest in the training of girl pupils at the Sakurai School in Tokyo *(Sakurai jogakko*, which was renamed *Jogakuin* in 1890). M.T. True then invited Anna Veitch, who had trained at the Royal Infirmary School of Nursing in Edinburgh, to join her; Anna Veitch worked in Japan from 1887 to 1888, training the Sakurai schoolgirls before working at Tokyo University Hospital (Kameyama, 1984c, p. 37-70).

In Kyoto, the American Congregational Church took part in setting up the Doshisha hospital and the Kyoto nursing school in 1887. Two eminent American nurses engaged in training Japanese nurses from 1887 to 1897: L. Richards, who had trained at the New England School of Nursing, followed by H.E. Fraser, who had trained at the Bellevue School of Nursing in New York (*ibid.*, p. 71-129). These British and American teachers were no doubt very familiar with the Nightingale system of professionalization.

All these attempts at implanting more modern training models in Japan were short-lived, however; the Sakurai School for girls in Tokyo closed down in 1907; and the links between the Kyoto nursing school and the American Congregational Church came to an end in 1895.

Failure to introduce the British and American model for professionalization was partly due to the fact that the American pioneers' efforts were strongly opposed by male American missionaries such as J.C. Hepburn (Kohiyama, 1992, p. 212-240). On the other hand, the Japanese doctors responsible for introducing Western hospital practices contributed importantly to setting up the nursing profession in this country. It should be mentioned that it was easier for Japanese physicians than for their French counterparts to acquire a powerful status at the hospitals where they worked.

In France, physicians practising medicine on an independent liberal basis only gradually acquired some power at the hospitals to which they were gaining access, since these establishments were controlled by the State, the Catholic Church and the municipal authorities. However, during the Tokugawa period, hospital systems of the Western kind simply did not exist in Japan. As soon as the State introduced a hospital system which catered for medical training with a view to adopting Western practices, the Japanese physicians quickly took the administrative power into their hands. The model for professionalization adopted in the Western world therefore did not fit the situation in Japan in the late 19th century, when the administrative and medical logics prevailed.

During this time, another form of nursing practice based on visiting nurses, known as *hashutsu-kangohu*, developed in Japan: this eminently female occupation was created at the instigation of the privileged classes. In 1885, K. Takagi, a Japanese naval doctor who trained at Saint-Thomas' Hospital in London from 1875 to 1880, created the Tokyo-Yushi-Kyoritsu Hospital, which was subsequently renamed the Jikei University Hospital. The Japanese aristocratic and bourgeois classes subsidised the training of nurses in order to benefit from the services of visiting nurses. An American nurse called M.E. Reade was in charge of this training scheme from 1885 to 1887. However, no attempt was make in this case to transpose or adapt the famous Nightingale system, since these visiting nurses were not actually mobile nurses but employees who were personally recruited by affluent families (Kameyama, 1984d, p. 104-118).

THE DEVELOPMENT OF THE NURSING PROFESSION

During the first half of the 20th century, the professionalization of French nurses began to take shape when they themselves initiated specific vocational training schemes dispensed at nursing schools. C. Dubar and P. Tripier have described this development as an "associative model" rather than a "vocational model":

> "When competence is assessed by professionals themselves, based on a system of certification proving that mastery of a specialized technique has been acquired, it is obviously the 'associative' aspect of the profession which comes into play; this is the English equivalent of the masonic brotherhood." (Dubar & Tripier, 1998, p. 77)

As A.-M. Arborio has pointed out, this system of professionalization involving competence assessments carried out by nurses themselves led to those who obtained qualifications being differentiated from the auxiliaries:

> "During the 1920s, there was still some confusion between qualified nurses and the others, and the hospital administrators were the first to complain about this situation. The nurses' representatives were also intent on making the distinction between the ward duty staff, who deal with patients, and the nursing staff in the strict sense of the term, including State certified nurses *(IDE, Infirmière Diplômée d'État)*, nurses trained at municipal schools, and employees who called themselves nurses without having acquired any vocational training at all." (Arborio, 2001, p. 30)

In France, the professional logics of the nursing profession developed quite unobtrusively during the first half of the 20th century in the framework of the dual authority exerted at hospitals by the medical profession and the hospital administration. Since there was a shortage of qualified nurses, hospital administrators were bound to accept various levels of qualification among the nurses they recruited. The typically French compromise reached between professional and institutional logics eventually led to State certified nurses being differentiated from nursing assistants. Nurses' professional role was at last dissociated at that point from their gender, since the domestic tasks were delegated thereafter to the nursing assistants.

In Japan on the contrary, the "monocratic" power exerted by the medical profession along with that of the administrators made it impossible for the nursing profession to pursue professional logics. The army doctors were the first to tackle the question of nurses' vocational training. This interventionist model abolished the traditional social norm based on gender relations, whereby women were obliged to care for their family members, but it introduced another gender differential by defining nursing not only as a professional activity but also as a female activity. According to this interventionist model, nurses were not expected to take any initiatives: they were obliged to simply execute the task of assisting doctors with their work. In addition, these institutional logics did not lead to nurses' right to even relative autonomy being recognized, since they were relegated to a vague category of employees in which the boundaries between qualified professionals and auxiliaries was extremely fuzzy.

Professional logics in the case of French nurses

The Western model for professionalization and the feminist awaking

Contrary to the interventionist approach corresponding to the administrative and medical models, the model launched by Florence Nightingale was partly based on training carried out by people who were nurses themselves. When she was young, Florence Nightingale, who was born in 1820, visited the hospitals run by the Saint-Vincent-de-Paul Sisters in Paris and the Kaiserswerth Deaconesses in Germany. She was impressed by the "vocational calling" model on which these hospital institutions were based, and in 1857, she created the Saint-Thomas'

Hospital Nursing School in London with a view to giving nurses a proper "civil career" (Charles, 1979, p. 86-94). Some attempts were subsequently made by some pioneering women to copy this model in France at private nursing schools. In 1902, Anna Hamilton became Director of the School of care workers *(École de gardes-malades)* in Bordeaux, and in 1904, Léonie Chaptal founded the Nurses' teaching home *(Maison-école d'infirmières)* in Paris *(ibid.,* p. 112-113).

However, these logics focusing on the occupational group had to comply with the logics of the administrative and medical hospital authorities. This is what J. Saliba has called the "French compromise" between the approach initiated by Florence Nightingale and Dr. Bourneville's Republican model. In other words, French nurses, who were attempting to introduce "dynamics initiated from the inside by the nurses themselves", had to contend with the existence of "heavy handed interventions imposed from the outside by the administrative and medical hospital authorities" (Saliba, 1993, p. 39-40).

It is worth noting one particular difference which existed between the type of training recommended by the Bourneville system and Anna Hamilton's followers. As mentioned by Y. Knibiehler *et al.*, the training organized by Anna Hamilton was intended for "women of education", whereas the Bourneville was intended for girls of humble origin:

> "In connection with this question of education, which Anna Hamilton never defined, we can see the issues on which Bourneville and Hamilton were opposed. The former believed that all women with primary education and solid professional experience having a suitably high standard of conduct will make excellent nurses, since the requisite moral qualities are to be found in all honest circles. Anna Hamilton was convinced, on the contrary, that the class from which nurses were recruited was of the greatest importance." (Knibiehler *et al.*, 1984, p. 56)

In those days, although it was never explicitly stated, nursing was still thought of as something of a vocation, since one of the main prerequisites for becoming a nurse was being a spinster:

> "Anna Hamilton insisted on nurses being unmarried; she objected strongly to the fact that one of the First Lady Directors of the Salpêtrière School of Nursing was married: family responsibilities did not seem to be compatible with nurses' devotion to their patients." (*ibid.*, p. 56)

This image of nurses as "lay nuns" was perfectly in keeping with the physicians' wishes (*ibid.*, p. 77). As Y. Knibiehler *et al.* have pointed out, Anna Hamilton stressed the female qualities of nurses in her writings:

> "However, the three fundamental qualities of housewives – submission, housekeeping skills and devotion – underwent some interesting changes in hospital settings. As far as housekeeping is concerned, most contemporary works emphasized the fact that nurses' activities were essentially manual housekeeping and domestic activities, but these tasks were completely transformed by the introduction of hygiene, and especially by the need for aseptic conditions at hospitals." (*ibid.*, p. 58)

Anna Hamilton accepted the opinion of a special medical commission, which was appointed in 1899 to draw up a training programme for nurses; she even agreed with the idea that the nursing profession should be open to women alone:

> "Anna Hamilton took advantage of these proposals by declaring men 'naturally unfit for per-
> forming the work of caring for patients' *(gardes-malades)*, apart from a few special cases. The idea
> that women were superior to men in the field of care was indeed something of a dogma at the
> time." *(ibid.*, p. 59)

However, logics focusing on the occupational group were still driving the efforts of some
pioneering women. The "social Christianity" movement resulted in some training courses
run by nurses being set up at private schools *(ibid.*, p. 60). In 1902, for example, Anna Hamilton attempted to introduce the Western model for the professionalization of nurses by
breaking free from the authority of the doctors and hospital administrators:

> "At the Protestant school of health and the associated *École de garde-malades* which she directed
> as from 1902, she introduced the basic principles developed by Florence Nightingale. This school
> was set up at a hospital, where the pupils constituted the nursing staff; the hospital and the
> school were both directed by a woman (a matron)." *(ibid.*, p. 60-61)

Another pioneering woman who attempted to introduce the Nightingale model was Léonie
Chaptal, who was born in 1873 into a powerful Catholic family living in the Allier region.
After a visit to England, where she was impressed by the practices she saw, she founded a
private nursing school in Paris in 1904:

> "She acquired the patronage of some eminent personalities, including Baroness Rothschild and
> Mrs Taine, as proof that this was an honourable profession. Twenty-four pupils aged at least
> twenty-one were enrolled as boarders to take the two-year course, which included sixty hours
> of practical work experience at public hospitals, where they were placed under supervisors."
> *(Ibid.*, p. 61)

Social Christianity and the philanthropy of middle-class women promoted the cause of women, foreshadowing the forthcoming feminist movement. This is what J. Saliba says about
Léonie Chaptal in this connection:

> "Léonie Chaptal was associated with women from non-Catholic circles who were also liberals
> involved in promoting social progress. Other women from the upper classes were also frequen-
> ting these circles. These self-declared feminists wanted to improve women's position in society.
> Their action focused on the training and education of girls. They adopted Florence Nightingale
> as the outstanding example of a woman who managed to turn her feminine specificities to
> advantage in her life and work. The nursing profession seemed to be a suitable target for this
> project, since it could serve to promote the cause of women, while at the same time providing
> women with an occupational outlet." (Saliba, 1993, p. 64-65)

As M. Perrot has pointed out, these pioneering achievements already carry some embryonic
traces of gender awareness, and often of feminist stirrings (Perrot, 1991, p. 234). The pioneers
who espoused the Nightingale model for the professionalization of nurses attempted to introduce it into France via the "vocational calling" model on which the hospital congregations
and Protestant associations were based. They were therefore attempting to transform a vocation into a profession by providing the training required.

In late 19th century European society, some specifically female occupations, which were closely linked to the concept of "social motherhood", developed under the influence of Christianity. Catholics and Protestants – the former in a more directive way and the latter tending

more to favour women's autonomy – exhorted the women of the world to take steps to improve the material and moral situation of the most needy populations (Perrot, p. 228). The concept of "motherhood" kept women cloistered in their homes, whereas that of "social motherhood" brought them out into the public arena, while restricting their scope for action to the three-fold mission of teaching, dispensing care and providing assistance. Women therefore took the initiatives to which they were entitled in these three areas.

M. Perrot has described as follows the opposition between the logics of the occupational group and those of the medical and administrative powers:

> "The management of social issues was taken over by politicians and professionals. Physicians, men of Law and psychologists were quick to relegate women to the status of auxiliaries reduced to performing the work of subordinates: that of nurses and social assistants." (*ibid.*, p. 234)

The limits of professionalization

According to G. Charles, the two decades between the two World Wars were a decisive period in the history of the nursing profession. During this period, many efforts were made to have nurses' qualifications properly recognized and to create nurses' associations (Charles, 1979, p. 123-168).

The war "spontaneously" mobilized women, while accentuating the sexual division of labour. Knibiehler et al. have described as follows the question of payment which arose among the voluntary Red Cross workers who originated from three women's associations (*Société de secours aux blessés militaires*, founded in 1866, *l'Association des dames de France*, founded in 1879, and *Union des femmes de France*, founded in 1891):

> "The women who volunteered in August 1914, unless they had sufficiently large personal resources, could not continue to survive as well as possibly providing for their families, while devoting their services on a voluntary basis." (Knibiehler *et al.*, 1984, p. 98)

These women's voluntary commitment to their work as nurses was therefore necessarily only a passing phase: it was not regarded as a real professional activity. These volunteers therefore contributed to the archetypal picture of nurses as voluntary workers endowed with qualities such as femininity, gentleness, devotion and obedience. The ideal nurse was therefore thought of as the mother, sister or wife of a soldier during the First World War: "the events occurring during five years of war led nurses to increasingly resemble the ideal imposed on them by the ideas circulating at the time" (*ibid.*, p. 106-107).

The mobilization of women during World War I nevertheless gave them access to public affairs and paved the way to the professionalization of nursing. As Y. Knibiehler *et al.* have pointed out, one of the more positive effects of the War was the fact that it enabled French nurses to gain social recognition:

> "In the aftermath of the Great War, the prestige acquired by female caregivers, and the high esteem and gratitude they had deserved enabled some strong female personalities to make the profession officially recognized." (*ibid.*, p. 109)

This social recognition led to the institution of the French State Nursing Diploma in 1922. This breakthrough was no doubt due to Léonie Chaptal and her group of women nursing-school directors. In a decisive text written in 1921, Léonie Chaptal insisted on the need for nursing studies to be accredited by diplomas:

> "Developments in medical science and asepsis have made it necessary for nurses to be trained as technicians. Devotion and a good-natured disposition no longer suffice. A proper training course involving both theoretical lectures and practical experience has become indispensable: the course should take at least two years and be based on an official programme; it should be approved by a State diploma." (*ibid.*, p. 112)

The professional competence certificate (in hospital nursing, visiting TB patient *(tuberculosis sufferer)* nursing and visiting children's nursing) instituted in the French decree of 27 June 1922 conferred on its holders the title of qualified State nurse. This decree also made provision for follow-up counselling at the nursing schools, in which Léonie Chaptal played a leading role. Another key event on the path to nurses' professionalization was the creation of the first association of State-qualified French nurses (the ANIDEF, for: *Association Nationale des Infirmières Diplômées de l'État Français*) in 1924. At the 1925 Helsinki Conference, this association became a member of the International Council of Nurses.

The process of professionalization was nevertheless limited by the fact that nurses' skills and their recruitment were not strictly controlled by either the French State or their professional association:

> "There were no laws obliging anyone to recruit only qualified nurses. The Ministry in charge certainly sent out circulars from time to time, asking the Prefects to exert pressure in favour of those with qualifications; and the Prefects duly forwarded these circulars to the establishments involved. However, the results were disappointing because for many reasons, the employers preferred to recruit unqualified nurses, who could be given lower wages and were more docile and malleable." (*ibid.*, p. 132)

In addition, since pioneers such as Léonie Chaptal accounted for only a minority of the French nurses at that time, the process of professionalization was not very widespread:

> "Women who were unmarried, militant and had highly demanding standards shaped the profession based on their own criteria. This is why the ANIDEF gained a hearing with the French Government although its membership was quite small (there were about 3,000 members in 1932). It is rather paradoxical that the rank and file nurses were quite unaware of the work being carried out and the diplomatic stakes being defended by the association." (*ibid.*, p. 123)

The process of professionalization was particularly evident in the case of the so-called "visiting nurses". The range of tasks for which these nurses were responsible increased, including the social aspects. However, visiting nurses featured only quite briefly in the history of French nursing: "they existed officially from 1922, when the specific State diploma was created, until 1938, when the visiting nurse's diploma was merged with that of social assistant and given the latter name" (*ibid.*, p. 140). However, as Y. Knibiehler *et al.* have mentioned, despite their short existence, visiting nurses contributed to the cause of women's liberation:

> "The battle to conquer the world of medicine [...] was supported enthusiastically by an increasingly large number of women. At the turn of the century, women from the aristocracy and the bourgeoisie were siding with the common people. Some of these unwitting feminists believed

charitable actions to be a means of breaking free from the narrow confines of domestic life and expressing themselves by taking action and personal initiatives. Many of them underwent training with Red Cross associations [...] and some of them were former nuns caring for the poor, who had either left their orders or were still dedicated to caring for people in their homes, such as the *Petites sœurs de l'Assomption*" (*ibid.*, p. 142)

A clash occurred between the proponents of this new approach based on the occupational group and the medical authorities. The leading hospital specialists in the fields of child care and phthisiology encouraged hospital practitioners to integrate this new female occupation, but it was rejected by the private practitioners *(praticiens libéraux)*:

"The nurses gained the support of the hospital practitioners. But they were violently opposed by those in private practice, who were supported by their unions. In the name of patients' right to privacy, for instance, they refused to declare patients with tuberculosis; in fact, this declaration was the prerequisite for a visiting nurse to be able to go to a patient's home." (*ibid.*, p. 160)

The professionalization of nurses therefore came up against the problem of defining the frontiers between the two occupational groups consisting of doctors and nurses. Y. Knibiehler et al. deplored the disappearance of visiting nurses in 1938, which "greatly impoverished the nursing profession" (*ibid.*, p. 164).

Administrative and medical logics

In the case of Japanese nurses, a model imposed by the administrative and medical authorities

Let us first attempt to explain why the Western lady pioneers' attempts to import their model for the nursing profession were thwarted by the Japanese administrative and medical authorities. We have an interesting first-hand report on this subject by C. Oseki, who was one of the very first nurses to graduate from the Sakurai School of nursing, where she studied under the English nurse Anna Veitch before working at Tokyo University Hospital, where nurses were trained within only 6 months. In 1890, the hospital reform proposed by C. Oseki was not accepted by her superiors and she gave up her job as a matron:

"Nurses' competences are essential to curing their patients quickly. Nurses must therefore master technical gestures as well as having a good mental attitude. We have to admit that they lack both of these qualities. However, it does not suffice to impose discipline on nursing staff. It is necessary to reform their training and the organization of their work. For this purpose, the number of nurses should be increased so that they are able to get enough sleep between shifts." (A letter from Oseki to Professor Sato, quoted by Kameyama, 1984d, p. 125-126)

The fact that C. Oseki's proposals were refused shows how difficult it was to apply the Nightingale model in Japan. M. Takahashi *et al.* have also addressed the question of nurses' training:

"With the help of teachers from other countries and under the influence of Christian missionaries, the Sakurai and Kyoto schools of nursing attempted to apply the Nightingale system. Florence Nightingale always stressed the fact that nurses should be nurses above all, and neither doctors nor assistants. A nurse is able to deal on her own with all the tasks that come within her scope [...]. This is why, despite the high goals pursued, the training dispensed at these two schools of nursing could not be easily integrated into Japanese social circles." (Takahashi *et al.*, 1973, p. 135)

The Nigthingale model for the process of professionalization, "initiated on the inside by nursing professionals themselves" was not compatible with the dictatorial interventions imposed from the outside by the administrative and medical authorities in Japan (Saliba, 1993, p. 40). After all these attempts to introduce the Nightingale system had failed, the interventionist model was firmly implanted at Tokyo University Hospital and then at the Red Cross Hospital, where nursing practices were regarded as "civic activities":

> "In the case of the Jikei Hospital in Tokyo (which was formerly called the *Tokyo-Yushi-Kyoritsu Hospital*), a system of visiting nurses was set up at the instigation of the bourgeois and aristocratic sectors of the population to care for patients in their homes, whereas at Tokyo University Hospital, where the focus was on medical training, nurses' activities shifted from caring for patients to carrying out medical prescriptions. [...] Later on, at the Japanese Red Cross Hospital, which had been devoted to caring for wounded wartime soldiers, nurses' training developed under the aegis of the imperial family and the military authorities, as often occurs after nursing staff have been mobilized in times of war. It has been estimated that the Japanese Red Cross nurses accounted for the largest component of the Japanese nursing profession." (Takahashi *et al.*, 1973, p. 134-135)

After coming into contact with the French Red Cross during a visit to Paris in 1867, T. Sano created the Fraternity Association *(Hakuai-sha)* in 1877 to care for Seinan civil war casualties. The Geneva Convention was ratified by Japan in 1886; the following year, the Fraternity Association became the Japanese Red Cross. This organization, which was subsidized by the imperial family and the State, quickly developed. Since it depended on State policy, unlike the French Red Cross Association, which was composed of volunteers, the Japanese Red Cross played a crucial role in the development of the nursing profession in Japan.

Contrary to what the Western pioneers had attempted to achieve by introducing the Nightingale system at the Sakurai and Kyoto schools of nursing, the Japanese Red Cross was under the banner of the interventionist model: the content of nurses' training was decided outside nursing circles, in line with the logics of the administrative and medical decision-makers.

It is worth mentioning here that at the 1887 Red Cross Conference in Karlsruhe, two army doctors, T. Hashimoto and T. Ishiguro, proposed to enrol a European nursing teacher, but this initiative failed. They therefore drew up the training programme for Japanese Red Cross nurses themselves (Kameyama, 1984a, p. 11-25). As M. Takahashi *et al.* have explained, it was difficult to transpose the Nightingale system to Japanese social and cultural circles in those days, and there was a feeling that nurses should be trained by doctors:

> "Since T. Hashimoto and T. Ishiguro did not manage to recruit a nursing teacher from another country, they decided that nurses' training would be carried out by army doctors. This was in fact quite in keeping with Japanese social and cultural practices. Ten army doctors were selected to be in charge of this training course, and were trained for this purpose under the supervision of T. Hashimoto and T. Ishiguro." (Takahashi *et al.*, 1973, p. 173)

The image of women as wives and mothers was not in keeping with investing in a career

In the name of the Confucian principle of piety, hierarchical relations between men and women were thought to be justified in the same way as those between the older and younger members of a family (Weber, 1989, p. 225-227 and p. 321-323). After governing family relationships, the moral principle of piety left the confines of people's homes and spread to the institutions (companies and State institutions).

As reported by M. Morishima, Japanese Confucian morality, which upheld the virtues of faithfulness and loyalty to the State (or the overlord), contributed greatly to the wave of social mobilization which contributed to the modernization of Japan during the Meiji period. This moral code favoured the development of a nationalist, capitalist economy based on the principles of seniority and lifelong employment. However, those who made the most fundamental contribution to setting up the new systems were men rather than women: bureaucrats trained during the Tokugawa period, "during which a samurai was a civil as well as a military officer" (Morishima, 1982).

The Confucian moral principle of piety responsible for the sexual division of labour and the fact that Japanese were confined to their homes was now called upon to mobilize them to go out to work[2]. The qualities acquired by women in their homes were now to be exported beyond the home. Their gentleness and submission were declared to be assets which would be useful not only at home but also at places of work institutions (Kameyama, 1984a, p. 111-116).

However, the new occupational status acquired by women was strictly limited by the administrative and medical powers that be, as shown by the following anecdote. In 1904, during the war with Russia, a team of American Red Cross nurses was sent to Japan on a humanitarian mission. The meeting between American and Japanese nurses brought to light the differences between their approach to their work. A.N. McGee, the leader of the American group, reported that Japanese nurses never took any personal initiatives: they only carried out the orders of their superiors to the letter (*ibid.*, p. 88-90).

At the 1909 International Council of Nurses Conference in London, a Japanese nurse called T. Hagiwara representing the Japanese Red Cross presented a paper ("Nurses and nursing practices in Japan"), in which she made some comparisons with nursing practices in other countries. She mentioned that the traditional gender relations based on Confucian ideas used to make it impossible for women to take up an occupation and to care for male patients other than family members:

> "In Japan, contrary to what occurs in Christian countries, women did not use to carry out the work of nurses. The status of our women is not that of nuns doing charity. This does not means that charity is unknown in Japan, but that Japanese Buddhism promoted care for patients as

---

2. The Confucian texts written during the Tokugawa period about women's moral obligations (*jokunsho*) praised the intrinsically female qualities and upheld the division of labour based on socio-sexual considerations (Kakehi, 1982, p. 310-324).

much as pity for the poor. On the other hand, up to quite recently, because of the social gap between men and women, women were not allowed to care for male patients outside the family circle. Only a servant paid by the family could care for the male members of a household. It was not out of charity but for financial reasons that women of lowly origin dispensed care to members of the upper classes." (The Japanese Red Cross Society, 1909a, p. 11)

The logics based on administrative and medical power therefore ended up by challenging the traditional Confucian divide between the sexes. However, the author of the above paper presented in 1909 pointed out the existence of some ambiguity between the morality which confined women to their homes and women's social mobilization:

> "Those in charge of the Japanese Red Cross attempted to abolish the traditional divide between men and women so that middle-class women could care for wounded soldiers. To further this goal, some upper-class women engaged in nursing activities and attempted to persuade their middle-class contemporaries that working as a nurse was a moral deed." (The Japanese Red Cross Society, 1909b, p. 12)

The Japanese branch of the Red Cross is an atypical branch in that its nurses are mostly permanent employees, who form the largest component of the Japanese nursing profession. It is particularly obvious how traditional gender relations have been reintroduced into this organization:

> "It was necessary for nursing activities to be carried out by women. This fact was widely recognized. In fact, all the hospitals employed nurses, and professional associations were created for purely lucrative ends. But the morality of the profession subsisted thanks to the Japanese Red Cross nurses, who consisted of two categories: voluntary nurses and 'relief nurses', who had permanent work contracts. The four thousand Japanese Red Cross relief nurses constituted a sold hub on which the whole nursing profession was based. The Japanese Red Cross nurses differed greatly in this respect from their counterparts in other countries." (*ibid.*, p. 16)

Unlike the volunteer Red Cross workers in European countries, the Japanese Red Cross nurses were therefore wage-earners with permanent contracts, although they stopped working as soon as they got married. The process of social mobilization which extracted women from their homes resulted in a shift towards an "occupational morality", especially during the war with Russia. The occupational moral obligations imposed by administrative and medical logics were associated with the rise of nationalism, which demanded "devotion to the nation and assistance to its soldiers" *(hokoku-juppei)*:

> "The Japanese Red Cross nurses' professional moral code differed from that obeyed by nurses in other countries. Although charity was traditionally held to be a virtue in Japan, nursing practices in this country focused more on 'devotion to the nation and assistance to its soldiers', whereas nursing practices in the Western countries were completely rooted in the Christian principle of charity." (*ibid.*, p. 17)

Confucian morality reverted, however, towards women being relegated to the role of wives and mothers *(ryosai-kenbo)*. It was again thought to be essential that the main goal of girls' education, especially at secondary schools *(koto-jogakko)* should be to give them the feminine qualities required to equip them for family life. This revalorization of the role of women in their homes obviously restricted their scope for professional commitment (Nagahara, 1982, p. 149-184).

As we have seen, the nursing profession developed on completely different lines between Europe and Japan. In Europe, the model for the professionalization of nurses was rooted in the "vocational calling" obeyed by hospital congregations and Protestant associations. This idea of the profession as a vocational calling conflicted somewhat with the administrative and medical authorities' power. In Japan, the image of nurses was directly inspired by the traditional role of women in their homes. Japanese nurses are trained by doctors to serve as their assistants, and even when they were mobilised in times of war, they were not able to develop their ideas as to how nursing should be practised.

However, the Japanese nursing profession is evolving these days and competence assessments are being introduced. According to the laws on nursing introduced by the Japanese Ministry of the Interior in 1915, would-be nurses have to undergo a 2-year training course after their primary education *(koto-shogakko)*, but women with work experience can sit a special examination with a view to obtaining the right to carry out the profession of nurses (Kameyama, 1984a, p. 162-166).

CONCLUSION

In France, nursing practices rooted in nuns' devotion to the principle of charity were challenged by the State administrative authorities as well as by the medical profession. The vocational calling model generated by hospital congregations and Protestant associations was eventually replaced by the "interventionist" model imposed by the administrative and medical authorities, which resulted in hospital nurses being classified as mere auxiliaries. Nursing practices subsequently developed into professional but strictly female practices. By opposing this picture of their profession as a woman's profession and demanding that training should be dispensed by "elite nurses", the French nurses transformed their calling into a real profession between the end of the 19th century and the mid-20th century.

The attempts made in Japan during the late 19th century to copy the Western model for nurses' professionalization failed because the Confucian principle "piety" required care to be dispensed within the family circle. The development of the nursing profession was also prevented by the monocratic form of authority exerted in the Japanese hospital system. When the State eventually introduced the Western approach to medicine and hospital administration during the Meiji period, the doctors became entirely responsible for hospital management. Up to the country's defeat in 1945, the "interventionist" model was therefore applied by the administration and the medical authorities, and women were no longer relegated to dispensing care in their own homes. However, traditional gender relations have continued to apply, since the right to practice nursing is still restricted to the subservient female sex.

REFERENCES

• Arborio AM. *Un personnel invisible. Les aides-soignantes à l'hôpital*. Paris: Anthoropos, 2001.

• Black N. Rise and Demise of the Hospital: A reappraisal of nursing. *BMJ* 2005; 331 (7529): 1394-6.

• Bradhaw A. The virtue of nursing: The covenant of care. *J Med Ethics* 1999; 25: 477-81.

• Charles G. *L'Infirmière en France d'hier à aujourd'hui*. Paris: Le Centurion, 1979.

• Cook C, Webb A. Reactions from the medical and nursing professions to Nightingale's "reform(s)" of nurse training in the late 19th century. *Postgrad Med J* 2002; vol. 78: 118-23.

• Currie G, Suhomlinova O. The Impact of Institutional Forces upon Knowledge Sharing in the UK NHS. *Public Adm* 2006; vol. 84, n° 1.

• The Japanese Red Cross Society (1909a), [The nurses of the Red Cross and other nurses in Japan] *(nippon-niokeru ippan-kangohu to sekijuji-kango-hu). Japanese Red Cross (nippon-sekijuji)* 1909; n° 264.

• The Japanese Red Cross Society (1909b), [The nurses of the Japanese Red Cross] *(nippon-sekijuji-kangohu). Japanese Red Cross (nippon-sekijuji)* 1909; n° 265.

• Dubar C, Tripier P. *Sociologie des professions*. Paris: Armand Colin, 1998.

• Hawkins S. From maid to matron: nursing as a route to social advancement in nineteenth-century England. *Women's History Review* 2010; 19.1.

• Kakehi K. [The texts of womens' morals in China and Japan] *(chugoku no jokun to nippon no jokun)*. In: Research group on womens's history (Josei-shi-sogo-kenkyu-kai) (ed.). *[History of Japanese women] (nippon-josei-shi)*, t. 3. Tokyo: Tokyo University Press, 1982.

• Kameyama M. (1984a), *[Modern history of the Japanese Nurses] (kindai-nippon-kango-shi)*, t. 1. Tokyo: Domesu-shuppan, 1984.

• Kameyama M. (1984b), *[Modern history of Japanese nurses] (kindai-nippon-kango-shi)*, t. 2. Tokyo: Domesu-shuppan, 1984.

• Kameyama M. (1984c), *[Modern history of Japanese nurses] (kindai-nippon-kango-shi)*, t. 3. Tokyo: Domesu-shuppan, 1984.

• Kameyama M. (1984d), *[Modern history of Japanese nurses] (kindai-nippon-kango-shi)*, t. 4. Tokyo: Domesu-shuppan, 1984.

• Kameyama M. (1993), *[History of nursing] (Kango-shi)*. Tokyo: Mejikaru-furendo, 1993.

• Knibiehler Y, Leroux-Hugon V, Dupont-Hess O, Tastayre Y. *Cornettes et blouses blanches ; les infirmières dans la société française*. Paris: Hachette, 1984.

• Kohiyama R. *[The 19ᵗʰ-Century American women's foreign mission and its encounter with Meiji Japan] (amerika-hujin-senkyoshi,rainichi-no-haikei to sono-eikyo)*. Tokyo: Tokyo University Press, 1992.

• Morishima M. *Why has Japan "succeeded"?* Londres: Cambridge University Press, 1982.

• Nagahara K. ["Ie" and women's occupations in the education of future wives and mothers] *(ryosai-kenbo-shugi-kyouiku niokeru "ie" to shokugyo)*. In: Research group on womens's history *(Josei-shi-sogo-kenkyu-kai)* (ed.). *[History of Japanese women] (nihon-josei-shi)*, t. 4. Tokyo: Tokyo University Press, 1982.

• Perrot M. *Les Femmes ou les silences de l'histoire*. Paris: Flammarion, 1991.

• Petitat A. *Les Infirmières. De la vocation à la profession*. Montréal: Boréal, 1989.

• Poisson M. *Origines républicaines d'un modèle infirmier*. Vincennes: Éditions Hospitalières, 1998.

• Saliba J, Bon-Saliba B, Ouvry-Vial B. *Les Infirmières. Ni nonnes, ni bonnes*. Paris: Syros, 1993.

• Sarkis JM, Connors VL. Nursing research: historical background and teaching information strategies. *Bulletin of the Medical Librarians Association* 1986; 74 (2): 121-5.

• Smith FT. Florence Nightingale: early feminist. *The American Journal of Nursing* 1981; 81 (5): 1020-4.

• Smith HL. Two lines of authority: The hospital's dilemma. *Modern Hospital* 1955; 84 (3): 59-64.

• Steudler F. *L'Hôpital en observation*. Paris: Armand Colin, 1974.

• Sugano N. [Health practices and care] *(yojo to kaigo)*. In: Hayashi R. (ed). *[Women during the Tokugawa period] (josei no kinsei)*. Tokyo: Chuo-koron-sha, 1993.

• Sugaya A. *[Japanese hospitals] (Nippon no byoin)*. Tokyo: Chuokoron-sha, 1981.

• Takahashi M. *et al. [Japanese nurses in the early modern era] (nihon-kindai-Kango no yoake).* Tokyo: Igaku-shoin, 1973.

• Vianden HH. La Refonte de la médecine à l'ère Meiji. In: Siary S, Benhamou H. (ed). *Médecine et société au Japon.* Paris: L'Harmattan, 1994.

• Weber M. (1989), *Confucianisme et taoïsme.* Paris: Gallimard, translated from *Konfuzianismis und Taoismus in Gesamelete Aufsätze zur Religionzoziologie, III*, 1921.

• Wildman S, Hewison A. Rediscovering a history of nursing management: From Nightingale to the modern matron. *Int J Nurs Stud* 2009; 46: 1650-61.

2. Gender issues addressed

Since it first came into existence, nursing has always been a predominantly female profession although it gradually became open to men. In France, men accounted for 6.7% of the nursing profession in 1975, and this figure increased to 11% by 1991 and 13% in 2009 (Feroni, 1994, p. 148-149; DREES, 2009). At the moment of acquiring a diploma, men accounted for 15.4% of French nursing graduate in 1998 (DREES, 2005 et 2009). In Japan, the percentage of male nurses increased from 1.3% in 1982 to 3.3% in 1993, and to 4.0% in 2000 (Japanese Nursing Association, 1995, 2004)[1].

The gender differentials involved in this essentially female occupation began to be challenged during the second half of the 20th century. The fact that nurses were expected to be constantly available made the pursuit of a career incompatible with raising a family long after the "vocational calling" model had been abolished. The prerequisite for women was therefore willingness to make "a short investment in time and space", *i.e.*, to separate their careers completely from their personal lives (Kergoat, 1992, p. 62-63).

Unlike Japanese nurses, whose working lives generally continue only as long as they are unmarried, their French counterparts are now able to pursue continuous occupational trajectories. French nurses have acquired the right to feel that they are normal wage-earners ("it's just like any other job") rather than carrying out a vocational calling, whereas Japanese nurses are "extraneous" to the institutions which employ them, to use D. Kergoat's expression: they are unable to pursue a coherent occupational trajectory and they are outsiders in the world of work they frequent (*ibid.*, p. 59).

The fact that gender issues came to the fore in France during the 1960s resulted in nurses' vocational qualifications no longer being confused with women's "natural" qualities (Hirata & Kergoat, 1988).

The comparisons made between France and Japan in this chapter will be based on the three main roles of nurses defined by I. Feroni in her doctoral thesis: the role assigned to nurses by doctors, nurses' own specific role, and the role of adapting the way work is organized (Feroni, 1994, p. 166-167).

---

1. In 2004, the percentage of female doctors in Japan was the lowest of all OECD countries; 16% as compared with 38% in France and the UK and 28% in the USA. But among the young Japanese doctors, under 29 years of age, the rate of feminization increased from 10%, in 1970, to 21%, in 1994 (OECD, 2006).

Once French nurses had dissociated their working lives from their personal lives, they were able to start thinking about the importance of qualifications. However, their occupational identity was still split between the role assigned to them by doctors and their own specific role, *i.e.*, between the requirements of the latest medical technology and their ideas about the professionalization which can be acquired at nurses' training schools. Japanese nurses still tend to give up their careers as soon as they get married or start having children. In addition, since no distinctions are made between nurses and nursing assistants in this country, they have difficulty in seeing the point of undergoing vocational training (*cf.* Hirata & Kergoat, 1988).

On the other hand, in addition to performing both domestic and technical tasks, nurses have to act as coordinators by solving the organizational problems arising at the workplace. French nurses therefore focus on personal initiatives and their relationships with their patients (corresponding to nurses' specific role), whereas the main role played by Japanese nurses is that of adapting the way work is organized.

FRENCH NURSES TORN BETWEEN THE ROLE ASSIGNED BY HOSPITAL DOCTORS AND NURSES' OWN PROFESSIONAL ROLE

Continuous occupational trajectories

Even as recently as the mid-20th century, it was difficult for French women to pursue a career. As soon as they got married and had children, they had to stop working:

> "Being a career woman was not felt to be very feminine; it was thought to be out of place for a woman to be ambitious, which is an intrinsically male quality. In any case, it meant giving up marriage and other things. Although there were no legal bars to marriage in France, such as those existing in other European countries, many occupations, from mining to hospital nursing, were open only to unmarried women. In 1900, nurses were housed at the establishments where they worked and closely supervised, whereas their male colleagues were allowed to take board and lodging elsewhere. Two thirds of the post office workers were 'young ladies'; and so were more than half of the secondary school teachers in 1954. The eldest daughter in a family owning a passementerie-manufacturing company in Saint-Étienne had to remain a spinster or marry late in life to be able to stay on with the firm." (Perrot, 1991, p. 204)

According to the latter author, spinsterhood was required in many walks of life so that women would be at their employers' complete disposal:

> "It seemed perfectly in order for female postal workers to take no holidays, nurses to be on duty on Sundays, and secretaries to have no closing hours. There was something religious about this expectation that women were devoted to their work, like housewives with their fluid, infinitely elastic working days, strictly regulated timetables." (*ibid.*, p. 204).

For D. Kergoat, the fact that women had to be completely at their employers' beck and call prevented them from dissociating their personal lives from/with their working lives, and thus from becoming fully involved in the "wage-labor nexus" (Boyer & Saillard, 1995), even when the "vocational calling" model was no longer in vogue (Kergoat, 1992, p. 62).

In addition, this requirement was liable to trigger a process of exclusion. This resulted in what Y. Knibiehler *et al*. Have called the "evaporation" of nursing staff which occurred in the 1960s because of nurses' poor living and working conditions:

> "Overburdened with many different tasks, nurses fled whenever they could into either marriage and private life, specialized jobs resulting from the latest technological innovations, or other occupational fields. In 1961-1962, the mean duration of nurses' working lives was only five years (or less than fifteen years, according to the most optimistic estimates). This exodus only worsened the burden placed on the shoulders of those who stayed behind." (Knibiehler *et al*., 1984, p. 275-276)

This process of exclusion from the world of employment was obviously due to the requirement made by hospital establishments that nurses should be at their complete disposal, which ran contrary to women's personal inclinations:

> "It may be worth mentioning here that the members of specifically female professions suffered from a particular handicap: they lacked the will to defend themselves. The laws of supply and demand should have come into play at this point: the shortage of nurses should have improved nurses' wages and their prestige, but this was not the case. Rather than fighting to improve their living and working conditions, the victims tended to flee into private family life, since working was only a makeshift occupation. This is what the so-called 'freedom of choice' granted to women actually amounted to." (*ibid*., p. 278)

During the events which occurred in France in May 1968, the upheavals which involved the whole of French society naturally had some effects on nurses. R. Magnon has described how the measures taken from then on to improve their working hours and conditions contributed greatly to decreasing the shortage of nursing personnel. Nevertheless, the greatest ever shortage of nurses occurred in France from 1960 to 1970 (Magnon, 1982, p. 89).

Since 1970, French nurses' working lives have lengthened considerably:

> "The mean duration of hospital nurses' working lives increased from 5 years in 1974 to 9.9 years in 1986 [...] although nurses were being recruited at an older age." (Feroni, 1994, p. 145)

However, in comparison with other professions, French nurses' working lives were very short. In 1989, only 44.7% of nurses with State diplomas had been working for more than 10 years, as compared with 69% in the case of primary school teachers (*ibid*., p. 145). I. Feroni attributed the subsequent lengthening of nurses' working lives to the introduction of part-time work, which made it easier to balance work and family life, as well as to the general tendency for women to have more continuous careers (*ibid*., p. 147). It was henceforth easier for women living with a partner to continue to pursue their careers:

> "Nurses' matrimonial status was beginning to resemble that of women in other walks of life. In 1986, only 29% of nurses were unmarried, as compared with 48% in 1975. [...] Based on a survey conducted in 1985, one out of every four nurses was a spinster between 40 and 49 years of age. It is worth noting that six out of ten of the nurses in this age-group are now living with a partner." (*ibid*., p. 148)

During the 1980s, French nurses therefore tended to strengthen their commitment to their careers, and most of them were pursuing more continuous occupational pathways.

Nurses as technicians: The role assigned by hospital doctors

During the second half of the 20th century, French doctors adopted a new attitude to hospital administration, which has been called a "participative" or "rationalizing" attitude (Steudler, 1974, p. 217). While the central administration was gradually acquiring greater power and drawing up rational health economics policies, the members of the medical profession were tending to participate more in decision-making processes at hospitals in order to apply their own professional logics (*ibid.*, p. 225). This relationship between the administration and the physicians might have been expected to prevent the process of nurses' professionalization from developing in France. However, the nurses' demand for their competences to be assessed by an elite body of peers was actually supported by the administrative and medical authorities as long as State qualified nurses continued to carry out the technical tasks assigned to them by the doctors, while being relieved of their more domestic tasks. This compromise was reached after the 1914-18 War:

> "Although nurses were still domestic servants in some respects in view of the tasks which fell to them, whereas the ward attendants were still performing tasks which would come under the heading of 'nursing' these days, the idea began to emerge that it was necessary to set up a hierarchy in order to obtain a stable group of hospital employees who were keen to pursue a career, as well as to rationalize the organization of work, since training nurses for technical jobs paid off better when their subordinates relieved them of the more domestic tasks." (Arborio, 2001, p. 31)

This "French-style compromise" therefore led to nurses with State-approved qualifications being differentiated from nursing assistants; this resulted in discussions about gender issues because nurses were being freed of the domestic tasks traditionally entrusted to women.

Immediately after the Second World War, progress in the field of medical technology transformed the content of nursing care: from 1945 to 1960, caring for patients switched from "mothering" to "technology" (Knibiehler *et al.*, 1984, p. 278-279). Some new types of medical intervention developed particularly fast:

> "Biological tests were being used to complement and confirm clinical findings. Making diagnoses and administering drugs require the ability to perform intravenous injections, draw blood, measure patients' pulse rate and blood pressure and handle the drips and probes." (*ibid.*, p. 280)

Now that all these technical activities were becoming so routinely practiced, it seemed to be possible to delegate them to nurses:

> "Since doctors could no longer be the only people performing these increasingly routine tasks, they handed them over to nurses. As one nurse recalled, 'before 1946, a very kind doctor taught me how to perform intravenous injections and then in 1950, the first arterial perfusions. I was only responsible for supervising patients undergoing blood transfusions because it was the doctor himself who set them up'." (*ibid.*, p. 280-281)

Before hospital physicians' status changed as the result of the Debré reforms passed in 1958[2], nurses had their own private working spheres with respect to that of the physicians:

---

2. The 1958 reform created the French University hospitals; it was pushed forward by Robert Debré, an eminent physician who had strong connections with political spheres.

> "Between the two World Wars, doctors used to be recruited by hospitals only on a part-time basis: they started to be given full-time contracts only between 1945 and 1958. At that time, the nurses, who were permanently on duty (like mothers looking after their children in their homes), were relatively autonomous." (*ibid.*, p. 292)

The 1958 reforms which made doctors' presence more strongly felt at hospitals favoured the "team approach" between nurses and doctors:

> "The full-time presence of doctors reduced the nurses' freedom and their responsibility, some-times in exchange for the team approach. The advent of new therapeutic methods and the risks involved created strong collective efforts among nurses to carry out their tasks successfully." (*ibid.*, p. 293)

In addition, because of the latest technological advances, nursing practices tended to revolve around a much more highly specialized and technical approach to medicine, especially at University teaching hospitals (or CHUs for *Centres Hospitalo-Universitaires*). These changes were referred to by I. Feroni as the "mutation of the nursing profession". In the first place, technical progress led to differentiating between various categories of hospital workers, na-mely between nurses, nursing assistants and ward attendants:

> "Three professions gradually emerged, starting in the fifties: nurses with State qualifications, who became the only members of staff entitled to call themselves nurses from 1946 onwards; nursing assistants; those belonging to the category of auxiliary nurses created 1949; and ward attendants (ASHs, *Agents de Service Hospitalier*), who carried out the heavy jobs" (Feroni, 1994, p. 71).

The numbers of health professionals, especially the numbers of State-qualified nurses, shot up at that time:

> "State-qualified nurses and psychiatric nurses numbered 305 000 in 1988, as against 77 000 in 1955. All the male and female nurses of all categories accounted for 40% of the county's total intermediate healthcare and occupational health workers." (*ibid.*, p. 74)

The mutation undergone by the nursing profession in France gave nurses the status of tech-nicians handling patients' bodies via potentially harmful instruments. The content of nurses' work therefore evolved in line with the activities delegated to them by doctors:

> "The changing medical practices led to a shift in the distribution of tasks between doctors and nurses, which had repercussions on all the other grades of hospital workers in turn. As the work of the doctors became increasingly complex, involving delicate exploratory and therapeutic interventions, other less complex and more everyday medical tasks extended the range of nurses' competences." (*ibid.*, p. 85)

These developments undermined the picture of nurses' feminine qualities. However, this picture was not completely shattered because the nursing profession was still a predominantly female profession, which had been based from the start on womanly qualities:

> "The reason why this was a woman's professional calling was that in the eyes of the pubic, women rather than men have the qualities one would like to encounter if one fell ill. One would be glad to find a smiling, kindly, pleasant, friendly, amiable, available, gentle person at one's bedside – in short, somebody with the qualities inherent to women as much as to nurses." (Charles, 1981, p. 25)

The fact that men have been joining the profession might seem to contradict the idea that it requires typically feminine qualities. However, the fact that the nursing profession is becoming mixed has led to another form of differential: "[...] although it is now recognized that men can join this profession, they are not perceived as being equipped to carry out the same tasks as female nurses" (*ibid.*, p. 25). Male nurses tend to be given the more technical tasks, whereas female nurses are again being pushed into the more domestic ones. However, when nurses demanded to have their qualifications recognized, they defined themselves as technicians and thus abandoned their claim to feminine qualities:

> "This rather pallid, outdated image did not reflect the many activities and roles of present-day nurses. In the days of women's liberation and their necessary integration into the technical world, nurses themselves were rightly rejecting this image of bigots which the public too frequently held up to them." (*ibid.*, p. 27)

As I. Feroni has suggested, men entered the nursing profession at the very moment when it was undergoing a technical mutation. It was only in the 1960s that this highly feminine profession became accessible to men, apart from those who were military and psychiatric nurses:

> "The fact that men became eligible in 1961 to study general nursing care at schools of nursing, which was confirmed by law in 1984, did not result in a radical change in the sexual structure of the profession. Male nurses accounted for 6.7% of the State-qualified nurses working at public hospitals in 1975, and this figure had increased to only 11% by 1991." (Feroni, 1994, p. 148-149)

R. Magnon has insisted on the need for the nursing profession to be mixed so as to put an end to the myth that the profession was based on feminine qualities:

> "Male nurses destroyed the parental image projected by the doctor and his nurse and that of the devoted female nurse endowed with exceptionally kind and gentle qualities [...]." (Magnon, 1982, p. 85)

The process of professionalization: Nurses' own professional role

As we have seen in the sphere of hospital practices, the advent of medical technology has led to nurses having to play the role delegated to them by doctors: nurses have become technicians. In the training sphere, however, the accent was placed on developing the nurses' own professional role and the important relational aspects involved.

In the early 1950s, the training dispensed by French schools of nursing was focusing on illnesses, and little attention was paid to the role nurses were supposed to play:

> "Nurses are technicians dispensing care. They have to carry out prescriptions. The definition of nursing given in the 1946 Health Code's definition of nursing reflects this picture quite well, and the 1951 training program was based directly on the previous text. It is significant that the preamble to this program contained no mention whatsoever of the respective occupational aims which ought to be pursued by student nurses, student nursing assistants and student midwives, who pursued the same curriculum [...] during their first year of study." (Charles, 1981, p. 39-40)

As the latter author pointed out, the lack of a specific function deprived the nursing of its significance:

"From this point of view, nurses existed only in terms of disease. But disease means consulting a doctor. [...] In addition, the way tasks were distributed, which obliged hospital nurses to work 'piecewise', and the lack of emphasis on the human aspects of nursing care exacerbated nurses' impression of being nothing but inconsistent parasites. After losing their religious aura, the reduction of their work to simply performing technical tasks which often had to be performed in a piecewise way with the emphasis on the disease stripped the nurses' function of its significance." (*ibid.*, p. 40)

During the 1950s, further education for nurses was flourishing in France. Many schools training nursing staff were created between 1950 and 1960, starting with the Red Cross school in 1951 and the Public Assistance school in Paris, which opened in 1954. By 1970, every region in France had a school of nursing.

The concept of the nurses' specific role was introduced into the training programme in 1961. This was defined as follows:

"Nurses had to be first and foremost healthcare technicians, but the training they receive enabled them not only to dispense care appropriately but also to take on certain responsibilities by looking after their patients from the point of view of their comfort, their daily requirements and the course of their disease, etc., or how they were withstanding their treatment, in order to be able to detect in good time any changes indicating that the treatment needed to be adjusted." (Charles, 1981, p. 41)

The definition of the nursing profession therefore evolved, and began to include the idea of providing patients with psychological, moral, and even pedagogical assistance. This new role of health trainer gave nurses some independence with respect to the hospital physicians.

As the years went by, the training programmes were revised, the duration of nurses' training became longer and nurses' "specific role" was eventually recognized. In 1972, their period of training was extended to 3 years and in 1979, the nursing profession was defined in terms of this specific role (Duboys Fresney & Perrin, 1996, p. 65-70).

The specific role of nurses which was officially defined in the 1978 Act was widely accepted by the nursing and teaching staff and used to promote the professionalization of nursing.

"The new image of the profession was transmitted at two levels:
– first among hospital nursing staff, especially among those with the highest grades, where it led to the development of policies promoting the idea of nurses' specific role, as well as promoting efforts to improve the quality of hospital care;
– and at the schools of nursing, where it contributed to changes being made in the curricula and the modes of practical assessment, which now focus on the ability to apply a genuine nursing process." (Feroni, 1992, p. 403)

French nurses' professional identity has therefore sometimes been split between the role attributed to nurses by hospital physicians and their own specific professional role. It is worth noting that the opposition between nurses' two roles led to an effective collective move to set up the nursing profession when the "Coordination" movement was created in 1988 (*cf.* Magnon, 2001, p. 106-109).

A survey on the New York health establishments (acute-care and long-term care hospitals and community healthcare centres) depending on the Health and Hospital Corporation (HHC) gives an idea of what this movement was about in comparison with what was going on in the USA. The HHC was founded in 1970 for the purpose of operating New York's City Hospitals. The New York City HHC, at which this survey was conducted, is the largest non-profit making hospital system in the USA[3]: it covers all the districts in New York (Manhattan, Bronx, Queens, Brooklyn, Staten Island).

The section of the HHC survey in which the various qualitative and quantitative components of nursing care are examined shows by comparison what scope for improvements existed in the French APHP (*l'Assistance Publique des Hôpitaux de Paris*) system at that time and what reforms would have to be carried out in the future.

In 1987, the HHC had already implemented all the projects relating to the organization of nursing care which were still in the embryonic phase in France (recognition of the nursing profession, defining nurses' responsibilities, providing patients with individual care, improving nurses' career paths and nurses' training); the one problem which still remained to be solved in New York was the shortage of nurses.

The conditions under which the nursing profession was carried out at the HHC hospitals in 1987, where the main principles adopted were optimum service to patients, tightly controlled budgets and internal and external risk management, confirmed that the lines on which the IDEs were working in France were sound. The new methods adopted involved keeping traceable written records, systematically recording and assessing all the procedures used, and promoting nurses' ability to contribute to all the stages (nursing diagnoses, keeping nursing records) in the process of in-patients' and outpatients' treatment.

In addition, nurses have been acquiring cross-departmental functions since some members of the profession have been acquiring specialized skills (as clinical nurses, nurses trained in the reception and dispatching of patients, emergency nurses, etc.): the existence of these specialities motivated many nurses to pursue their profession.

The existence of cross-departmental functions of this kind had effects in terms of governance. Each establishment was headed by an Executive Director, who was appointed by the hospital's General Director, with the assistance of the Medical Advisory Board, of which the Head Nursing Manager was a full member. The Executive Director was responsible for defining the

---

3. At that time, the HHC included 11 acute care hospitals, 5 long-term care hospitals, 5 local family healthcare centres and a set of satellite centres, some of which were specialized (in the abuse of drugs or alcohol, mental disease, etc.), as well as dealing with emergency patient transport. These hospitals had signed many contracts with University medical departments and other leading hospitals on joint healthcare and research projects. The HHCs account nowadays for 11,000 beds, including 6,100 at short stay units and 1,350 at psychiatric units: their capacity has therefore decreased by 2,000 beds in comparison with 1975 as the result of the economic crisis, and especially the financial crisis which recently hit the City of New York. It is also worth noting that external consultations, emergency care and home healthcare play a particularly important role in this healthcare system. These data were collected by Maryse Boulongne-Garçin.

healthcare philosophy and the goals to be achieved, drawing up the hospital budget, recruiting nursing staff, maintaining the healthcare monitoring system, and organizing the development and implementation of nurses' training and continuing vocational training programmes.

However, these responsibilities were shared out because of the highly structured hierarchy which existed at Hospital Nursing Departments. In addition to the classical hierarchical scheme, responsibility for specific hospital teams and/or patients was allocated as follows:

– The Head Nurse Instructor was responsible for training nurses and "licensed practical nurses" working at specific units such as coronary care units;
– Clinical nursing specialists were nurses with appropriate training and experience for dealing with specific groups of patients, such as cancer patients in particular and more recently, patients with AIDS.

These nurses were responsible for assessing patients, choosing appropriate interventions and assessing the outcomes; they were also in charge of training and informing staff nurses and assisting patients' families.

Their role was therefore three-fold: providing patients and their families and healthcare teams with expertise and advice; and dispensing information to specific communities (such as colleagues, firms and groups at risk).

Other nurses were responsible for dispatching emergency patients: the emergency wards at these hospitals were always overrun. These specialized nurses were in charge of collecting administrative information about incoming patients, noting their observations about their state of health and directing them to the appropriate emergency unit as quickly as possible to ensure that they would be given the best possible attention.

However, the recruitment of nurses was setting decision-makers a serious problem at that time in the USA, because the nursing profession was not sufficiently attractive. There was a high rate of turnover in hospital teams, the numbers of students enrolled at schools of nursing decreased by 20% from 1984 to 1986, and the numbers of school pupils enrolled in initial vocational training programmes for future nurses decreased by 13.6% during the same period. In 1986, 15% of the budget allocated to nurses' wages was not spent. This situation raised questions about the quality of care and led to attempts to re-organize the management of healthcare and improve hospital employees' careers by increasing their responsibility for patients' treatment in exchange for extra bonuses. The changes made on these lines focused mainly on staff nurses, who were subdivided into 3 levels, depending on their experience: this incited nurses to pursue their careers further and since they were able to obtain promotion within a shorter period of time, this had stabilizing effects on the nursing profession as a whole.

As in France, the distribution of nursing staff to the various facilities depended on the medical specialities involved and the way the establishments were organized, as well as on the diseases treated, the healthcare standards, the levels of qualification required, and on specificities such as nurses' ability to work in emergency wards, outpatient units and operating theatres. A system of patient classification was set up in order to identify the staff requirements of each type of hospital department. For this purpose, the nursing time required by each patient per 24 hours was defined on the basis of a set of indicators: the administrative time per patient, the modes of treatment (basic nursing care, technical interventions, patient training, personal contacts), and a set time was also allowed for the indirect activities devoted to the patients.

This system of classification was assessed regularly in order to determine what changes had occurred in terms of new pathologies (AIDS), new modes of treatment resulting from the latest medical findings and the latest modes of organization (such as outpatient care and hospital stays lasting less than 24 hours).

Research on nursing time management had only just started in France during that period, based on the Canadian Nursing Research Programme (PRN) and the Individual Patients' Nursing Care Programme (SIIPS) launched in French nursing research circles.

At a time when it was thought to be out of place to mention the introduction of nursing care plans, the HHC hospitals became aware that hospital nursing teams could contribute importantly to the organization, assessment and provision of care. Incoming patients were diagnosed by the nurses in terms of their own skills, the actions required were defined and the outcomes were subsequently assessed. The nursing care plan became an integral part of the patient record and served as a basis for assessing the methods of treatment and following patients' progress. The various health insurance systems obliged hospitals to assess the quality of the services they rendered to their "customers". Healthcare units, therefore had to develop relevant standards for dispensing care, systematically apply quality assurance methods and justify the care dispensed, as well as defining the healthcare models adopted using generic indicators in order to reduce the financial liabilities. In 1987, hospital institutions in New York were subject to three levels of control: those exerted by the JCAH at national level, the State of New York, and the HHC Corporation.

The last point worth mentioning is that at all levels of responsibility, the healthcare procedures used were regularly assessed on the basis of standards defined in documents which could be readily consulted by all healthcare professionals; these assessments were followed when necessary by recommendations and adjustments, in which all the actors in the healthcare process were involved. These procedures dynamised nursing research, were integrated into the content of nurses' training programmes and featured among the objectives defined by the hospital departments. In parallel, nursing colleges' programmes were accredited by the National League of Nursing (NLN), which organized symposia and programmes on relevant topics, published several journals and trained nurses to carry out research.

In France, by comparison, since nurses did not keep systematic records and few if any formal nursing procedures were used, healthcare activities were not assessed and nursing research was in its infancy. On the other hand, it was only after the turn of the century that healthcare establishments began to be subjected to a national system of assessment (thanks to ANAES, and later to HAS) in this country.

JAPANESE NURSES' DIFFICULTY IN ESTABLISHING THE IMPORTANCE OF QUALIFICATIONS

Career paths disrupted by marriage

In the mid-1970s, French women's working lives were almost a long as those of men. The occupational trajectories of those born in the 50s, who arrived on the labour market during the 70s, were practically continuous (Battagliola, 2000, p. 81-83). Based on the OECD statistics, 25% of female French employees in the 20- to 54- year-old age-group were working part-time during the years 1985 to 1987 (OECD, 1994, p. 95); whereas the curve describing Japanese women' activity rates between 1979 and 1989 showed a trough, corresponding to the fact that they stopped working at the birth of their first child (*ibid.*, p. 64; see also Chapter 5 of this book). In addition, part-time work, which accounted for only about 15% of female Japanese employees in the 20- to 24-year old age-group increased to more than 30% after the age of 25 (*ibid.*, p. 96). The occupational trajectories of Japanese women were therefore much more discontinuous than those of their French counterparts.

Based on the statistics published by the Japanese Ministry of Labour (the Department for Women and Children), M. Kaneko noted that in 1950, 70% of Japanese nurses had been working at the same establishment for less than 3 years. The average working lives of nurses in the lower grades was only 2 years and 6 months, whereas that of matrons was 8 years and 2 months (Kaneko, 1992, p. 207). Since nurses' working lives, like those of other categories of female employees, were not compatible with their family lives, they were unable to pursue continuous careers. Nurses' working conditions at that time indeed constituted a very real social issue:

> "According to the stipulations of the Japanese Labour Code, the legal working day consisted of 8 hours of work, and since workers were entitled to one day off per week, they worked 48 hours per week. The Code allowed nurses to work up to 9 hours per day, amounting 54 hours per week. However, nurses' average working week often amounted in fact to 56.2 hours. In other words, they worked more than 9 hours per day. [...] Nurses were therefore putting in longer hours than factory and office workers (who worked 48.3 hours per week in the public sector and 45.6 hours in the private sector)." (*Ibid.*, p. 200-201)

The number of working hours was therefore challenged, and so were the nurses' night shifts. At that time, most Japanese hospitals had adopted a three-shift system of rotation: the daytime, afternoon and night shifts:

> "Working at night was extremely problematic, especially for married nurses, since it made it difficult for them to look after their children [...] In 1963, the national union of healthcare workers demanded better night work conditions at public hospitals. They asked to have the number of night shifts reduced to six nights per month per nurse, and to have at least two nurses on night shift duty in each ward (consisting of less than 40 beds). In 1965, the Commission responsible for settling problems arising in the civil service concluded that the number of night shifts should first be reduced to eight per month and that the work schedules should be reorganized so that more than one nurse would always be on night duty in each ward." (*ibid.*, p. 203)

This Commission's recommendations were not legally binding, however. They simply consti-tuted a long term project which was submitted to the hospital establishments. In 1968, the nurses all over the country went on strike, demanding that these recommendations should be applied. This demand was referred to as the "two eights" *(ni-pachi)*, meaning that two nurses should be on duty every night, and each nurse should be on night duty only eight nights per month. The recommendations of the Commission were eventually adopted by the hospital establishments *(ibid.,* p. 203-204).

However, Japanese nurses' conditions of work still had not improved sufficiently for their career paths to be continuous. Based on the statistics published by the Japanese Nursing Association, the mean age of Japanese nurses of both sexes was only 35.7 years in 1992, and that of the auxiliary nurses of both sexes was only 35.2 years. In terms of their family status, 63.4% of Japanese nurses of both sexes were married, and 55.3% had children. Japanese nurses were therefore still tending to give up their occupational activities at a certain point in their family lifecycle. The careers of Japanese nurses therefore come to a stop when they marry or when they start to have children. Based on the results of a survey conducted by the Japanese Nursing Association, marriage and childbirth are the main reasons why Japanese nurses stop working either temporarily or for good. Those who return to work later on opt for part-time jobs:

> "[...] the main reason for giving up nursing is marriage (42%), and the second reason is to raise a family (38%). 93% of those who gave up their nursing career had children: 50% of this group had children under two years of age and 73% had children under six years of age. 16% had worked for more than 10 years and 52% had worked for more than 5 years. When asked whether they intended to go back to work, 48% stated that they would like to work on a part-time basis, mainly in order to be able to choose the days and hours on which they worked and to avoid having to do night shifts." *(ibid.,* p. 12-13)

The nurses employed at the large Japanese hospitals mostly have full-time contracts. Those looking for part-time jobs after a period of inactivity therefore have to apply to the small hospitals and clinics. Stopping work for family reasons therefore reduces the range of jobs available.

Lack of distinction between nurses and nursing assistants

To describe the evolution of the nursing profession in Japan during the second half of the 20th century, it is necessary to recall the traditional Japanese approach, whereby patients were cared for by members of their own family. As we have seen above, nursing was intro-duced into Japan only at the end of the 19th century, when Western medical practices were adopted as part of the process of modernization. The fact that the nursing profession has a very short history in this country has affected the development of this profession and the way it is practised. As far as "basic care" was concerned, the Japanese nurses had to rely up to 1994 on patients' family members and the external care workers *(tsukisoi)* engaged by patients' families. This explains why there are no nursing assistants at Japanese hospitals. M. Kawashima has explained as follows why the use of external nursing staff fitted in with traditional Japanese customs:

> "According to Japanese customs, anyone who is sick is supposed to have a personal career. Even if there are hospital nurses in charge, patients expect to be accompanied by a relative or a personal attendant. That's the Japanese tradition." (Kawashima, 1997, p. 75)

After the 1945 defeat, the occupying Allied Forces' General Headquarters proposed to reform some sectors of Japanese society. Grace Elisabeth Alt, an American nurse who had the rank of Army Captain, made an important contribution to reforming the health care system (Kaneko, 1992, p. 2-6). At the center for hospital administration research *(byoin kanri kenkyu-jo)* set up in Tokyo in 1948, it was attempted to introduce the American system of hospital administration (Kaneko, 1994, p. 91-94).

An American physician called C.F. Sams, who was Head of Public Health and Social Assistance at the Allied Forces' General Headquarters from 1945 to 1951, reported that hospitals were organized differently in Japan and the United States. Unlike their American counterparts, Japanese physicians were employed on a full-time basis and were strongly involved in hospital administration work. The fact that hospital directors were physicians themselves shows how strongly the medical authorities were involved in the running of the hospitals (Sams, 1998, p. 122).

This situation was not at all favourable to the professionalization of Japanese nurses. As C.F. Sams also pointed out, Japanese doctors did not feel it was essential for the hospital staff to include nurses.

However, the idea of abolishing the practice of having patients accompanied by relatives or nurses engaged outside the hospital was eventually taken up in 1950, when a system of "complete nursing care" was instituted. This system failed to work, however:

> "The system of 'complete nursing care' *(kanzen-kango)* set up in 1950 meant that the external care workers *(tsukisoi)* were banned from the hospitals. But the requirements for nursing staff were not defined in this system. Nurses' conditions of work therefore deteriorated and unpaid trainee nurses were recruited to dispense basic care." (Kawashima, 1997, p. 64)

In 1958, a so-called standardized system of nursing care *(kijun-kango)* was at last introduced, which defined the standard requirements by imposing the ratio of one nurse for every four patients, but since auxiliary nurses were included in this staff ratio, this meant that the numbers of properly qualified nurses could be reduced *(ibid.,* p. 64-65).

Modern medical technology began to put in an appearance at Japanese hospitals during the 1960s; but the nursing staff was too small to be able to cope with the increase in the number of tasks which resulted from these innovations. The plan to abolish recourse to external nurses was therefore not put into practice:

> "In principle, external care workers should have disappeared from the scene, but they actually continued to accompany patients as they had always done, on the grounds that the patients needed them. The hospital nursing staff certainly did not suffice to provide the patients with their requirements." *(ibid.,* p. 66)

Nevertheless, the practice of recruiting nurses outside the hospitals was eventually abolished. In the new nursing system *(shin-kango-taikei)* launched in 1994 (after the 1988 social movement), the advanced University teaching hospitals employed one nurse for every two patients. But because of the lack of differentiation between nurses and nursing assistants, Japanese nurses did not challenge the idea that feminine qualities are associated with dispensing basic care. They found it difficult to establish a fair qualification nexus, whether in playing the role attributed to them by hospital physicians or whether they were playing their own specific role as nurses. In response to the increasing number of technical tasks arising without any corresponding increase in the numbers of hospital staff, nurses tended to focus on how to adapt to hospital organization.

In a comparative study on the nursing profession in Japan and other countries, C. Arai has described how the density of hospital beds increased in Japan as the economy ruined by the 1945 defeat gradually recovered. At the same time, however, the density of the nursing staff has remained fairly low:

The number of nurses per 10 000 inhabitants is relatively low in Japan. This ratio amounted to 84.6 in Sweden in 1985, as compared with 83 in the United States in 1984, 66 in France in 1977, and 63.4 in Japan in 1988. (Arai, 1992, p. 8-9). As we will see in Part III, this situation has not changed very much since then.

It is worth noting, however, that in these comparisons, C. Arai took only the number of qualified nurses into account. If assistant nurses were included, the density in France and other Western countries would increase two-fold, whereas the figure would remain almost unchanged in Japan. C. Arai has described as follows the problems focusing on the number of nurses employed at hospitals:

> "For instance, one nurse may be assigned to care for two patients regardless of the kind of care require. Whereas patients must have 24 hours attention, it is impossible for any one nurse to put in 24 hours of work. A nurse therefore, would have to care for six patients by simple calculation taking into consideration, three shifts per day. With introduction of five-day work-week from 365 days a year, nurses take more than 120 days off. In other words, only about 70% of all nurses are on duty on any given day. This means a nurse must care for eight or nine patients. In reality, the nursing personnel is sometimes reduced on night shifts, with just two to three nurses on duty. This reflects an effort to maintain the level of daytime nursing care by assigning more nurses during the day." (*ibid.*, p. 9)

The American approach to the organization of nurses' work partly solved these problems. *Functional nursing*, as it was called, involved nurses being specialized in specific tasks (applying bandages, for example). This system was then replaced by *team nursing*, where the work was divided into a hierarchy of simple and complex tasks, executive tasks and responsibilities[4]. This led to the development of the group leader's role:

> "A nurse who has been working on the site for some years obviously perform superior work compared to one fresh out of school, both in terms of quality and quantity of work. When experienced nurses leave and the same number of less experienced nurses are hired in their place, this will increase the burden of senior nurses who must supervise new nurses in order to maintain the quality of patient care." (*ibid.*)

---

4. See Petitat, 1989, pp. 151-180 for an explanation of the content of nurses' work system.

Unlike French nurses, who delegate the domestic tasks to assistant nurses, Japanese nurses, whose work is not differentiated from that of assistant nurses, experience a permanent dichotomy between the domestic role and the role attributed to them by the hospital doctors. The proposal put forward by the Allied Forces in their hospital reform project that the practice of recruiting external care workers should be abolished did not lead to introduction of nursing assistants, but forced nurses to find ways of adapting their activities to the organization of hospital work.

As reported by M. Kaneko, who was responsible for nursing practices at the Japanese Ministry of Health during the early 1950s, the idea of adopting two categories, "nurses with State diplomas" and "assistant nurses", was refused; but in 1951, it was decided to introduce the two levels of training proposed by the medical profession: nurses with the State diploma and auxiliary nurses. However, no distinctions were made between the tasks allotted to each of these two categories although they did not undergo the same training:

> "The administration decided to examine the numbers of nurses required and their levels of competence. Note that there was a shortage of qualified nurses (nurses who had undergone 3 years of vocational training after their secondary schooling). The question of the financial cost of nursing staff also had to be solved. In Japan, two-thirds of the medical care is dispensed at private clinics and consultancies, which absorb large numbers of nurses. The medical profession therefore strongly supported the existence of nurses with low levels of education and training (primary schooling + 2 years of vocational training), who are still performing the work of nurses these days, in line with the regulations adopted in 1915. It was only after the departure of the Allied Forces' Headquarters that debates at the National Assembly led to the category of auxiliary nurse *(jun-kango-hu)* being instituted." (Kaneko, 1995, p. 54)

As we can imagine, the fact that separate vocational training led to performing a single function required considerable flexibility on the part of nurses to be able to adapt to the hospital institutions' logics. The fact that no distinctions were made between the two categories of nursing staff meant that nurses were not relieved of the domestic tasks, which made it difficult for them to tackle the issue of gender relations in what was generally regarded as an exclusively feminine walk of life.

The diversification of basic vocational training for nurses

The Japanese Nursing Association was created in 1947, when the legislation on the nursing profession was being revised under the aegis of the Allied Forces Headquarters. The law on public health nurses, midwives and nurses was promulgated in 1948, and the regulations on the training of these professionals came into force in 1949. In comparison with the 1915 regulations, which allowed for various levels of vocational training, the 1948 regulations improved the levels of training by extending the period of training to 3 years:

> "The regulations on the training of public health nurses, midwives and nurses in general made provision for a 3-year course of basic vocational training: to qualify for this course, applicants had to have obtained the secondary school-leaving diploma. In addition to this basic training program, further 6-month courses were run for public health/hospital nurses and midwives." (Japanese Nursing Association, 1993, p. 14)

At the departure of the Allied Forces in 1951, the Japanese Ministry of Health, with the support of the Japan Physicians' Association, created another lower vocational training course for auxiliary nurses. This 2-year course was open to applicants who had completed their primary schooling (Kaneko, 1992, p. 216-242, and Japanese Nursing Association, 1993, p. 14). In other words, after the reform introduced by the Allied Forces' Headquarters with a view to improving the level of training, the Japanese and medical powers-that-be succeeded in maintaining dual vocational training paths. Auxiliary nurses *(jun-kangohu)* and fully qualified nurses *(sei-kangohu)* all performed the same tasks despite the difference between their levels of education and vocational training. The hospital establishments distinguished between the two categories, however, in their recruitment practices: nurses who had undergone the 3-year training course were recruited by large hospitals and less highly trained auxiliary nurses obtained jobs at small private clinics.

The vocational training reform in the field of nursing was not only a matter of legislation. Under the aegis of the Allied Forces Headquarters, three schools of nursing (two in Tokyo and one in Okayama) were raised to the rank of pilot schools. The pilot school in Tokyo (Tokyo Demonstration School of Nursing), for example, was created in 1946 at the initiative of four American teachers of nursing with a view to creating links between the Japanese Red Cross and the Saint-Luke's School of Nursing, which was created in 1920 with the help of the American Episcopalian Church (Kaneko, 1992, p. 50-56). S. Takahashi, who carried out several périods of internship in the States in 1948-1949 before becoming involved in the training of nurses at the pilot school in Tokyo, mentions the meetings or "conferences" which were arranged between the members of a team and the spirit of "team nursing" with which not only trainee nurses but also nurses at the start of their hospital careers were inculcated at that time:

> "At the 'conferences', trainee nurses described their patients' cases and discussed how they should be treated and why. These 'conferences' were therefore intended to teach them several things. [...] Sometimes it was the teacher who presented a problem arising at the hospital ward; on other occasions, the physician was asked to explain a particular medical diagnosis." (Takahashi, 1998, p. 9-14).

The introduction of these group meetings can be said to have been the starting point in the development of hospital nurses' vocational training in Japan. These privileged moments of communication served not only to acquire knowledge but also to carry out "nursing research". The directors of the large Japanese hospitals supported the development of these groups promoting "reflection, projects, direct experience, quality, etc." (Dubar & Tripier, 1998, p. 233).

In 1967, the basic vocational training programme was reformed by the Japanese Ministry of Health. The training dispensed up to then at Japanese schools of nursing had been similar to what was learned on the job, in that the emphasis was placed on the practical rather than the theoretical aspects. Practical work experience, which often meant that students were serving as unpaid nurses, accounted for two thirds of the teaching hours. The new programme adopted in 1967 reduced the proportion of the time devoted to acquiring practical on-the-job experience (Ujiie, 1998, p. 198-219). On the other hand, after acquiring this initial vocational training, would-be teachers of nursing had to train for a further 6 months in 1966 as compared with 3 months previously, and this period of training was extended to one year in 1976 (Kaneko, 1992, p. 61-62).

Just as many young Japanese youths were gaining access to higher education, training in nursing was gradually integrated into University curricula: first at University institutes (which ran 3-year courses), and subsequently at the Universities themselves (which ran 4-year courses). Training courses for nurses therefore became quite diversified, since there was a choice between University, University institutes, training schools for nurses and training schools for auxiliary nurses. This pattern of diversity has been described as follows:

> "The existence of licensed auxiliary nurses has been a hindrance to the development of nursing as a profession. The Japanese Nursing Association among others had long worked to abolish the auxiliary nurse education. They have been able, however, to stop the training of nurses who can be easily hired at low pay. Due to the overwhelming collective power of medical doctors, Japan's nursing education remains backward even by the standards of many developing countries. In 1991, nearly 20,000 nurses graduated from the 478 registered three years courses. In the same year, nearly 15,000 students graduated from 412 extension courses, mentioned earlier. Around 3,500 graduated from 58 three year junior colleges, and a mere 487 or less than 1.3% of all graduates, completed the four years college course in that year. It is difficult to call nursing a profession when only 1.3% of the fresh nurses are college graduated." (Arai, 1992, p. 7)

In the end, the training dispensed at Universities and University institutes has not generated a new approach to vocational qualifications among nurses. In the first place, like those with diplomas delivered by schools of nursing, most University graduates do not manage to pursue continuous careers. Holding University qualifications has not speeded up the rates of promotion, even among those in the higher hierarchical grades *(cadres)*. Giving qualifications a real meaning can be said to require challenging the "extraneous" status of Japanese nurses and dissociating their work from their personal lives, which is a prerequisite for nurses to enter the wage-labor nexus (Kergoat, 1992, p. 59 et p. 62).

CONCLUSION

Since the 1960s, the role of nurses has become increasingly technical because of the development of advanced medical technology. Since nurses have accepted this role, they have had to delegate the nursing jobs to nursing assistants, so that their gender is no longer tied up with their occupational image. At the same time, in order to be able to respond to the needs of patients and their families, nurses felt the need for greater autonomy and specific know-how setting them apart from the medical profession while giving them a complementary role to play. The development of initial and continuing vocational courses leading to the acquisition of proper qualifications strengthened these two aspects of the profession by making them more widely accepted and put into practice.

Up to the 1945 defeat, the "interventionist" model imposed in Japan by the administrative and medical authorities predominated, abolishing the former gender differentials resulting from the fact that women were traditionally supposed to dispense care only to members of their own families. Traditional gender relations were subsequently restored, however, when nursing came to be strictly associated with women's domestic role.

From the reforms introduced by the Allied Forces up to the present day, as hospital patients gradually ceased to be accompanied by members of their family, Japanese nurses were obliged to act as "quasi-nursing assistants". The administrative and medical authorities' heavy-handed management prevented even qualified nurses from being differentiated from nursing assistants, especially as the institution of University training courses for nurses did not result in the promotion of those who obtained these vocational qualifications. As a result, Japanese nurses did not succeed in improving their conditions of work in order to be able to forge and maintain continuous career paths.

The following hypothesis might be put forward to explain the existence of this difference between France and Japan: in France, the need to reach a compromise between professional and institutional logics abolished the idea that nursing required typically feminine qualities, which opened the doors of hospital wards to male nurses as well as enhancing the social image of the nursing profession. In the case of Japan, the former institutional logics predominated and resulted in the sexual division of labour being maintained. It was therefore extremely difficult to set up a profession devoid of gender connotations.

REFERENCES

• Arai C. Problems of nursing in Japan: basic education, shortage and adapting to changes. *NWEC Newsletter* 1992; IX (1), Tokyo: National Women's Education Centre.

• Arborio AM. *Un personnel invisible. Les aides-soignantes à l'hôpital.* Paris: Anthoropos, 2001.

• Battagliola F. *Histoire du travail des femmes.* Paris: La Découverte, 2000.

• Boyer R, Saillard Y. *Regulation theory, the state of the art.* London: Routledge, 1995.

• Charles G. *L'Infirmière en France d'hier à aujourd'hui.* Paris: Le Centurion, 1979.

• Charles G. *Quel avenir pour l'infirmière française ?* Paris: Le Centurion, 1981.

• DREES. Les cinq premières années de carrières des infirmiers sortis de formation initiale. In: Marquier R. DRESS, *Études et Résultats* 2005; n° 393.

• DREES. *Démographie des Professions de santé*, novembre 2009.

• Dubar C, Tripier P. *Sociologie des professions.* Paris: Armand Colin, 1998.

• Duboys Fresney C, Perrin G. *Le Métier d'infirmière en France. Du métier d'infirmière à l'exercice professionnel des soins infirmiers.* Paris: PUF, 1996.

• Feroni I. La Rhétorique de la profession d'infirmière, le cas de la formation. *Gestion Hospitalière* 1992; n° 316.

• Feroni I. *Les Infirmières hospitalières*, Ph D Thesis. Nice: Université de Nice Antipolis, 1994.

• Health and Welfare Statistics Association (Kosei-tokei-kyokai). *[Patients and medical institutions in Japan] (nippon no kanja to iryo-shisetsu).* Tokyo: Health and Welfare Statistical Association (Kosei-tokei-kyokai), 1995.

• Hirata H, Kergoat D. Rapport sociaux de sexe et psychologie du travail. In: C. Dejours (ed). *Plaisir et souffrance dans le travail*, t. 2. Paris: Éditions de l'AOCIP, 1988.

• Japanese Nursing Association *(nippon-kango-kyokai)*. *Nursing in Japan.* Tokyo: Japanese Nursing Association Press *(nippon-kango-kyoukai-shuppan)*, 1993.

• Japanese Nursing Association. *[Statistical Data on Nursing in Japan] (kango-kankei-toukei-shiryo).* Tokyo: Japanese Nursing Association Press *(nihon-kqngo-kyoukai-shuppan),* 2004 (1ˢᵗ edition 1995).

• Kaneko M. *[The administration of nursing care after the war] (Shoki-no-kango-gyosei),* Tokyo: Japanese Nursing Association Press *(Nippon-Kango-kyokai-shuppan),* 1992.

• Kaneko M. *[The light of nursing care] (kango-no-hi-takaku-kakagete).* Tokyo: Igaku-shoin, 1994.

• Kaneko M. [The past, the present and the future of the law of public health nurses, midwives and other nurses] *(Hokenhu-josanhu-kangohu-ho-no-kako-genzai-mirai). The Nursing care (Kango)* 1995; n° 12, Tokyo: Igaku-shoin.

• Kawashima M. *Questioning the hospital nursing care today (Ima-byouin-kango-wo-tou),* Tokyo, Keiso-shobo, 1997.

• Kergoat D, Imbert F, Le Doaré H, Senotier D. *Les infirmières et leur coordination, 1988-1989.* Paris: Lamarre, 1992.

• Knibiehler Y, Leroux-Hugon V, Dupont-Hess O, Tastayre Y. *Cornettes et blouses blanches ; les infirmières dans la société française.* Paris: Hachette, 1984.

• Magnon R. *Le Service infirmier ces trente dernières années.* Paris: Le Centurion, 1982.

• Magnon R. *Les Infirmières. Identité, spécificité et soins infirmiers, le bilan d'un siècle.* Paris: Masson, 2001.

• OCDE. *Les Femmes et le changement structurel.* Paris: OCDE, 1994.

• OCDE. *Plus de femmes médecins.* OCDE, 2006 (web site: observateurocde.org.juillet).

• Perrot M. *Les Femmes ou les silences de l'histoire.* Paris: Flammarion, 1991.

• Petitat A. *Les Infirmières. De la vocation à la profession.* Montréal: Boréal, 1989.

• Sams CF. *Medic, the mission of an American military doctor in occupied Japan and Wartorn Korea.* New York: An East Gate Book, 1998.

• Steudler F. *L'Hôpital en observation.* Paris: Armand Colin, 1974.

• Takahashi S. *[The dawn of the modern Japanese nursing] (nihon-kindai-Kango no yoake).* Tokyo: Igaku-shoin, 1998.

• Ujiie S. [The reform of the training program for nurses in 1967] *(kango-kyoiku-karikyuramu no 1967 nen kaisei).* In: *[The Japanese society for the history of nursing] (nihon-kango-rekishi-gakkai), [The evolution of nursing profession, 50 years after the war] (kensho, sengo-kango no 50 nen).* Tokyo: Mejikaru-Furendo, 1998.

Part II
The social worlds of French and Japanese nurses

In this part of the book, it is proposed to analyze two surveys carried out twenty years apart on French and Japanese nurses, based on interviews and questionnaires, with a view to documenting the main changes undergone by the nursing profession during this period. The aim is to determine the processes at work and how they have affected nurses' identity, as well as to describe the underlying logics and how they are perceived by nurses, who have also been involved themselves in setting up their profession. The accent will mainly be placed here first on nurses' commitment to their profession and their training and secondly, on their working relationships. These two important aspects depend on individuals, their attitude to their work and the strength of their links with the hospital institutions which employ them. Chapters 3 and 4 will focus on surveys conducted in France and Japan, respectively. In each case, the similarities and differences encountered in the recent history of the nursing profession in the two countries of interest will be briefly pointed out. However, the main comparisons between the French and Japanese nursing profession's relationships with hospital institutions will be made in Part III.

3. French Nurses' Social World: Setting up a fuzzily defined social group

As we will see in this chapter, the processes whereby French nurses have forged a professional identity have been based mainly on their commitment to their profession and their training, and on their work relationships and their social demands. But these processes have not led to any internal segmentation of the profession, for instance between nurses and matrons. Although they have resulted in a truly professional group, its solidity is due to tension between centripetal forces imposing homogeneity and centrifugal forces imposing heterogeneity.

It is worth mentioning that the first of these surveys was conducted in 1987-1989, when French nurses' social movement, known as *coordination infirmière*, was starting up, whereas the second survey was conducted in 2007-2008, in the context of the move to rationalize and restructure the hospital system which led to the introduction of the "new hospital governance" regime (including the re-organization of hospital departments into associated groups, known as "poles", or clusters).

The first survey was based on interviews with more than forty nurses and matrons working at two public hospitals in Paris. The characteristics of the population interviewed (their seniority, rank and sex) are given in *table 3.1*.

The interviews were homogenised to ensure that the findings obtained could be compared. When discussing the convention he called the "comparability convention" which is implicitly accepted by participants, E.C. Hughes stated that there is no point in conducting interviews unless they form a really comparable series of encounters (Hughes, 1996, p. 287).

At the time of this survey, it was naturally not planned to carry out a second survey twenty years later. But the fact that the interviews were directive gave the respondents' discourse a high level of comparability, both between the respondents in each series and between the two series. The same can be said of the Japanese surveys.

The interviews were carried out at the nurses' place of work. They lasted for one hour on average and the questions were planned in advance, based on formal guidelines (Glaser & Strauss, 1967, p. 105-113). The interviews were recorded and re-transcribed for future analysis.

For the sake of comparability, the 2007-2008 survey was conducted at the same hospital departments as the 1987-1988 survey. For reasons focusing on the nurses' availability and time, the second survey was based on questionnaires which were distributed to 73 nurses and matrons. The characteristics of this population are given in *table 3.2.*

Although the questionnaire used in 2007 was slightly more formal than the 1987 interview, it focused on the same items and the same aspects of the nursing profession. It also included some open questions: the responses to these questions could therefore be treated practically as if they were excerpts from interviews.

Table 3.1. *Sample included in the survey in 1987-1988.*

Seniority	Rank		Sex		Total
	Nurses	Matrons	Women	Men	
12 years or less	20	2	20	2	22
13 years or more	13	11	20	4	24
Total	33	13	40	6	46

Table 3.2. *Sample included in the survey in 2007-2008.*

Seniority	Position		Sex		Total
	Nurses	Matrons	Women	Men	
12 years or less	36	2	36	2	38
13 years or more	27	8	33	2	35
Total	63	10	69	4	73

COMMITMENT TO THE PROFESSION AND CONTINUING VOCATIONAL TRAINING

Dedication to hospital work in 1987-1988

Most French nurses speak about their career paths in terms of alternatives: they had to either attempt to find a balance between their work and their family lives or embark on a properly planned career. At the same time, their opinions about their relationships with hospital institutions and their profession consistently included references to the best place for obtaining the vocational training which would give them the additional skills required.

Nurses in the less senior group: Working to achieve a balance between family life and promotion at work and vocational training within the establishment

In the youngest age-group interviewed, in which the nurses had 12 years' seniority or less, the great majority of the respondents presented arguments in favour of achieving a balance between their work and their family lives. However, this was more of an ideal than a real-life situation. Whether or not they had children, they mentioned the need to find this balance, although this was not necessarily a problem with which they had to deal personally at the moment.

These nurses' statements about promotion and their careers and were on similar lines. They spoke about the possibility of being promoted and said they hoped for it (being upgraded or becoming specialized in child care, anaesthetic assistance or surgical nursing), especially by obtaining the necessary qualifications, but they perceived this promotion as something liable to occur only in the distant future.

Only one of the nurses interviewed said she regretted her choice of occupational mode and was considering adopting a different mode of operation. None of them said they wanted to leave the profession.

The nurses consistently stressed problems with their work schedules, both in connection with achieving a balance between their work and their personal lives and when talking about setting up career paths. The youngest nurses questioned had nearly always started off doing afternoon or night duty. They only obtained daytime shifts later on, depending on two criteria, namely their seniority and their family situation (whether or not they had a family to raise).

This was so in the case of D.N, a nurse with 7 years' seniority living with a partner, who had no children. She was on duty at the neurosurgical ward from 15:00 to 23:00. When asked how she planned to further her career, she gave a short answer, showing that although this was a concern, it was not yet of great personal importance:

> "Working as a matron, no, it does not appeal to me because it means taking up administrative work. Matrons are not constantly in charge of their patients. I would rather become specialized later on, in child care perhaps. Because you are still in touch with the patients."

This respondent had more to say on the subject of nurses' work schedules: she hoped to find a balance between her work and her personal life. Although the problem had not yet arisen, reaching this balance was already an objective which she planned to achieve by juggling with her timetable in the future:

> "I will have to change my working hours. But I don't want to work during the daytime. I prefer working between 13:00 and 21:00, because that's when the new team come on duty. At hospitals like this one, there are many married people on the staff. That means that in theory, three quarters of the people working in the morning are married and have children. Those on night duty are the most recently qualified and unmarried nurses. Those who are married like me don't mind working those hours at the beginning. But when you have children, it's hard to go on working up to 11 p.m. Because the hospital *crèche* [nursery] closes at 9 p.m. When I first arrived here, I heard that 25% of the nurses gave in their notice after five years. I don't know whether that's still true. But it probably is. When you have children at home, you have to be there occasionally during the day. Baby-sitters are too expensive."

When other nurses spoke about pursuing a career, the mentioned how difficult they expected to find balancing their personal lives and their work.

D.C., for example, who had 6 years' seniority, was living with a partner and had two children, spoke about her career prospects. She was working during the daytime in a surgical ward and was managing to achieve a balance between the requirements of home and work: *"Compatibility with family life is not a problem for me. I find my work perfectly compatible with my personal life."*

Unlike D.N., who mentioned the need to find a compromise between work and family life, D.C., who was preparing to sit the entrance examination to the matrons' training course, expressed her hope for promotion at work. She felt that promotion to the status of matron was a sign of progress in her career as well as providing an opportunity of *"having slightly different tasks and greater responsibility"*, while keeping to the same occupation: *"matrons also dispense care, after all."*

It should be mentioned here that being promoted to the rank of matron requires some sacrifices on the side of family life, since it is difficult at the beginning to find jobs on daytime shifts. Although D.C. was hoping to become a matron, she was aware of this problem:

> "[...] nurses start by doing night shifts. Later on, they obtain jobs with better hours. It's just the same with matrons. At the beginning, they will never be given daytime shifts (from 8 a.m. to 4 p.m.) and they have to take a night duty job. What attracts people mainly to the nursing profession is dispensing care and having direct contacts with patients. There is therefore a gap between nurses' profession and that of matrons. And once you have trained to be a matron, you have to do night shifts for 5 to 7 years before getting back to having a daytime job. Being a matron and fitting in your family life is not easy when you are married and have children."

The dynamic picture which emerged from nurses' statements, which took the form of descriptions of their projects, usually included a fairly clear description of the place where vocational training should be dispensed to those who hope for promotion, which needs to be made compatible with family life. Among the most recently qualified respondents, there were two ways of picturing the updating of knowledge.

Although the majority of the nurses interviewed said how much they had learned from practising their profession, especially in terms of the specific techniques used at the hospital unit where they were working, others attached some importance to qualifying vocational training courses.

Like other participants, B.R., who lived alone, had no children and had been on the afternoon shift at a rhumatological unit for 3 years, mentioned the gap between what one learns at nursing school and the skills required on the field. While recognizing the importance of learning the job by working with a team, she stressed how important it was for individual nurses to master the specific techniques used at a given hospital ward. She said it was essential to adapt to the latest technological developments applied at the ward, which is a matter of practice, although she did not minimize the theoretical bases acquired at nursing schools:

> "We work as a team. Whenever I have a problem, or my colleague has a problem, we put our heads together. We try to find what's best for the person involved. Theories are the same for everyone, but practices differ from one ward to another, and even from one nurse to another. The aim is to obtain the best possible results and the most hygienic conditions possible. Once we have learned

that during our studies, we cannot throw it overboard. Our work has to always take a continuous path. Then there is always the need to update knowledge. A lot of techniques keep on changing. After learning one thing, you have to learn something else six months later."

C.N., who was living with a partner but had no children, was on the afternoon shift at a neurosurgical unit. She had 6 years' seniority and was in favour of continuing vocational training being dispensed at the nursing school in order to become a nurse anaesthetist, a children's nurse or a matron, although she regretted that it was so hard to gain access to this training. Contrary to the previous respondent, C.N. attached particular importance to possibility of obtaining promotion via the continuing vocational qualifications dispensed at French public hospitals. She expressed the opinion that this pathway was a means of obtaining social recognition:

> "Some people think nursing is nothing at all, just like being a domestic help. In my opinion, we should continue our training after becoming a nurse, develop other occupational skills, learn to do other things. In France, there are schools for becoming nurse anaesthetists, operation theatre nurses [so-called *panseuses*], children's nurses and matrons, but there are not very many of them. Nurses who want to go on specializing often cannot do so. In my opinion, there should be more specialized courses and more continuing vocational training courses. And to enable people to attend these courses, they should be given time off work."

Nurses in the more senior group:
Attachment to the profession and the parent establishment

Nurses with some seniority who already had children did not find the idea of becoming a matron particularly attractive. They had chosen working hours and schedules which left them time to look after their children and they were well aware that if they acquired further qualifications, they would go back to being the last to choose their shifts.

The discourse of nurses with the status of matrons included many arguments focusing on the question of promotion (whether they were satisfied or disappointed with the situation), but very few of them mentioned the problem of balancing the requirements of their work and their family. This probably means that they had given priority to pursuing their careers and had no regrets.

Nurses with some seniority, whether or not they were matrons, tended to express their attachment to either the public hospital institution or the nursing profession itself.

These two poles of reference are not in fact incompatible. The large French public University teaching hospitals have always been at the summit of the French hospital system. It is therefore natural that belonging for many years to one of these institutions strengthens nurses' feelings of attachment, especially in the present context, where they are free to choose their place of work.

Let us take the example of G.R., a male nurse who had worked in three different sectors during the previous 22 years: at a private clinic, then as a free-lance nurse, and lastly, at a public University teaching hospital. Upon comparing the three experiences, he expressed a positive opinion about University teaching hospitals, which he referred to as being like "a great big home", which reflects his strong attachment to this institution. He was therefore greatly in favour of internal mobility within the public hospital system:

"I have worked both at a private clinic and as a free-lance nurse. So I have had three different statuses. If you leave the public hospital sector to work in the private sector, you are liable to lose your retirement pension rights. Nurses at private clinics have to be in with the surgeons. Free-lance nurses are working to earn money. At public hospitals like mine, we have an advantage which private clinics do not provide: we form a team consisting of doctors, nurses and nursing assistants. The public hospital system is like a great big home. We are not specially qualified in surgery, general medicine or rheumatology. We can move to another ward if we want, if there is a space available. There are places which have jobs for nurses. After 10 or 15 years in activity at public hospitals, female nurses have many opportunities of working in the private sector. They can earn huge bonuses."

Nurses whose career has led them to work in various sectors and capacities tend to commit themselves each time to the profession itself. This was so in the case of J.G., a daytime matron with 17 years of experience working in a gastroenterological unit, who was at least as attached to her profession as to the institution which employed her, if not more so.

J.G. had worked for 5 years at an emergency department and then in an endocrinological unit; after taking a teaching job for 2 years, she trained to become a matron. At the time of the interview, she had been a matron at a gastroenterological unit for 10 years. After obtaining internal promotion to her present job, which some people might have called taking a step towards administrative work, she felt on the contrary that she was working with the patients, which in her opinion was the essence of nurses' work. In this way, she felt she had pursued a perfectly coherent trajectory via several different commitments within the same profession:

"If you stay in the Paris area, there are many public hospitals, so you can make a change of job without leaving the system. The work of matrons is different from that of nurses. But when you are a matron, you are still very close to the patients and the paramedical staff. I feel really involved in the hospital unit where I work. I feel it's essential. Therefore, even if you move to a different job, you are still involved in caring for patients. That's what I have done. I have been working as a matron for 10 years now. I could easily undergo further training to become a head matron but I haven't done so. Frankly, it doesn't appeal to me. That would really be the end. It would mean simply becoming a manager."

Nurses' commitment to their profession therefore centres on their dealings with their patients; they see the possibility of moving to a purely managerial position as giving up the key to their profession. The barrier placed by nurses between themselves and their immediate superiors (the matrons) is similar to that placed by the matrons between themselves and the head matron. This goes to make up an overall picture of the profession which is both stratified and unified.

This may explain why nurses who have acquired some seniority tend to be in favour of collective learning. Most the respondents said they approved of learning processes involving several nurses or nurses and physicians working together at the same hospital ward. Some of them expressed the opinion that vocational training can take place in a wider collective setting, as long as it is a properly approved setting. This is so in the case of the nurses' research groups which are currently developing at hospitals and in the framework of some associations.

E.G. had acquired 16 years of experience as a nurse and was working at a gastroenterological ward on a daytime shift. She said she had stopped working at the birth of her child and refused to envisage advancing her career so as not to lose her daytime job. She had no wish to take qualifying continuing vocational training courses since she did not want to be promoted.

However, as she was very keen to go on developing and learning, she naturally tended to grasp all the opportunities available for undergoing further training; in her opinion, nursing research was one of the many ways of acquiring knowledge. Becoming an active member of a research group (an association for nurses specialised in liver disease) was therefore not part of a plan to obtain promotion, but rather a means of distancing herself from her everyday work. The network in question was both inside and outside the hospital. The wish to belong to a network outside the hospital walls was explicitly described by his nurse as a means of obtaining social recognition for specialized nurses' specific skills:

> "Continuing vocational training is fine. It means keeping up with technical progress. Because we are highly specialized. I feel that newly qualified nurses should move from one department and one speciality to another. I have worked in general surgery, orthopaedics and surgical cardiology, including intensive care. Now I am at the gastroenterological ward. I intend to stay here for several years. At the public hospitals, there are training courses on specific subjects. We are entitled to training leave, but it depends on whether the department can do without us. I attended the course on hepatology last year. Continuing vocational training is not compulsory, but it's not always possible to attend the classes. It depends on the department, which has to go on functioning smoothly. When I was working at other public hospital departments, I never attended any vocational training courses. I always applied, but my application was not forwarded, whereas here, I have enrolled to attend the congress later on this year. There are discussion groups for nurses with various specialities. They are trying to keep up. There is one on cardiology. There is one on neurology. There is one on hepatology. It's at national level."

Another matron, J.C., provided another example of the efforts made by nurses to improve their skills by turning to professional networks outside the traditional healthcare service-providers. This matron with 16 years' seniority was in charge of a daytime shift at the general surgery ward. In response to the question about her relationships with her colleagues at work, she moved on to the topic of acquiring knowledge as part of a team. She mentioned the latest care procedures (based on *technical files*) designed to set up an inter-professional research network including not only nurses but also doctors.

Collective learning as a means of adopting suitable procedures for keeping up with the latest technological advances was said by this matron to be in line with her institution's policy on the length of patients' hospital stays:

> "We discuss surgical techniques and how to prepare the patients. In this case, it's the digestive surgery ward; it's all about the colon and the intestines. There are special preparatory techniques. We have therefore drawn up technical files for each surgeon. All the methods used vary, especially depending on the equipment used. We are automatically obliged to work differently, depending on the equipment, the cotton wool and the type of syringes used. During the past 20 years, everything has changed. Here we feed the patients quite soon after their operation. It's part of a technique, a policy adopted in this department. The latest products and equipment are presented to us by the laboratories, in other words, by the manufacturers. It's the head matron

who decides first. The matter is then discussed between the doctors and the matrons like me. Then we try out the new syringes, for example, and if they suit us, they are adopted. It's mainly the nurses who decide in the long run. The changes are made gradually. We don't make any sudden breaks. When we are working in the same department, using satisfactory methods of treatment, we simply go on improving them."

Summary of the findings obtained in the first survey

The respondents' feelings about their commitment to their profession are summarized in *table 3.3*. Among the 22 respondents with less than 12 years' seniority, 10 hoped to succeed in their family lives while continuing their occupational activities under good conditions, and 6 were more interested in gaining promotion. Half of the 24 more experienced nurses gave priority to family life, and the other half expected to evolve professionally while working during the day or achieving the rank of matrons. Most of them declared that they were attached to the *grande maison*[1] and that caring for patients was central to their profession.

In 1988, very few of the nurses interviewed (in both age-groups) said that their careers were blocked and that they therefore intended to leave the profession. As we will see below, some of the nurses interviewed in 2008 said they were considering this possibility.

The various ways in which nurses in the two age-groups updated their knowledge are presented in *table 3.4*.

Nurses in the less senior group mentioned on-the-job vocational training and training acquired among colleagues, as well as qualifying hospital vocational training schemes. By contrast, nurses in the more senior group and matrons were more in favour of training acquired at the establishment or in the department as a member of a hospital team.

Table 3.3. *Nurses' commitment to their profession (1987-1988).*

Seniority	Promotion to the position of matron	Achieving a balance between work and family life	Attachment to the institution or the nursing profession	Blocked careers or departure from hospital work	Other considerations	Total
12 yrs or less	6	10	2	1	3	22
13 yrs or more	1	9	11	3	0	24
Total	7	19	13	4	3	46

---

1. Here, the *grande maison* ("big house") is the named given to the APHP (Assistance Publique des Hôpitaux de Paris); it is actually a set of around forty public hospitals brought together under the same administration.

Table 3.4. *Means of updating knowledge (1987-1988).*

Seniority	Public Hospitals' vocational training plan	On the job training, training with colleagues	Congresses run by associations	Other	Total
12 yrs or less	6	15	0	4	25
13 yrs or less	1	21	3	2	27
Total	7	36	3	6	52

Twenty years later: A wide range of career paths

At the time of the 2007-2008 survey, a novel approach to internal restructuring, involving the formation of clusters of services *(pôles)* was being applied at French public University teaching hospitals. These groups, which were intended to replace the previous departments (which were said to be irrationally designed from the medical point of view and economically unsound) actually consisted of superimposing a further level of organization on the pre-existing levels. At the time of the survey, there was therefore some confusion as to where exactly the medical, nursing and economic control was carried out. One of the hospital establishments involved in the survey was even on strike for this reason. The feelings of the nurses interviewed were therefore strongly influenced by this state of affairs. They feared in particular that the restructuring might result in staff reductions and impose patterns of mobility within the various newly formed *pôles* or clusters. Later on, although the creation of these *pôles* was still setting problems, the emphasis had shifted to more economic and financial considerations (delegating responsibility, signing contracts on behalf of *pôles*, etc.). The restructuring was less directly perceived in terms of employment, especially in the case of matrons.

Documenting these events made it possible to detect the processes underlying the setting up of a new professional identity among French nurses. The climate of change by no means prevented them from mentioning their projects, their careers and their relationships with the institution which employed them, just as their predecessors had done. Although the need to balance work and family life was still mentioned, this problem was obviously less serious, and several ways of finding solutions had become available.

Nurses in the less senior group: Promotion or specialization

Hospital work is usually organized in three shifts. Nurses without children usually work at night, whereas the day shift workers are mostly women with children.

Day care hospitalization, which developed more strongly in France in 2008, also increased nurses' chances of obtaining rotations (6.30 a.m. to 2.30 p.m; 10 a.m. to 6 p.m.; and 12 p.m. to 7 a.m) which were more in keeping with their families' requirements than the traditional successive 8-hour shifts. On the other hand, the respondents deplored the fact that the introduction of day care had been accompanied by staff reductions.

In the end, nurses manage to make adjustments during their careers between their working hours and their family's requirements by exchanging good turns among themselves. These adjustments are facilitated by the large number of hospital establishments and the diversity of the sectors of activity in which French public hospitals are involved: mobility and special arrangements are therefore favoured by the great diversity of nurses' occupational situations. This characteristic also comes into play at the level of nurses' careers and how they are pursued.

In response to the question about their future career, 25 of the 38 nurses in the less senior group gave details which showed that they were more interested in this question than the previous cohort. Nine of the latter group pictured their future in terms of career advancement, and many nurses in the 1987-1988 survey also mentioned the possibility of being promoted to the status of matron *("becoming a matron in the future")* or becoming specialized *("continuing to undergo vocational training and possibly specializing" ; "becoming a coordinating nurse" [infirmière coordinatrice]).*

Contrary to what was observed in 1988, however, many of this group mentioned mobility within the public University teaching hospital system. These nurses felt that pursuing their career might involve mobility: *"making a change of department"* or *"making a change of establishment"* in order to *"find out about other specialities".* Making changes of this kind is compatible with undergoing vocational training, and some of the nurses interviewed equated mobility with the acquisition of skills. In response to the question "How do you perceive your future career?", one young nurse declared, for example, that she imagined it *"evolving thanks to continuing vocational training courses and/or making a change of establishment."*

Some other nurses predicted that their future career would follow a linear pattern *("still working as a nurse").* They hoped for stability for purely professional reasons, but one of them said the wish for a stable career was motivated by the need to *"devote more time to my family."*

This nurse was an exception, since the young nurses interviewed in the 2000s were more interested than their predecessors in the various pathways to advancement in their profession, which they regarded as a real career and not just a stable occupation.

However, the responses to the question about intra-hospital mobility suggest that staff adjustments are made on the basis of competence. The nurses themselves were of the opinion that beginners should *"work for about 5 years in the same ward"* before making a change.

Now the fact that French hospital units have been re-arranged into clusters *(pôles)* instead of separate wards and the numbers of staff have been reduced is liable to put an end to continuous, linear careers. The nurses interviewed said they perceived this change as a being liable to upset the balance between the three areas in which they had invested: family life, their profession and the institution for which they worked. Performing multiple tasks or alternating between various functions had become a constraint imposed by the administration and was no longer a matter of personal choice.

The uncertainty created by the latest situation has resulted in a state of polarisation. On the one hand, the younger nurses, who are more in tune with the aims of the hospital reforms than their elders, are able to grasp the opportunities these reforms have opened up; and on the other hand, the least mobile or least well informed nurses have these changes imposed on them without realizing the real career perspectives available, although the range of possibilities has actually been extended.

The so-called "exit" strategy (Hirschman, 1970)[2] is therefore sometimes being adopted these days because of the feeling that hospital nursing is becoming increasingly hard work due to the chronic shortage of staff. This was not case in 1987-1988. There still exists a link between nurses' careers and their conditions of work, but some of them see this link in a purely negative light: *"the demands made by the organization are increasingly hard"*; *"the conditions of work are not right (permanent understaffing)"*. To the extent that nurses are opting more frequently and cold-headedly than 20 years ago for giving up hospital work. They are still strongly attached to their profession, however: *"I hope to be able to work as a free-lance nurse"*; *"[I am thinking of becoming] a trainer at the Institute of nursing"*; *"[I think I will] go and work abroad"*.

Nurses in the more senior group:
Less attachment to their institution and/or the nursing profession

In this context, older nurses who have become socialized within a stable organization, whether or not they opt for mobility, might be expected to be destabilized by the fact that the winners from now on are going to be the organization's most mobile employees.

The responses of the more senior nurses show that they were aware of this change and knew about the scope for upward or horizontal mobility. Seven of the 35 nurses with more than 13 years' seniority hoped to pursue their careers by being promoted to the status of matrons or by specializing or moving elsewhere in the public hospital system, whereas only 3 preferred continuous careers and continuing to work as nurses at their present department.

What is new here is that nurses talking about their career prospects mentioned the possibility of obtaining a matron's position by moving transversally from one department to another in the same hospital cluster: *"[I imagine] progressing transversally within this cluster"*; *"[I know] it is possible to be appointed to the position of matron within the same cluster, where I would be responsible for a wider range of tasks."* This wider range of tasks would include administrative ones, which used to be regarded as being practically beyond the scope of nurses' occupational world: *"[I could carry out] administrative tasks."*

---

2. According to A.O. Hirschman, "exit" occurs when a "customer who, dissatisfied with the product of one firm, shifts to the product of another, uses the market to... improve his position". Therefore, "to resort to "voice" rather than "exit" is, for the customer or member [of an organisation] to make an attempt at changing the practices, policies and outputs of the firm from which one buys or the organisation to which one belongs. Voice is here defined as any attempt at all to change, rather than to escape, an objectivable state of affairs" (Hirschman, 1970, p. 30).

The more senior nurses were therefore well informed about the possibilities open to them, and those who had career projects formulated them clearly and thoughtfully. It is worth mentioning here that the transversal positions available within a cluster include those of clinical nurse, specialized hygiene nurse, and specialized pain management nurse. Specialization therefore goes hand in hand with organizational change and enlarges nurses' occupational scope: *"becoming a clinical nurse or acquiring therapeutic trainers' skills."*

Many of the more experienced nurses typically showed the same attachment to their profession *("I am still as enthusiastic as ever")*. However, their discourse about their commitment no longer focused on the same three points (balancing work and family life, attachment to the profession and attachment to the hospital institution). In this older group, the main point was their attachment to the nursing profession, especially as the profession is evolving and it is necessary to preserve its most positive aspects: *"to go on being a good nurse"; "keeping up with the changes"; "I hope to go on enjoying my work."*

It emerges that the latest organizational and technical changes have accentuated the differences between those who have been able to spot the positive opportunities and those who view these changes as a threat to their careers; however, among the latter, only one nurse mentioned the possibility of making a change of occupation.

The 6 nurses out of the 35 in the more senior group who felt their careers were blocked were convinced that this situation was directly due to the new organizational arrangements: *"Since the advent of the hospital reform and flex time [...], the future has been looking completely chaotic. I can no longer imagine having a future in the public hospital system."* Another nurse said how demotivated she had become: *"I cannot picture my future career very clearly because the nursing staff have become demotivated by the many changes occurring in the department"; "however hard I try, [I can't help seeing] the problems ahead."*

One of the nurses interviewed suggested that these problems might jeopardize the profession as a whole: *"one wonders what is going to become of the nursing profession"*. Another respondent said she was *"worried about the future of her occupation."*

The nurse who envisaged making a change of profession linked her family situation to this decision, since she confirmed implicitly that she had been able so far to reach a balance between her work and her family life: *"I am thinking of making a change of occupation as soon as my children are old enough."*

Summary of the findings made in the second survey

Almost half of the population of nurses interviewed had less than 12 years' seniority and one or several children. In the more senior group, more than two thirds (24 out of 35) fitted this description *(cf. table 3.5)*. The responses recorded show that these nurses' work and family life were compatible only thanks to their flexible conditions of work: they were able to work part time when necessary, and the working week was reduced by law in the 2000s to 35 hours

(Bouffartigue & Bouteiller, 2003). As we will see in Chapter 4, Japanese nurses, whose working week is sometimes as long as 60 hours, find it much harder to juggle with the time spent at work and outside work.

In comparison with the late 1980s, French nurses' working conditions in 2000 were much more flexible, which has made it possible for them to adapt their working hours so as to be able to look after their families properly as well as having a job. In the 1980s, most French hospital nurses were working full time at a rate of at least 39 hours per week, whereas some nurses are now working only during 80% of the present 35-hour full time week (see *table 3.6*).

Although only 4 of the 73 nurses in the present sample were working on a part-time basis, the numbers are known to be much higher (approximately 25%) at national level, even in the public hospital system. According to the administrative staff questioned, however, the rate of part-time work was approximately 10% at the two hospitals at which the present survey was conducted.

During the 1980s, the main question arising for French nurses wanting to engage in a career was whether or not they would be able to preserve the quality of their family life. For this purpose, some of them opted for a monotonous nursing career enabling them to juggle with their working hours and schedules, whereas others deliberately chose to move up the ladder. During the 2000s, French nurses could choose between various modes of advancement. Those who felt their hospital careers were blocked often decided to take jobs elsewhere.

The nurses participating in the second survey agreed that the various vocational training courses available, whether or not they led to obtaining approved qualifications, were essential to building a career. It had become possible for nurses to find ways and means of raising a family without giving up their occupational ambitions because of the greater scope and the various options available for pursuing a career. It is rather paradoxical, however, that in an economic context governed by the principle of rationalisation, these various opportunities are not always more readily grasped (see *table 3.7*).

In parallel with these changes, patterns of mobility have also changed. During the 1980s, nurses' professional commitment mainly took the form of hoping to spend their whole career at the same establishment, or even at the same department. During the 2000s, however, after the *pôles* were instituted at French hospitals, the scope for career advancement extended to include the whole public University teaching hospital system. Here we have another paradox, since nurses had meanwhile begun to specialize in medical activities, whereas they were expected to perform multiple tasks in the *pôles*. Their method of resolving this contradiction consisted of accepting the idea of mobility, no longer within a single establishment, but within the whole public hospital system which employed them.

It is therefore not very surprising that in response to the question about how they updated their knowledge, half of the nurses interviewed mentioned continuing vocational training dispensed within the public hospital system *(Table 3.8)*. The previous cohort focused on continuing vocational training dispensed at the establishment or in the department itself, whereas the 2000 respondents intended to advance their careers by taking advantage of the whole range of possibilities provided by the French public hospital system.

Table 3.5. *Nurses with and without children (2007-2008).*

Seniority	No children	One or more children	No reply	Total
12 years or less	20	17	0	38
13 years or more	8	24	4	35
Total	28	41	4	73

Table 3.6. *Nurses' working hours (2007-2008).*

Seniority	Full time	Part time	Total
12 years or less	36	2	38
13 years or more	33	2	35
Total	69	4	73

Table 3.7. *Nurses' commitment to their profession (2007-2008).*

Seniority	Promotion to the position of matron	Specialization or intra-hospital mobility	Balancing work and family life	Attachment to the institution or the profession	Career blocked or they intended to leave the hospital system	Other responses and no reply	Total
12 years or less	4	5	1	4	7	17	38
13 years of more	4	3	0	3	7	18	35
Total	8	8	1	7	14	35	73

Table 3.8. *Means of updating knowledge used by nurses (2007-2008) (several responses could be given).*

Seniority	The public hospital vocational training plan	Training at the establishment, in the department, among colleagues	Congresses	Documents, journals, Internet	Total
12 years or less	31	18	0	7	56
13 years or more	23	21	3	7	54
Total	54	39	3	14	110

Work relationships and nurses' social demands

Technical versus relational work and nurses' social demands in 1987-1988

The participants' responses to the questions about their relationships at work clearly showed that nurses took this to mean their relationships with patients, other nurses, nursing assistants and doctors. More specifically, these findings are in line with the results of other studies published both at that time and more recently, showing that French nurses tend to stress the opposition between technical work (consisting mainly of the work delegated to nurses by physicians) and relational work (nurses' own specific work), and on the adjustment between the two.

Nurses in the less senior group: Recognition of initial vocational training

The interviews with the 22 nurses having less than 12 years' seniority showed that 4 of them felt it was important to meet all their patients' needs, whereas 3 others stressed the difference between nurses' relational and technical roles. On the other hand, 4 of the nurses in this group expressed the opinion that teamwork is possible among nurses as well as between nurses and doctors; whereas 6 other respondents said it was difficult to work as a team. Five members of this group felt that relationships with patients depend closely on teamwork among hospital workers, whether or not this is possible to achieve.

The following excerpts from four interviews illustrate these perceptions: in three cases, the respondents made the distinction between relational and technical hospital work, and the other respondent had difficulty both in establishing good relationships with patients and in working together with the other members of the hospital team.

D.N. was working on the afternoon shift at a neurosurgical ward. She had been employed in the intensive care unit for 4 years before joining the post-intensive care unit, where she had been working for 3 years. In response to the question about her relationships with patients, nurses and doctors, this respondent described the difference between the intensive care and post-intensive care units as follows:

> "After 4 years at the intensive care unit, I asked to be moved. The patients are in a coma. You have to do everything for them. After 4 years, I was suffering from the lack of communication. When these patients wake up, they are much better and so they are immediately transferred to the post-intensive care unit. In the intensive care ward, you have to do everything, make all the vital functions work and try to wake up the patients, working closely with the anaesthetists. The nurses working there often move elsewhere. I myself missed the possibility of communicating with patients. As soon as they improve, off they go. All you see is patients in a coma. I couldn't take it any longer."

In the post-intensive care unit to which she moved, this nurse devoted herself to helping patients get back to normal life. By pointing out this difference, D.N. was stressing the difference between relational and technical work; working under these extremely demanding conditions made her realize the importance of relational work:

> "Here in post-intensive care, the patients have had brain surgery and so on. They don't know exactly how it went. They are anxious. So you have to explain things and reassure them and after that, help them to recover their autonomy. For example, here we have people who have had car accidents, who can't remember what has happened. So it's good to help them get back to normal life. Of course, it's much less technical. Some people may say it's technical, but it's not just that: it's 50% technical and 50% relationships. We don't perform many life-saving gestures here, but we do relational work. There are many patients who are paralysed after the operation. So you have to try and cheer them up. I have problems with the doctors sometimes, with the surgeons, who are not always very available because they are so busy. At times, the patients don't know what's going on. Their families don't understand what is going to happen. It's often we who are in the middle, helping patients, families and doctors to communicate."

According to this nurse's picture of her work and the relationships involved, the nurse's role consists of alternating the two registers, which she distinguishes very clearly. As we will see in the next chapter, Japanese nurses cannot and do not make this distinction.

Another nurse, C.N., who was thinking of becoming a matron, spoke about the routine hospital work she carried out. She had worked at a surgical reanimation unit, and then at a paediatric neurosurgical unit. The opposition between relational and technical work featured prominently in her discourse. Like the previous nurse, she mentioned the contrast between work of a technical kind (intensive care) and work of a relational kind (at the paediatric unit). Technical tasks *("injections and dressings")* seem very monotonous to nurses, and make them feel *"like robots"*.

On the other hand, the emotional aspects of nurses' relationships with their patients in the intensive care unit are very strong; their attachment to a patient is sometimes greater than their satisfaction at seeing their health improve, however paradoxical this may seem. This is due to the intense focus on the patient's motionless yet still reactive body which occurs during this crucial stage in the treatment:

> "There are times when I felt physically and mentally exhausted. In fact, I moved to another unit after 2 years. When I was at the intensive care unit, the work was very technical. I was giving injections, doing bandages and having no personal contact with the patients and their families. I didn't like that at all. I said to myself, I did not become a nurse to be a robot, to become a robot. That's why I wanted to move to another department. When I was at the reanimation unit, I could no longer stand it when patients started to move again. It's really awful. If that's what they are doing, they will have to go elsewhere. Some nurses say *'the patient has moved.'* I couldn't stand it; I wanted them to stay where they were."

What was even worse according to this nurse was the fact that once nurses' working habits had been acquired, they became automatic, not only in the case of technical tasks but also at relational level:

> "At the paediatric unit, I get on very well with the children. You see personal contacts, emotional states. But now that I have been there for 4 years, I sometimes think I am fed up with it because I have seen it all in this unit. It's going to become just a routine. When you go on working in the same department, it becomes monotonous. Then you start to get blasé. I would rather something unusual happened from time to time. If nothing special happens, you just go on feeding them, and this and that... I am not going to stand it much longer."

However, this state of real or imminent boredom does not cause nurses to consider leaving the public university hospital system, and even less, giving up their profession.

This preference for stability seems to be often due to the priority given at hospitals to technical tasks because of the conditions under which they work, as in the case of B.R., who was working on an afternoon shift at a rheumatologic unit. When asked about her relationships at work, this nurse described the specificities of the work in this department. She explained that since pain is generally the main problem in rheumatology, the nurses speak about it openly with both the patients and the physicians:

> "There are often two of us, a nurse and a nursing assistant, or three of us, two nurses and one nursing assistant, in charge of 32 patients. It depends on whether any of our colleagues have a day off or have gone on holiday. Well there are no problems with the patients. For example, here in rheumatology, pain is the main thing we have to deal with. The patients complain when they are in pain. We try to find out where it hurts, and in what way. Then we speak to the doctor, saying: *'So and so is feeling the pain more today than yesterday, maybe we should do this or that.'* The patients are often anxious. No problem. If a problem arises, we tell the doctor."

In addition to describing the attention paid to pain, this young nurse said the tasks associated with medical prescriptions were too heavy. Here she compared the nurses' relational tasks with the technical jobs delegated to nurses by doctors. She stated that priority was given to the technical work, since *"the main thing is to make sure the prescriptions are carried out properly"*:

> "I chose this profession. I like my work. You are responsible after all for a whole lot of things. When you are setting up a patient's chemotherapy or a drip, it's a responsibility. So the main thing is to make sure the prescriptions are carried out properly. That's not always easy from the technical point of view. When you install a drip, because people are often put on a drip, it's not always easy. In addition, the conditions are not always ideal for the hospital staff. There are so many things to be done. I do as much as I can. Sometimes I am not pleased because I haven't had time to do all I wanted to do. The patients are anxious. They need to be reassured. They need us to speak to them. Unfortunately, spending three minutes talking to somebody is not enough to reassure them. We do our best, but we have all sorts of other jobs to do as well. In that case, I am not pleased because I don't manage to spend more time speaking to the patients. I talk to them though when I am handing out their medicine."

C.C, a young surgical nurse, spoke on similar lines:

> "When you are doing dressings, you speak [to the patients] all the time. But here we are not always available when a patient feels most like talking. This morning, I did three rounds of dressings, and then the surgeon and the anaesthetist came round the ward. It is difficult to find time for conversation with the patients. It's embarrassing."

However, C.C. compared the time devoted to patients with the time spent working with the doctors:

> "You see, here I feel there is something that's not right. It's the fact that the interns do their round, then the surgeon does his round and then the anaesthetist does his round. That amounts to three consultations every morning, but they rarely coincide. So each doctor sees the patients separately and often none of them say the same thing. They all give their opinion, and we the nurses try to fit the three messages together. But we don't have all the information. There are meetings between surgeons and nurses and the surgical nurses. But here there are no meetings

at which nurses are included. Patients who are not doing well, who are demoralized, or dying, have to be comforted. There are no meetings about that. Patients who undergo operations don't even know why. Why not? Because there are no meetings [about it]."

This criticism links up with the comments quoted above about the role of vocational learning within a team and its importance to the younger nurses. These statements express the need to work more actively as members of a team in order to have their contribution to managing patients and their families properly recognized.

The discourse of the nurses with less than 12 years' seniority included references to the upgrading of their wages, but these statements were always associated with the need to have their initial vocational training (involving a 3-year course of study after the *baccalauréat*) properly recognized. This demand was also linked to the idea of improving the status of the whole profession.

Another nurse, D.N., argued in favour of nurses' wages being made proportional to their level of training. The duration of nurses' initial vocational training has been extended from 27 to 36 months after the secondary school-leaving certificate (the *baccalauréat*). But this nurse expressed the opinion that social policies giving people with no *baccalauréat* access to higher occupational spheres had degraded the status of the intermediate occupations. She stressed the need to defend the idea that initial vocational training should be a prerequisite for obtaining a salary equivalent to that of technicians:

> "Everyone agrees that our work is of great importance, but our wages are not in line with this idea. When I was a student nurse, the course lasted 27 months. Now it takes 3 and half years. It can therefore be said to constitute higher education just like any other higher education. Actually beginners' wages in nursing do not nearly correspond to higher education. It's true that studying for 3 and half years after secondary school corresponds more or less to the duration of technicians' training. But then, nurses do not earn nearly as much as technicians when they start off. Our status is going to be depreciated because of a decree that is going to be issued. It means that if you can prove you have been employed anywhere at all for 5 years, you are eligible to sit the general knowledge test to obtain entry to nursing school. I don't agree with that. I prefer this profession a hundred times to others. That's why I am not doing a different job."

The social debate on the issue of initial vocational training levels naturally led to some discussion about the changes in nurses' training which had occurred since *nursing care science* was introduced. According to C.R., a nurse with 3 years' seniority in rheumatology, nurses have to update their knowledge more than members of other professions in order to prevent their profession from becoming depreciated:

> "Nowadays we want to make our profession evolve, to give it an identity. In any case, the only way of giving it an identity is via higher education. I fell the nursing profession is being depreciated. The trouble is that if you are depreciated, if you are underestimated by other people, and you lose your own self-esteem. In a way, it is to fight processes of that kind, to show that we are not less clever than doctors, that we too can pursue further studies, that nursing care science was created."

Women's access to the intermediate occupations has brought up the question of working hours and work schedules. In her discourse, C.C. criticized shift work (day shift, afternoon shift and night shift) arrangements because they favour women with children, which prevents the others from learning what nursing is all about:

"Newly qualified nurses are not put on morning shifts like the one I am on just now. In other words, they are obliged to work at night. But night shifts are not very active. Well the nurses here are active at night, but it's not the same work. They don't have to change surgical dressings, the patients are asleep, and the nurses can't ask the doctors to explain things to them. I myself have been on a morning shift for two and a half years because have a baby. I was lucky to get this shift. But there are some bachelors who work for 3 years at night. When they are on night duty, they tend to forget everything they have learned. You stop evolving. At some hospitals, the shifts follow a rota. But that's no good from the family point of view."

Another point raised was nurses' conditions of work, which were mentioned by A.C., a nurse who had been working on an afternoon shift in a general surgery ward for 2 years. This nurse said the reduction of staff and equipment resulting from the latest "global budget" approach to hospital accountancy had also reduced the quality of care:

"Of course we are not well paid for the work we do. It's very tiring. From the point of view of the equipment, the public hospital system does not always provide the necessary means because they are expensive. We have to work under poor conditions. It's a great pity. From the point of view of the staff, there are not enough of us. When an emergency occurs, we have difficulty in coping."

Nurses in the more senior group: The forms of compromise between relational and technical work and the recognition of competences

Like the younger nurses, their elders were happy to talk about their work relationships and about what their role should essentially consist of; but they spoke about team-work in more positive terms than their younger colleagues.

Eleven of the 24 more senior nurses interviewed discussed the overall care dispensed to patients, and 7 of them did not mention the difference between relational and technical work (as compared with only 3 out of 22 in the younger group).

These nurses with at least 13 years' seniority, who had obtained daytime positions, tended to work in close collaboration with the doctors. Nine of them were very much in favour of this situation, which according to them can be easily achieved. Five of these nurses criticized the way the work was organized, but they all attached great importance to teamwork relationships.

The following excerpts from interviews with one male nurse and two female nurses illustrate the older group of nurses' representations and opinions. The male nurse mentioned that the main aspects of his work were the relational and technical ones, since the more "household" jobs can now be delegated to nursing assistants; all three nurses expressed the opinion that patients' overall care can be managed by working as a team.

G.R., the male nurse, mentioned how nurses' work has changed; since they are now relieved of the *"more domestic, household tasks"*, they are able to concentrate more on the *"relational tasks"*:

"A few years ago, I felt ill at ease because I didn't have time to care for my patients properly. Now I feel this way less frequently because we can spend more time with patients. The various tasks are distributed, which gives us more time. We used to have to perform all the tasks. Now

> we only carry out those specific to nurses. Well, we no longer serve breakfast because the nursing assistants are there to deal with the more domestic, household tasks. It's not our speciality. We sometimes do it out of a spirit of teamwork, but we are not obliged to do so. The time saved can be spent on other more specific services to the patients, such as providing relational care. There are four nurses and three assistant nurses in our team. The quality of care has improved on the whole, luckily."

In this nurse's discourse, nurses' technical skills and nurses' own specific role were enhanced by qualifying the more lowly tasks he disliked as *"domestic tasks"*. This point of view is particularly relevant in the French context, where there are almost as many nursing assistants as nurses, and where nursing assistants have a distinctly lower status than nurses. As we will see in the next chapter, this distinction was completely meaningless at Japanese hospitals during the 1980s, and although it is beginning to emerge nowadays, it is not of great importance in terms of either the nursing profession or nurses' identity.

The second nurse in the more senior group, E.G., was on a day shift in the gastroenterological unit. She had a positive opinion about her work relationships, stressed the distinction between nurses', nurses assistants' and physicians' roles, and said she appreciated nurses' autonomy:

> "The nursing profession has evolved but the mentality of people outside the profession has not changed. When they talk about nurses, they think of a person holding a syringe, that's all. In other words, it's the person who is dispensing the care prescribed by the doctor. Whereas it's not that at all. Nurses are people who have to look after patients and carry out prescriptions, I quite agree. But they are definitely people who manage to be in the middle of everybody, between the doctors and the patients. Then there are all kinds of things: a psychological side and an educational side. Nowadays there are nurses and nursing assistants. Nursing assistants distribute meals, which is not really meant to be part of their work. They spend a lot of time on routine care, which means washing and changing patients. The routine care is important. Nurses should participate in it."

However, unlike her colleagues, she did not compare nurses' relational work with the technical tasks delegated to them by doctors: according to this respondent, both kinds of work fit together and complete each other and are not mutually exclusive. More specifically, the quality of the fit depends on that of the teamwork between nurses, physicians and patients:

> "Nurses are the people who spend the most time with a patient. Therefore, it is they who see the patient most, who notice the changes, the improvement or deterioration of the patients. I feel it is necessary to speak to the patients. One must never forget that there are doctors and nurses, that we don't do the same job, we don't have the same qualifications, but we have the same goal. It's working together, teamwork. As far as relationships between doctors and nurses are concerned, it's very personal. I think it's the doctors who want to create and foster a barrier between the nurses and themselves. But I feel it's up to the nurses to make themselves respected, to show what they are capable of doing, show how they work in order to be accepted and become part of team. The nursing profession needs to be recognized, both officially and unofficially; nurses' role should be recognized. We must stand up for ourselves. We must show what we can do, show how we work. There are prescriptions. We have to carry them out, but we must also be capable of weighing them up."

According to this nurse, the fight for recognition is driven not by a spirit of competition but by a spirit of cooperation, which is also the goal. This respondent's discourse focused on the differences between the various categories of work, not only between nurses and doctors but also between nurses and matrons:

> "The ideal 'supervisor' is one who sees everything and intervenes when she has to, but lets people get on with their work. People must be made to feel responsible. That's a huge problem at the public hospitals: people don't feel responsible for the whole job. Each of us plays the role of nurse, looking after the patients, dispensing care. When you are competent, you don't need to have somebody supervising you. Supervisor isn't the right word. In my opinion, I don't need to be supervised."

The question of teamwork and supervision was addressed in different terms by J.G., a matron at the gastroenterological unit, who emphasized nurses' need for support because of the emotional demands made on them at work:

> "Nurses have a lot of technical work; they keep getting more tests to carry out. But they have to deal as well with all the aspects of the patients' comfort, their needs, their vital requirements, their need to eat, drink and be clean. But being ill makes patients anxious. You have patients who are anxious and families who are anxious. Nurses have to respond to all that. Nurses too are anxious. We are in an anxious environment. A nurse, when her working day is loaded with strong emotions, can become attached to a dying patient. It's hard psychologically. I can't imagine thinking 'Let's go home and forget about all that'. It's just not true. I know there are little details which occurred during the day at the hospital, which go on obsessing me at home. I know it's difficult to get over that anxiety, but I believe we should discuss it together. That's what teamwork is all about. If we manage to keep going, it's because we work as a team. We give each other mutual support that way. When we accompany people who are dying, people often say they get used to it but I don't think that's true. It's not something you can get used to. We don't wear armour just because we are nurses. We are just as sensitive as other human beings. I discussed this the other day with a doctor. There is a woman dying of cancer. The nurses had been asking for several days for treatment to relieve her but he couldn't make up his mind about it. In fact, from his point of view, the treatment was finished, since nothing more could be done to save that woman. But for us, this wasn't the end. We were in there with her. We have to stay with our patients right up to the end. We have to help them."

According to J.G., performing multiple tasks has nothing to do with being available or not. Likewise, J.C. (on daytime duty at the general surgery unit), who did not mention the problem of making contact with patients despite nurses' lack of time due to the hospital institution's policies. This point featured more prominently in the responses to the 2007-2008 survey. But in the 1988 survey, the process of hospital rationalization was not very advanced. In this case, J.G's opinion about teamwork was positive:

> "There are people who are always short of time. I think it's a question of one's personality. On some days, there is lots of work, so we can't listen to the patients. Sometimes it's worth knowing that listening to patients for five or ten minutes is good listening, whereas spending half an hour with them does not always amount to good listening. In my opinion, these are two different things. When you are listening to someone, you are attentive. You must pay attention; you must be able to give time. Of course there are days, on Mondays, for example, when a lot of new patients arrive. We nurses cannot listen to people on those days. But on other days, when things are quieter. We work increasingly to a programme. If there are no emergencies going on, then you must start listening. Personally, I believe that if you want to, you can do it."

On the other hand, this nurse stated that good relationships among matrons, nurses and doctors are really possible to achieve. Although nurses cannot all attend meetings with doctors, there can be meetings during coffee-breaks: informal meetings where the matron has a mediating role to play - *"These meetings make it possible to make connections between the tasks of the nurses, assistant nurses and doctors"*:

> "There is a regular Monday meeting with the doctors, which lasts for an hour or an hour and a half. We discuss all the patients due to arrive that week and draw up an operating schedule. The nurses can participate if they want, but they often don't come because they have too much work to do. A lot of patients are admitted on Mondays. There are three nurses in this unit. None of them can free themselves to go along to the meeting. Afterwards, I tell them, such and such patient is having such and such an operation. In my unit, we speak quite openly. In the first place, we have lunch together. A great deal goes on at that time. We talk a lot about the patients, all three grades of nurses together. Sometimes the doctors join us for coffee. I am there, the nurses are there, and the nursing assistants are there. The head surgeon and the interns are often there too. We are all there together. It doesn't last very long, a quarter of an hour or half an hour at most, but much is said during that time. We discuss the treatment, the patients, the patients' lives, and the patients' social problems."

Teamwork therefore seems to be feasible despite the difficult working conditions. People learn to listen to each other during the short breaks available when they manage to juggle with time. In some places such as surgical units, where the treatment can be closely planned, these breaks easier to arrange. However, all over the hospital, nurses have to set up suitable conditions for preventing emergency situations from arising, since emergencies are known to result less frequently from patients' condition than from a lack of foresight and organization.

Contrary to the less experienced nurses, those with more than 13 years' seniority suggested that the nursing profession could be improved by focusing on the quality of the work from both the relational and technical points of view, rather than on the length of nurses' initial vocational training.

In the discourse of H.N., who had been working for 15 years on a daytime shift in the neurosurgical department, the need for social recognition was associated with the need to improve the quality of nurses' work by doing away with the concepts of charitable work and nursing as a selfless calling; *"The nursing profession has changed. In the old days, it used to be benevolent work and a personal calling... Now it is all technical. It needs to be recognized as such"*.

The changes undergone by the nursing profession have nevertheless been won as the result of conflicts and negotiations. The problem of nurses being deprived of all initiative in the technical sphere cropped up in a conflict with the medical biologists in 1981-84, which was mentioned by E.G. in connection with the diversity of the tasks nurses have to perform:

> "A few years ago, some medical biologists wanted to practically abolish a large part of our work, everything to do with drawing blood. We were in danger."

L.C., a matron at a general surgery unit who had been in the nursing profession for 32 years, mentioned that nurses' wages had not been upgraded as the result of the trend towards more technical work which she had seen developing throughout her career:

"Nurses feel they are underpaid for the work they do and the knowledge they have acquired. Our work is poorly understood. Nowadays we do jobs (such as drawing blood and handling various kinds of technical equipment) which used to be carried out by doctors. Dealing with intravenous injections, catheters, administering chemotherapy, etc. I think nurses would like to have their wages reviewed because we are not really very well paid."

J.G., another matron, discussed the opposition between technical work and basic nursing care. According to this matron, the motivation required to solve these issues is not a matter of nurses' wages but depends rather on their "professional conscientiousness":

"In the hospital field, many demands are made on nurses. They are expected to have technical skills, to work faster, and the number of tests they have to carry out is on the increase. They are also being asked to adopt a holistic approach to their patients, *i.e.*, not to forget that they are caring for people. But their wages are ridiculously low. It's no joke. People who work hard and are justly rewarded go on working hard. I can say at least that I myself am fed up at times. I have been doing this for 10 years since qualifying as a matron but I'm still on the basic pay. That's not at all encouraging. Nurses have nothing left at the end of the month, except for the satisfaction which comes from their professional consciousness. They are conscientious. It's perfectly true that I am sometimes fed up. I realize how much effort I have put into it, and yet at the end of the month, I get the same amount of pay as those who have made no efforts. As long as I go on working in the hospital system, I will feel I have a moral commitment towards the patients."

As we can see, this matron's discourse included some criticisms about the various conventions: the technical convention, the holistic convention, the reward convention, and the professional convention.

On the other hand, G.R., a nurse working on an afternoon shift, objected to the working hours and the way beginners start off because of the way in which the work is divided into permanent shifts:

"The teams should be much more homogeneous. I mean, there should be a rota so that we don't have either a daytime shift, an afternoon shift or a night shift but a team which moves from one shift to another. That never happens here at the public hospitals, but they do it at some other hospitals. If you put a young nurse on night duty, she is not going to learn anything and she will forget everything she knew. It's disastrous."

The demand for higher wages was not mentioned by all the nurses in the more senior group. I.N., for example, who was a daytime nurse with 18 years' seniority working at the neurosurgical unit, moved from Brittany to Paris, where she married a policeman originating from the same part of the country as she did. She did not regard herself as a "technician" but simply as a worker. Because of this image and the differences between Paris and the provinces, she made no reference to wage claims, since she felt she was fairly well paid.

L.R., a nurse with 24 years' seniority working at a rheumatologic unit, who had lived through the social upheavals of May 1968, when she was already working as a nurse, stated that the situation was *"calm"* at the time of the interview in spring 1988. As the following excerpt shows, she did not foresee the emergence of the so-called "coordination" movement which was about to explode and continue to develop as from the autumn of that year:

"Actually it's not easy to become properly recognized by the administration and by the doctors, to make a place for oneself. Since May 68, we have had a lot of problems. Our relationships have changed. I myself completed my nursing studies before 1968. The members of the medical profession were on the one side, and the paramedicals were on the other side. We didn't mix very easily. After 68, there were huge changes, which also changed our relationships. But in any case, nurses are operatives. It's calm at the moment."

Summary of the findings made in the first survey

As can be seen from *table 3.9*, multiple responses occurred more frequently in the discourse of the most senior nurses (the 24 respondents in this group produced 38 differently coded responses) than in that of the less experienced nurses (the 22 respondents in this group produced 26 differently coded responses). This means that the older nurses tended more readily to make several successive statements in response to a given question. Apart from this quantitative feature, this confirms that the younger nurses were less inclined than their elders to talk about their profession as a whole. Likewise, the question of a holistic approach to nursing and that of the need for teamwork were also more frequently mentioned by the nurses in the more senior group.

The fact that the more senior nurses referred more frequently to the holistic approach to hospital care is consistent with the idea that the younger nurses felt more strongly that the relational and technical aspects will be difficult to combine.

On the other hand, the statements made by the respondents about the other aspects of their work depended very little on their seniority. The findings made in the 2007-2008 survey, which will be presented below, were quite different.

In the case of the nurses with less seniority, 14 out of the 22 respondents in this group made statements about nurses' social demands. It is worth noting that the arguments presented by 5 of them focused on the need to upgrade their wages to match those of technicians, whose initial vocational training also lasted for 3 years after the *baccalauréat*. In the case of the nurses with more than 13 years' seniority, 14 of the 24 respondents in this group mentioned nurses' social demands: 6 stated that the status of the profession should be improved via the content of nurses' technical work and their work in general *(Table 3.10)*.

Table 3.9. *Work relationships (1987-1988).*

Seniority	Holistic approach to treatment	Technical *vs* relational aspects of care*	Contacts with patients		Teamwork		Organiza-tional constraints	Total
			Possible	Difficult	Possible	Difficult		
12 years or less	5	3	2	3	5	5	4	27
13 years or more	10	4	4	3	8	7	4	40
Total	15	7	6	6	13	12	8	67

Table 3.10. *Social demands (1987-1988).*

Seniority	Wages corresponding to 3yrs' study after the baccalauréat	Working hours and shifts	Staff shortages	Social recognition and/or techni-cians' wages	University training, nursing associations	Negative attitude towards social mobilization	Total
Less than 12 years	5	1	2	2	2	2	14
More than 13 years	2	1	1	6	0	4	14
Total	7	2	3	8	2	6	28

The new system of organization introduced in 2007-2008

The way nurses distinguished between technical work and relational work and compared the two kinds of work changed considerably from 1988 to the 2000s. In the second survey, they stressed the fact that the organization of hospital work is based nowadays on a hierarchical split between therapeutic care and basic nursing care. Another point often raised by the respondents in the second survey was the question of nurses' relationships with their patients and with the other members of their team.

Nurses in the less senior group: Some ambivalence about relationships with patients and recognition of nurses' initial training

When the nurses with less than 12 years' seniority spoke about patients' trajectories, whether in positive or negative terms, typically included references to the diversity of nurses' technical and relational tasks. Their responses to questions about this diversity showed that the overall care of patients was often seen in a positive light *("[I feel] motivated to help patients recover")*. In response to the question "On what occasions do you feel most motivated to do your work?", a large number of respondents mentioned some aspect of the quality of the overall care involving many aspects: whenever *"patients improve"*; whenever their *"pain is alleviated"*; *"when attending to patients in pain"*. Other aspects mentioned were palliative care and stomatotherapy. In these two cases, patients are treated using multidisciplinary methods which call for the personal commitment of both patients and nurses (listening to, supporting and educating patients).

The negative side emerged in response to the question "On what occasions do you feel your work is particularly difficult?". These nurses often answered *"when patients are about to die"*; *"when they are nearing the end of their lives"*; or when *"they are feeling bad"*. Although the "bad" disease itself was only rarely named, it was of the kind which called for close contacts: *"dealing with severe diseases such as cancer"*; or *"coping with pain"*.

On the subject of technical work, the younger nurses said they were motivated to dispense therapeutic care and stated that their satisfaction and their motivation were greatest when performing *"technical gestures"* such as *"applying dressings"* and *"tending surgical wounds."* Achieving success with their treatments, especially at crucial moments *("when the heart stops bea-ting" or fighting "to save a patient's life")*, were cited as times at which their motivation for their work was boosted. Only one member of this group said she was afraid of *"harming patients."*

On the other hand, the responses obtained confirmed that the quality of nurses' relationships with each patient was a source of great satisfaction. These nurses were *"keen on having close contacts with patients"*, and being *"by the patients' side."* They felt motivated *"when the patients are satisfied" or "pleased with our attention" or "cooperative."* One of them even stated that she felt encouraged in her work when *"patients come back to see us after being discharged from hospital."*

At the same time, these respondents described problems in their relationships with patients by expressing regrets about *"the lack of time to talk to patients"*, *"patients and families who don't understand the doctors' explanations"*, and *"patients' suffering."* They also reproached the pa-tients themselves for not behaving as the nurses felt they should: *"the patients are aggressive"*; *"the patients are unmanageable"*, *"impatient"*.

They also mentioned their relationships with the rest of the team: *"teamwork and mutual respect between professions"*; *"professional solidarity"*; *"the team atmosphere"*; *"progressing with the team on a project."* However, they also deplored the *"lack of communication among the staff"*, *"the lack of communication between doctors and nurses"*, having to *"take decisions alone"*, and *"carry out projects in a very short time."*

Although these nurses saw both sides of their work relationships, this was not the case when it came to their conditions of work: on this score, their opinions were largely negative. In particular, they complained of having problems due to the new work arrangements: *"under-staffing"*; *"being overworked"*; *"human resource management when disputes occur"*; *"the working hours."* These problems resulted from the move to rationalize hospital work which occurred when the *pôles* were created: flex time, for example, is difficult to cope with when there is a shortage of staff.

Respondents no long complained as much as their predecessors about the need to improve their wages and their occupational status. Most of their criticisms focused on the "new go-vernance" reforms, especially the quality of care and their career paths. However, these cri-ticisms were not expressed in terms of the usual demands (for better pay, working hours, etc.). The issues at stake had changed since 1987-1988. Nurses had acquired more recognition in general, and were able to balance their work and family lives more easily. The main ques-tion was now whether the reforms were liable to undermine this progress. It is worth noting that the second survey was conducted in Paris at the time when these reforms were being first implemented. In view of the context, these young nurses' criticisms about the organi-zational changes were not in fact particularly harsh.

In response to the question about the hospital reforms, five of the nurses with less than 12 years' seniority complained about priority being given to cost-effectiveness to the detri-ment of the quality of care:

"I am against it. The system is unfortunately focusing increasingly on financial efficiency rather than on the quality of care."

"We are moving all the time towards a dual healthcare system: those who can afford it will pay for their treatment, and the others will not have access to treatment."

"Too many budget restrictions are preventing medical practices from being carried out in good faith."

"All people see is the economics of hospitals. They don't care about humanity and the work the staff are doing."

"The reforms were needed but their implementation is laborious and they do not please the patients."

Two nurses criticised the hospital reforms because of their impact on the organization of work: *"the budget restrictions have led to a shortage of staff"*; *"with the clusters arrangement, the workload is liable to become heavier."*

Although some respondents qualified the hospital reforms as *"important"*, others objected that *"they never consult us"*, or refused to give an opinion at such an early stage: *"we will have to wait and see"* because *"I have not been well informed."*

In response to the question about nurses' associations and unions, the younger nurses expressed the opinion that they were useful at collective level, since the issues they addressed were broad ones: *"improving conditions of work and protecting our rights"*; *"since they defend the cause of our profession"*; *"defending the profession and those who work in it."*

To defend their individual interests, nurses turn more readily to the unions than to nurse' associations: *"in terms of the security of my job and if I have any conflicts with my superiors"*; *"the union is useful for individuals but not for the profession as a whole"*; *"providing support and assistance with problems."*

Some of these nurses expressed a lack of interest in this question: *"I am not particularly interested in these things and I don't know how they work"*; *"there's no contact"*; *"no comment"*; *"as little as possible"*. Those who adopted this passive attitude were neither for nor against the reforms; but most of them were not very militant, although changes have to be supported by all those involved if they are to last.

Nurses in the more senior group: Relationships with the team and powerless unions

Nurses with more than 13 years' seniority ore frequently complained about the hierarchy between hospital professions and focused on the relationships between professions and with patients.

In response to the question about patients' trajectories, like the less senior nurses, they mentioned both positive and negative aspects without making any hard and fast judgments. They said they were motivated, for example *"to take an overall approach to patients and give them personal attention"*; *"to look for other methods of working to make the treatment easier and adapt it to the patients in the best possible way"*; *"to bring back patients' autonomy"*; to alleviate *"pain"*.

Like their younger colleagues, they said they found their work difficult when patients *"die"*, when dealing with *"patients with severe diseases"*, or treating them *"with a view to relieving their pain."*

They said they were motivated to perform technical tasks, which they referred to in fairly general terms: *"technical gestures"*, *"getting patients through an acute phase"*, *"the outcome of a disease"*, *"curing patients."*

However, some of them said they preferred performing the tasks which are specific to a given unit: *"I like working in this speciality; I always feel motivated; it's a really interesting pathology"*; they were motivated because they were *"attracted to the speciality"* with which their unit dealt.

They also mentioned their motivation to build relationships with patients (*"contact with patients"*), and to satisfy patients (*"the patients are satisfied"*; *"the patients are pleased"*; *"the patients and their families are happy"*; *"the patients are glad to see me"*). The problems encountered in this respect were described as follows *"not being able to devote as much time to patients"*; *"problems in my relationships with patients"*; *"patients who are difficult to relate to psychologically"*; *"several demands made by patients"*; *"difficult to cope with family visits"*; *"dealing with the family when death occurs unexpectedly"*. However, unlike their younger colleagues, they did not use any very emphatic emotional terms (*"suffering"*, *"distress"*, *"aggressive"*).

They also spoke more explicitly than the less senior nurses about the fact that treatment should be based on teamwork. They were most highly motivated by *"getting on well with colleagues"* *"in a spirit of mutual trust"*, *"in close collaboration with the intern, which is conducive to verbal exchanges"*; they spoke about *"the quality of our work and the efficiency of the team"*, *"the nurses' attention and minding good practices."* They said they like being involved in team projects; one of them quoted *"the introduction of ambulatory care"* as an example of a project which brought the work collective more closely together.

However, teamwork can have a negative side when the conditions are not conducive to cooperation. In this case, the respondents described *"the bad atmosphere in the ward"*, and *"clashes between members of the team"*, when talking about the relationships between other members of staff.

Physicians were said to be partly responsible for these situations: cooperation among those working together was said to be difficult because of *"the doctor's irregularly timed visits, [which resulted in] disorganization"*. Some of them insisted on the term *"medical disorganization"*. One respondent deplored the fact that when there were no clear-cut medical prescriptions, she sometimes had to take on more responsibility than she was officially supposed to. In response to the question about particularly difficult work, one nurse mentioned a case where the diagnosis had been made and the problem identified, but *"the treatment to be applied in order to solve this problem was left to me although there was no medical prescription, which meant there was the problem of taking on that responsibility."*

In addition, the lack of coordination between physicians sometimes led nurses to make statements to their patients which put them in the wrong. One of them even spoke of lack of confidence and trust between herself and the patients, and the need to be able to align what she said with the treatment prescribed.

Like the younger nurses, the more senior ones mostly mentioned problems resulting from the constraints resulting from the new ay of organizing the work. The shorter hospital stay and staff reduction policies adopted when the clusters were created (*"we are permanently un-*

der-staffed") lead to complications *"when there is both a large flux of patients and a shortage of nursing staff"*; *"when the workload becomes really overwhelming"*; in addition, one matron responsible for regulating and attenuating the effects of staff shortages stated that *"managing the timetables is not easy because it's so difficult to find replacements"*.

Some of the nurses said the hospital reforms were entirely based on health economics criteria: *"focusing increasingly on cost-efficiency"*; *"we are moving towards separate medical systems for the rich and poor"*; *"a dual medical system, all at the expense of quality and our health"*; *"the healthcare supply is decreasing."* Other nurses stated (without referring to health economics)that the hospital reforms had simply reduced the quality of healthcare: *"I don't expect it will improve the quality of care"*; *"the patients are penalised, it takes such a long time getting to hospital"*; *"the only problems addressed have been medical ones, whereas no attention has been paid to paramedical issues."*

Half of the nurses in this group said that the hospital reforms imposed intra-hospital mobility on them while detracting from the quality of care: *"the problem with the new system of governance is that it means nurses are always being moved around in the cluster"*; *"the staff are going to become even more demotivated because they are being moved around by the administrators like figures on a chessboard"*; *"the impact on nurses is that they are afraid of being moved around in the cluster"*; *"it may be good for health economics but this moving around is not so good (being a stop-gap)"*; *"I feel setting up clusters and decreasing the numbers of staff are liable to affect the patients' treatment and the quality of the care and personal attention they receive"*; *"the lack of concertation can only detract from the quality of care"*; *"dehumanising the work, the team spirit is being undermined."*

Like their younger colleagues, some of these older nurses, either refused to assess the reforms for lack of information: *"it's hard to say, I don't know"*; or were unable to weigh up the pros and cons.

On the other hand, some of the more senior nurses took an interest in the efforts made by their unions to improve their conditions of work and by nursing associations to improve their social status: *"the unions are fighting for better working conditions; one nursing association is trying to improve our status"*; *"having our profession recognized"*; *"as long as they are able to stand up for us"*; *"to handle the 'hot potatoes' (tricky issues)"*.

Others said they took a personal interest in the nurses' unions and associations *"at the local level"*: *"when personal problems crop up in a unit, they deal with them; at the national level, they don't seem to do so much"*; *"to keep up with the latest laws and reforms"*; *"to support, defend and inform us."*

Some respondents mentioned the fact that unions do not make a stand on the quality of care or the organization of work, and wondered whether they were actually any good at negotiating: *"the unions are not very dynamic as far as hospital care is concerned"*; *"the unions don't do much about the way our work is organized"*; *"I don't think they have much power or many means of exerting pressure"*; *"they have very few means at their disposal."*

Summary of the statements made by nurses in the second survey

In this survey, the importance attached to the treatment dispensed by nurses and their contacts with patients featured more prominently in the discourse of the younger nurses than in that of their elders *(Table 3.11)*; whereas the more senior nurses were more interested in questions having to do with teamwork. However, contrary to those interviewed in 1980, the second group of more senior respondents surveyed no longer expressed the opinion that cooperation among those working at a hospital unit was a central issue. The latest ways in which the work is being organized, which have obliged nurses to move from one unit to another within a given cluster, are tending to reduce cooperation between nurses in comparison with the previous generation. And yet the younger nurses in the second survey stated that it was difficult for them to handle patients' "sufferings" without the support and cooperation of their team.

It therefore emerged from these surveys that the respondents expressed the opinion that the latest reforms were degrading the quality of hospital care. In addition, many of the most senior nurses considered that French nurses' world of work is being destroyed by the new system of work organization based on "poles" or clusters *(Table 3.12)*.

As shown in *table 3.13*, less than half of the nurses who participated in our second survey answered the question about nurses' unions and associations, and about one third of them took an interest in these matters only from the individual point of view, while another third said they were not interested because unions and associations do not deal with issues such as the quality of care and how nurses' work is organized.

Table 3.11. *Work relationships (2007-2008).*

Seniority	Diversity of the tasks	Therapeutic care	Contacts with patients		Teamwork		Heavy constraints due to the organiza- tion of work	Total
			Possible	Difficult	Possible	Difficult		
Less than 12years	14	10	15	13	6	3	27	88
More than 13years	13	6	12	7	11	12	28	89
Total	27	16	27	20	17	15	55	177

Table 3.12. *Opinions about the hospital reforms (2007-2008).*

Seniority	Quality of care degraded	Criticism of the *pôles* (clusters) arrangements	Simply a positive or negative response	Refusal to give an immediate appraisal	Total
Less than 12 years	5	2	6	6	19
More than 13 years	7	12	2	5	26
Total	12	14	8	11	45

Table 3.13. *Nurses' expectations about the role of unions and associations (2007-2008).*

Seniority	Defending collective interests	Defending individual interests	Not interested	Total
Less than 12 years	6	6	5	17
More than 13 years	4	5	7	16
Total	10	11	12	33

CONCLUSION

In the light of nurses' patent mistrust of the latest reforms and their lack of confidence in their institutional representatives, the picture which emerges as to the future of the classical forms of collective action is not a very optimistic one.

However, many nurses are placing their hopes on new forms of organization (such as those likely to be instituted by the new Order of nurses) and on new means of achieving recognition via vocational training levels or personal commitment to increase the autonomy of their team. This may in fact indicate that the nursing profession in France is now endowed with large, flexible qualification professional spaces, and that it has therefore become a fully-fledged profession.

After the present period of transition, once the *pôles* have settled down into more stable and efficient patterns, the individual trajectories open to nurses will no doubt become more clearly perceptible. At the present moment, these trajectories still focus on the units to which nurses are attached; but these stable links are now on the road to extinction.

The nurses' unions will only be able to recover even a small measure of utility if they are able to join the present move towards rationalization. This can be done by helping to define the contours of this change, thereby sustaining and possibly increasing the scope for nurses and other paramedical to take responsibility for carrying out projects and implementing changes. As shown by the 2009 decree reorganizing the governance of the

French hospitals, the present period is so open to innovation and experimentation means that all the members of hospital staff should think hard about re-defining their own activities and missions.

REFERENCES

• Bouffartigue P, Bouteiller J. Jongleuses en blouse blanche ; la mobilisation des compétences temporelles chez les infirmières hospitalières. In: *Actes des IXes Journées de Sociologie du Travail.* Paris, novembre 2003.

• Hirschman AO. *Exit, voice, and loyalty. Responses to decline in firms, organizations, and states.* Cambridge: Harvard University Press, 1970.

• Hughes EC. *Le Regard sociologique. Essais choisis.* Paris: EHESS, 1996.

• Glaser BC, Strauss A. *The Discovery of grounded theory.* Chicago: Aldine, 1967.

• Magnon R. *Les Infirmières. Identité, spécificité et soins infirmiers, le bilan d'un siècle.* Paris: Masson, 2001.

4. Japanese Nurses' Social World: Segmentation between those Integrated into the Organization and the Others

In this chapter, it is proposed to present the results of two surveys conducted in Japan in 1989 and 2007-2008, with a view to examining the evolution of Japanese nurses' identity, as done in the case of French nurses in the previous chapter. Here again we will focus on the following two aspects of nurses' social world: their commitment to their profession and their interest in continuing vocational training, and their work relationships and social demands. As we will see from the Japanese nurses' statements about their work, a sharp distinction exists in this country between those who are integrated into the hospital system and those who are not. In the case of Japan, this distinction has led to the existence of a large gap between the staff nurses and matrons.

In the first survey, which was conducted in 1989, interviews were conducted with forty-six Japanese nurses working at four large Tokyo hospitals[1]. At that time, Japanese hospitals were being classified as short stay or long stay hospitals as the result of a policy adopted in 1985. In addition to the fact that this policy led to the names of hospitals being changed, it also meant that the numbers of staff varied considerably from one hospital to another. Larger numbers of staff were being employed at University hospitals and hospitals with specific functions than at the other hospitals and clinics.

In this survey, "theoretical sampling" procedures were applied as differences between groups emerged. It is worth noting that the composition of both groups of nurses interviewed differed between France and Japan in terms of their seniority: the Japanese nurses had less seniority on the whole than their French counterparts. The two groups into which the Japanese sample, which included only one male nurse, was subdivided were composed as follows: the first group consisted of 24 nurses with less than 6 years' seniority, and the second group consisted of 22 nurses with more than 7 years' seniority (see *table 4.1*).

---

1. These four hospitals were Saint Luke's Hospital, Toranomon Hopital, Tokyo Ikashika University Hopital and Chiba University Hospital.

The interviews were conducted in the nurses' rest-rooms, which were located in or near the wards where they worked. The interviews, which lasted one hour on average, were structured on the basis of a formal guide and focused mainly on three subjects: nurses' commitment to their profession and their training; and their work relationships and social demands.

All the interviews were recorded and transcribed for further analysis. The attitudes of the nurses in the two groups defined above were then examined, using the same procedure as that adopted to analyse the French nurses' discourse (coding their statements into classes and analysing any variations observed),

The 2007-2008 took place at a time when the functional differentiation between hospitals had become more firmly established. This survey, which was designed to describe the evolution of the nursing profession in Japan, was based on the use of a questionnaire containing a set of open questions on the socio-professional topics mentioned above. The questionnaire was answered by 72 nurses working at the same four Tokyo hospitals as those involved in the previous survey.

The study population is presented in *table 4.2.*

Table 4.1. *Sample included in the survey in 1989.*

Seniority	Position		Sex		Total
	Nurses	Matrons	Women	Men	
Less than 6 years	24	0	23	1	24
More than 7 years	8	14	22	0	22
Total	32	14	45	1	46

Table 4.2. *Sample included in the survey in 2007-2008.*

Seniority	Position		Sex		Total
	Nurses	Matrons	Women	Men	
Less than 6 years	42	0	42	0	42
More than 7 years	13	17	29	1	30
Total	55	17	71	1	72

JAPANESE NURSES' COMMITMENT TO THEIR PROFESSION AND THEIR INTEREST IN CONTINUING VOCATIONAL TRAINING

The choice between giving up one's career and internal promotion in 1989

Most Japanese nurses who were not matrons in 1989 expected to give up their career when they got married, but they often decided to go on working if they were given the opportunity of being promoted to the rank of head nurse or matron. Their discourse showed that they wavered between these two possibilities.

Nurses in the less senior group: Incompatibility between professional and family life; gradual acquisition/updating of knowledge

Half of the Japanese nurses with less than 6 years' seniority questioned expressed negative opinions about their professional commitment: they expected to eventually give up their work, which they took to be incompatible with raising a family. This feeling of incompatibility can be attributed to the conditions of work at Japanese hospitals. Unlike the French nurses interviewed, who always worked on the same shift, Japanese nurses have to follow a rota between the night, afternoon and daytime shifts, which means that they work eight nights per month on average and their daytime shifts end as late as 19:00; in addition, they are practically not paid for any overtime work they do.

Three of these nurses mentioned the career prospects outside the hospital, and said they might get a teaching job at a nursing school or become a primary school public health nurse, no doubt because of the regular hours which go with jobs of this kind.

Let us take the case of one young unmarried nurse who mentioned the problem of reconciling work and family life: her response was typical of most of these fairly young nurses. Staff nurse A.T. was working at the Toranomon Hospital, and had only one year's seniority. Her discourse reflected her lack of commitment to her profession. She admitted that *"like most other people"*, she did not intend to commit herself for long to the nursing profession:

> "Many of us come from the provinces, and after working at the leading hospitals in Tokyo, they go back home. So they stop working after practising for 3 years. I don't intend to return to the province I came from. But I will see what I decide to do in 3 years' time. Last year, eight people left my unit. This is a mentally tiring job; so they needed a rest after working for a few years. It's hard to go on working at the same place."

Many nurses therefore invest in the profession for short periods, and only a minority make long-term commitments, either because they are resigned to spinsterhood or because they have hopes of obtaining internal promotion. A.T., another young nurse, explain how difficult it is to commit oneself to the profession after marriage because most Japanese husbands do not want their wives to work.

She said it was difficult to commit oneself to such a *"lowly"* profession with no status. However, this negative picture of nursing because of the *dirty work* involved was offset by a more positive definition in terms of the *"feminine and maternal qualities"* it requires and the *"sensitivity to other people which is specific to women"*:

> "Some people are able to go on working because they are willing to remain unmarried, but that is not my choice. If husbands did not object, we could go on working. It's true that we have to come in very early in the morning and get home very late at night. Some people look for good reasons for committing themselves to working as nurses, but I feel it is difficult. Most nurses find it hard to invest in their work. Working for 3 years is enough. It's a lowly profession. It consists, for example, of washing patients and dealing with self-centred people. I used to think it would be great to learn all about patients' psychology: that's why I decided to become a nurse. In this profession, you have to be sensitive to other people, which is a female, maternal quality that I didn't possess. I thought I would be able to become more sensitive to other people by working as a nurse. That's why I chose this profession."

Japanese nurses who have been working for at least 3 years are more prepared than their younger colleagues to pursue a career. Their negative opinions about the lack of compatibility between professional and family life were offset in the case of 4 nurses by hopes of promotion outside the hospital (becoming teachers) and in that of 4 other nurses, who expressed their attachment to the hospital institution.

Nurse C.C., who was working at Chiba University Hospital and had acquired 5 years of experience, was one of those who expressed hopes of promotion outside the hospital. Her freely chosen trajectory, consisting of moving back and forth between the provinces and the capital, between *"dispensing care"* and *"teaching"* was devoid of family constraints. In the following excerpt from her interview, she described her professional trajectory, which consisted of five parts: starting off as a nurse; going in for teaching; taking a continuing vocational training course; going back to nursing; and going back to teaching. The reason she gave for pursuing this zigzag trajectory was that she did not want internal promotion to a matron's position. Her present occupational project was *"teaching"*, i.e., making another break with her present commitment to *"dispensing care as a nurse"*:

> "It was not for family reasons that I came here. I am not married. It's rather complicated. After working for 3 years at the Surgical unit at the Kyushu University Hospital, I was fed up with surgery. At first I thought about working in a public health department because I have the public health nursing diploma. But I didn't find a job there. Then the head nurse told me about a job going at a nursing school in Tokyo. So although I had no teaching qualifications, I went in for teaching for one year. As I was keen (on teaching), I enrolled at a further educational college to obtain the teachers' diploma. And I was thinking about whether to return to Kyushu. But since I was sent to the Chiba University Hospital when I finished the teacher-training course, I decided to work at that hospital and go back to nursing. At that point, I was in the General Internal Medicine department. That experience would be useful if I became a teacher. I don't expect to become a matron or to go on working in the same place. If I stayed on at the same hospital, I would be promoted to the position of matron, but that doesn't appeal to me. As long as I am in nursing, I want to be in touch with the patients. I don't want to go on nursing all my life. One day or another, I would like to go back to teaching."

Unlike the staff nurses, who expected to give up their jobs when they were married, those promoted to the position of matron whom we interviewed were glad to have obtained internal promotion. F.T. was a typical example of those in the group of young nurses who had been promoted to the rank of matron.

F.T., who was unmarried, was working as a matron at Toranomon Hospital. She had 5 years' seniority. She said her professional commitment was partly due to her liking for hospital work, and partly due to the fact that she was promoted unexpectedly, after being briefly attached to the Intensive Cardiology unit, where she had made a good impression: this promotion enabled her to *"carry out a project."* The position of matron was in fact her first choice. This internal promotion was an important point in her career, which made her want to *"go on working"* at the same hospital. Internal promotion was therefore a means of integration into the institution, from which those not promoted are excluded. The latter tend to give up their jobs because they are not compatible with their family lives:

> "Many of them go back to their provinces after working for 3 years at a large hospital. So they give up hospital work. I myself like the work and although I was having problems, I didn't think about leaving the hospital. So here I am. After 3 years, people are often fed up with their job. Personally, however, after working for 2 years – that means before I started getting fed up – I moved to the intensive care unit and worked there for another 2 years. It's true that last year, I was getting fed up and I was thinking: 'If I stay on here, I am going to be in a difficult situation'. That wasn't because the work was hard, but I had been learning for long enough and I was already the most senior member of the team. I couldn't see how I could carry out a project. That is why I was in a difficult situation. And then I was offered the job of matron. That was my first choice [...]

> After acquiring 5 years' seniority, it's not possible to go on working without thinking about one's career. After 5 years on the job, you have to make a choice. Some people expect to be able to balance their professional and family lives. Some can only fulfil themselves professionally and others invest in family life. In my case, I was given an option. I don't think it can be easy to manage work and family life because of the way the work schedules are distributed. But I am not yet engaged to be married."

On the other hand, among the 24 younger nurses (those with less than 6 years' seniority) interviewed about how they had updated their knowledge in the field of nursing, 16 spoke about the practical experience acquired while working at the hospital. Nurses' acquisition of skills is often interrupted after 3 years of experience because their commitment to their profession is not very strong. Although 3 nurses said they were interested in nursing research, 3 others expressed doubts as to whether doing research was worthwhile.

Nurse A.L., who was working at Saint Luke's Hospital, had only one year of seniority. She stated that each year of practical experience constituted a stage in the acquisition of competences, which she described as a gradual process:

> "Our objectives during the second year at work are still quite rudimentary, and my level of competence depends directly on the position I hold this year, which is not the same as last year. Here there is a system of competence assessment: the matrons make technical and psychological assessments and we also have to assess ourselves. Every six months, we have an interview with our matron to determine our level of competence."

The gradual acquisition of knowledge was also mentioned by nurse A.I., who had been working for 2 years at Ikashika University Hospital. She explained how, after learning the *"basic techniques"* during the first year, nurses start to *"deepen their knowledge about some diseases"* before taking an interest in *"patients' psychology"* during the third year:

> "I now realize that what I have been learning during my third year has been different from what I learned during the first two years. The first year, I improved my ability to perform basic techniques such as injections. Then I improved my knowledge about some diseases. Now I am learning how to understand the patients' psychology. I am taking an interest in the patients' lives since I have already progressed in other fields. Up to now, I simply couldn't imagine what the patients felt."

Given the low level of commitment of most newly qualified nurses, A.L. stressed the difference between *"those who plan to stay on for a long time"*, who acquire a very high level of competence with a view to achieving internal promotion, and *"those who do not intend to stay"*, who will never reach this level:

> "I would say that those who plan to stay on for a long time will acquire competences which those who do not intend to stay will never acquire. It depends on the person. But there are some people who may be judged to be more competent than others although they behave in the same way. The assessment is therefore not really fair. The assessment doesn't mean anything."

As far as nurses' "quality circles" and "nursing research" at the hospital or within the unit itself are concerned, some of the younger nurses expressed negative opinions about these group activities. D.T., who had been working as a nurse for 2 years at Toranomon Hospital, explained this attitude as follows:

> "Some people attend continuing vocational training courses, conferences and study groups, but not everybody does so. Those who participate are highly thought of. It's hard to do research when you are short of time and I doubt whether the research is really worthwhile. Finding a topic or taking part in a research project is very hard because it means working overtime without any additional pay."

I.I. was the first male nurse ever employed at Ikashika University Hospital. He was a bachelor who had been working for one year at the operating theatre. He explained how he had come to choose this profession by chance after taking a part-time student job at a hospital. On the one hand, he admitted that nursing is a predominantly female profession, since both male and female patients prefer to be tended by female nurses. But he had a good argument supporting his choice of profession, based on the difference between sexes: *"men see patients differently from women"*:

> "A short while ago, a new male nurse arrived at the operating theatre. I believe women are better nurses than men. But people say men are needed in the theatre to do the heavy physical work. It's true, I carry out only physical tasks. However, men see patients differently from women. The arrival of men is not a bad thing. But the patients certainly prefer to be tended by female nurses. Both male and female patients prefer female nurses. The doctors too prefer to work with female nurses. But maybe men are going to gradually enter the profession from now on.
> When I was studying natural science at the University, I had some part-time office jobs at this hospital. That made me think about working in the field of healthcare. And I watched the nurses working, which led me to choose this profession. I am new here, but I am older than most of the others."

This male nurse believed that it is essential to acquire practical skills by spending some time at the same institution *("I want to gain experience")*. However, unlike most of the younger female nurses, who expected the learning phase to be quite short (3 or 4 years), he looked much farther ahead:

> "I can give my point de view to the other members of the team. But there are some more senior colleagues who have been there for 10 or 20 years, whom I cannot convince, simply because I have acquired only one year of experience. However, experience can be acquired only through practice; and theories count too. But I want to gain experience. To achieve leadership, I will have to wait until I am at least 30 years old."

Nurses in the more senior group:
Attachment to the hospital institution and practical training

The nurses in the older group had between 7 years' and 40 years' seniority: most of them expressed positive opinions about nurses' commitment to their profession. Out of the 22 respondents in this group, 13 were pleased with the internal promotion they had obtained, and 4 placed the accent on the length of time they had spent working at the same hospital and seemed to have managed to balance their work and their family lives.

To study this more experienced group of nurses, extracts from the discourse of two of the respondents were analysed: one spoke favourably about her internal promotion to the position of matron, and the other about reconciling her career with her family life.

G.I. was an unmarried nurse with 19 years' seniority working at the Ikashika University Hospital. She had become a matron 4 years previously. She spoke of her promotion as a means of integration into the hospital institution. Her commitment to the nursing profession was therefore entirely based on this internal promotion. She specified that all the matrons were recruited within the hospital. It is worth mentioning here that in Japan, internal promotion to the rank of matron is based on an assessment of the candidates which is conducted by the matrons themselves:

> "I have often thought about giving up my job. But when I was promoted to the rank of matron, I decided to stay here. When nurses are promoted to being matrons, they usually decide to stay on at the same hospital. They go on working until they retire. Once you become a matron, you have no chance of being recruited at other hospitals. So there is no way out. In addition, you become attached to the place of work once you have been there for years. One acquires a feeling of responsibility.
> The matrons suggest candidates for the position of matron. Once the candidates have been assessed by the matrons themselves, the head matron makes the appointments. You therefore cannot be promoted if your assessment is poor, even if you have been working for many years. Therefore, I feel it is important for nurses to find a matron who will give them practical training with a view to being promoted up the career ladder."

It is worth noting that the most senior matrons who participated in this survey said it was possible to reconcile work and family life. H.I., for example, was married with children and had been a matron at Ikashika University Hospital for 2 years. She had 25 years' seniority in all. As she explained, she had managed to balance work and family life because she was working in the operating theatre when her children were small, which meant doing very little night shift duty:

"I graduated in 1964. At first I worked for a few years at a hospital in the Hokkaido region. Then I got married and my husband was appointed by his company to the region of Kyushu. I therefore worked at Kyushu Hospital for 3 years and acquired some experience in the operating theatre. Then I followed my husband again when he was moved to Tokyo. I came with him to Tokyo. There was a job available at the operating theatre at Ikashika University Hospital and I took the job. When my children were small, I didn't often have to work at night because I was working in the operating theatre. That was a good thing. But at the hospital's inpatient wards, the nurses have to do rotas, working alternately at night, in the afternoon and during the day. I have been working at the general surgical unit for 5 years. When you have been working for many years, you can be promoted to the rank of matron. You can choose whether to become a matron or not. But people who are offered promotion generally accept it. I have been a matron for 2 years now. I would no longer like to return to the operating theatre because what is interesting about being a nurse is dispensing care in the inpatient departments.

After acquiring experience at a University Hospital, many young nurses go to work in the provinces. That causes problems for the matrons. However, with their experience, they may be a good influence at other hospitals. I am married and I am still working. I hope they will go on working too after they are married. Their husbands should allow them to work."

On the other hand, two thirds of the 22 of the nurses in the more experienced group expressed definite interest in research. They tended to prefer doing research on the hospital premises outside their working hours. Seven of them mentioned the value of acquiring practical learning with other colleagues. The following interview illustrates the interest in research shown by many of the experienced matrons and the idea that matrons should set an example to the members of their team by engaging in research projects.

H.L., who was a matron in charge of a children's ward at Saint Luke's Hospital had 11 years of seniority. Her statements show how keen she was to develop relational skills in the younger nurses: according to her, these take 3 or 4 years to acquire. This matron also mentioned her role as a trainer of the members of her team:

"I would say all nurses do not have contacts of the same quality with their patients. Some of them are able to make good contacts and others seem to lack something. I esteem those who are gentle and friendly towards their patients. But that does not always suffice, because to be a good nurse, you also have to adapt to the patients' sensitivity. It takes 3 or 4 years of experience to be capable of handling both aspects: observing children's relationships with their parents and understanding children's psychosocial development. They are therefore not capable of handling the whole nursing process single-handed until they have acquired 3 years of experience. I hope they learn to apply these skills in a gentle and friendly way. Since becoming a matron I have had no time to dispense care and make contact with the patients. But I do talk to patients occasionally all the same. In the old days, I used to apply the whole nursing process and I was in touch with the children and their families. I enjoyed doing that. I no longer have any direct contacts with patients, but I do enjoy making suggestions to the nurses in the team about how to plan their activities. And as I am a matron, it is up to me to explain to the families the rules which have to be obeyed while their children are in hospital. From that point of view, I'm afraid have a rather unpleasant role to play towards the families.

We are trying to introduce the primary nursing care system here. And I make suggestions to the nurses about how to apply the whole nursing process to patients single-handed. I am responsible for coordinating the nursing of the patients. This system makes them feel more responsible for what they do. I suggest to some nurses that they should look into ways of handling a particular case. I run a nursing research group which focuses on caring for children with leukaemia. We are studying the use of various treatment protocols in aseptic chambers, patients' diet and how to train children's families. The nurses in my team and I are increasingly motivated to take part in research groups. It's the best way of training ourselves."

In this matron's opinion, the transmission of technical and scientific knowledge to nurses requires first developing qualities which are practically innate and "naturally" feminine. This is one of the main characteristics which goes to make up the public image of Japanese nurses' social world.

Summary of the findings made in the first survey

This sample of 46 nurses was subdivided into two groups, based on the nurses' seniority and the type of position (staff nurses or matrons) they held *(Table 4.3)*. The younger nurses expressed little desire to engage in a proper nursing career because they thought it was too difficult to balance work and family life. The only young male nurse interviewed spoke about his decision to go in for nursing and his awareness of the difference between male and female nurses. The more experienced nurses interviewed, many of whom who had been promoted to the rank of matron, had succeeded, on the contrary, in reconciling their professional activities with their family lives and hoped to continue working indefinitely for the same institution.

Table 4.4 shows the answers given about the various forms of further learning, depending on the nurses' seniority. The less senior nurses tended to prefer training on the hospital premises, whereas their elders preferred "quality circle" nursing research groups within the hospital precincts.

Most of the staff nurses felt that acquiring professional experience was of little importance because they were likely to give up their jobs when they married or started to raise a family.

Nursing research initiated by matrons with the support of their hospital nursing management and the hospital management was found to result in segmentation: those who participated in research projects could be promoted to the rank of matrons, whereas the others were either not promoted or gave up their jobs.

Table 4.3. *Nurses' commitment to their profession (1989).*

Seniority	Balancing work and family life not possible	Leaving the hospital	Achieving balance between work and family	Attachment to the profession and/or the institution	Other	Total
Less than 6 years	12	4	0	3	5	24
More than 7 years	4	0	4	13	1	22
Total	16	4	4	16	6	46

Table 4.4. *Means of continuing vocational training (1989).*

Seniority	Training at the hospital, at the ward or among colleagues	Lack of interest in nursing research	Interested in nursing research	Undergoing continuing vocational training outside the hospital	Total
Less than 6 years	22	3	3	1	29
More than 7 years	13	0	15	0	28
Total	35	3	18	1	57

Career advancement via external vocational training in 2007-2008

Nurses in the less senior group: Future prospects outside the hospital

None of the 42 nurses with less than 6 years' seniority had children, and half of them were working more than 56 hours per week, which breaks down into a 40-hour week plus 16 hours of mainly unpaid overtime.

During the 2000s, as in the 1980s, the hard conditions of work were preventing Japanese nurses with children from pursuing continuous careers.

However, in response to the question "How do you picture your future career?", the younger nurses questioned in 2007-2000, unlike those questioned in 1989, only rarely mentioned the problem of balancing their profession with their family lives. Three of them certainly mentioned family reasons for giving up their careers, however: *"I will not be able to go on working here after getting married."*

Almost half of this group intended to move to another place of work: *"I (often) change my place of work but I go on being a nurse"*; *"I plan to work for another 3 or 4 years at the same place, but after that, I will go to work elsewhere"*. Others stated that their future lay outside the hospital: *"I am interested in caring for elderly people, and I want to work at an old people's home. I am working here to advance my future project"*; *"I want to work as a visiting nurse, outside the hospital"*; *"I would like to become a public health nurse at a company"*.

In order to advance their future career, 3 nurses planned to leave the hospital to pursue further studies: *"I plan to do University studies"*; *"I intend to study at the University up to Masters' level"*; *"I would like to do periods of work experience abroad in order to go on being a nurse in the future."*

Only one third of the younger nurses expected to continue working at the same place: *"I will continue to work at the same hospital"*; three of these respondents also said *"I would like to work at a different unit"* at the same hospital.

Within the space of 20 years, Japanese nurses' career prospects have therefore completely changed: the majority of the younger nurses declared that they planned to pursue their nursing careers outside the hospital, whereas their 1980 counterparts imagined that they would give up their careers as soon as they got married.

What they said about their future projects was purely speculative, however, since most of the nurses in this group had not really had to make any real choices so far. The turning-point which usually occurs at the birth of the first child had not yet arrived. However, this event was likely to affect their career paths before very long.

On the other hand, the nurses questioned in the 1980s stated that continuing vocational training, in the form of the quality circles known as "nursing research", should be dispensed at their units or at least at the hospital where they worked, whereas those questioned in the 2000s stated that most continuing vocational training courses were being run outside the hospital.

In response to the question "How do you update your knowledge?", half of the younger nurses mentioned the continuing vocational training courses run outside the hospital by associations such as the Japan Nursing Association, which organizes courses in clinical nursing as well as congresses. One third of this group mentioned training within the unit itself or at the hospital where they worked. The two possibilities available to nurses for updating their knowledge (either inside or outside the hospital) therefore corresponded to the two possibilities open to them for pursuing their careers, namely either inside or outside the hospital.

Nurses in the more senior group: Feeling blocked

Only 5 of the 30 more senior nurses versus 18 of the 42 younger nurses were working more than 56 hours per week. The more senior nurses, many of whom had been promoted to the rank of matron, were exempted from night duty. In addition, only 5 of the nurses in the more senior group had children: 4 of them were matrons doing a 50-hour week, and one was a staff nurse doing a 48-hour week. These nurses managed to juggle with their work schedules in order to balance their professional and family lives by making arrangements with the other nurses in the team.

Two of the more senior nurses expressed their attachment to the present institution as follows: *"I am still working at the same hospital."*

However, their attachment to the institution may not be destined to last very long, because most of them were unmarried and childless at the time of the survey. Only one of these nurses mentioned the problem of balancing work and family life: *"I will not be able to go on working under these conditions when I am married: I am thinking about changing my place of work."*

Others were thinking about moving to another place of work because of the long hours, while continuing to be nurses: *"I am planning to change my place of work because the workload is too heavy here"*; *"there is a lot of overtime here and I want to work elsewhere, where I will be properly recognized as a nurse."* The more senior nurses frequently stated that working for more than 7 years consistently doing overtime was more than they could stand physically: *"I want to move to another place of work because the workload is too heavy here, it's very hard physically."* It is worth mentioning that being promoted to the rank of matron meant being exempted from night duty: *"It's hard to go on working without being promoted to a matron's position"*. Only one of the older nurses specified where she would like to work: *"I would like to become a visiting nurse or do palliative care at the hospice."*

Unlike their younger colleagues, who planned to pursue their careers outside the hospital, the more senior nurses who said it was difficult to go on working felt they were blocked and stressed the heavy workload they had to put up with; and yet they did not envisage leaving the hospital.

In response to the question about updating their knowledge, the more senior nurses, like their younger colleagues, mentioned the vocational training schemes run by associations outside the hospital as well as those run at the ward or elsewhere within the hospital. The question arises here as to whether these two ways of updating knowledge are liable to lead to the pursuit of careers outside the hospital as well as to continuous hospital careers.

We do not have sufficient hindsight at the moment to determine the impact of the qualifying continuing vocational training schemes set up by the Japan Nursing Association on nurses with a view to having cross-departmental positions created for hospital nurses specialized in hygiene or stomatotherapy, for instance. These positions require high levels of competence as well as the ability to adapt to the complex task of combining relational and technical work. Here again, the outcome will depend on whether hospitals and their management are able to respond to this challenge.

Summary of the findings made in the second survey

In the sample of Japanese nurses included in the second survey carried out in 2007-2008, most of the respondents (67 out of 72) were childless (see *table 4.5*). In Japan, the standard working week was reduced from 48 to 44 hours in 1961, and then to 40 hours in 1997. However, as can be seen from *table 4.6*, 23 nurses out of the 72 were doing more than 56 hours per week. The nurses with less than 6 years' seniority were doing more overtime than those with more than 7 years' seniority.

The statements made by the nurses in both groups about their commitment to the profession are summarized in *table 4.7*. Unlike the nurses questioned in 1980, those questioned in 2007-2008 did not frequently mention the problem of balancing their work with their family lives when explaining why it was difficult to pursue a career. Only 18 out of the 42 younger nurses planned to pursue their future careers outside the hospital, whereas 21 out of the 30 more senior nurses pictured a future career outside the hospital. Unlike their younger colleagues, the more senior nurses tended to feel they were blocked, since they were unable to specify where they were going to work in the future.

The ways in which the respondents said they updated their knowledge are given in *table 4.8*. Two different approaches were used by those questioned in the 1980s: undergoing training within the hospital or at the ward itself, or by joining "nursing research" quality circles. This duality had disappeared by the 2000s, when the two approaches to continuing vocational training were perceived as having merged into a single category: half of the participants in the 2000 survey mentioned the continuing vocational training courses launched by nursing associations.

Tableau 4.5. *Nurses' family situation (2007-2008).*

Seniority	No children	One or more children	No response	Total
Less than 6 years	42	0	0	42
More than 7 years	25	5	0	30
Total	67	5	0	72

Table 4.6. *Number of hours of work per week (2007-2008).*

Seniority	Less than 45 h	Between 46 and 55 h	More than 56 h	Total
Less than 6 years	5	19	18	42
More than 7 years	3	22	5	30
Total	8	41	23	72

Table 4.7. *Nurses' commitment to their profession (2007-2008).*

Seniority	Difficulty in balancing work and family life	Planning to leave the hospital to become visiting nurses or work at hospices, firms or schools	Attachment to the institution	Undertaking University studies	Other	Total
Less than 6 years	3	18	13	3	6	43
More than 7 years	1	9	21	0	0	31
Total	4	27	34	3	6	74

Table 4.8. *Means of updating knowledge (2007-2008).*

Seniority	At the ward, within the hospital, among colleagues	Continuing vocational training courses and congresses held outside the hospital	Journals and Internet	Total
Less than 6 years	18	24	16	58
More than 7 years	21	20	12	53
Total	39	44	28	111

NURSES' WORK RELATIONSHIPS AND THEIR SOCIAL DEMANDS

A marked hierarchical gap between those performing manual and supervisory tasks in 1989

In the Japanese nurses' discourse, their work relationships featured mainly in terms of contacts with patients and cooperation with the other members of the team. It is worth noting that the distinctions made by the French respondents as regards hospital workers' rank were not referred to by the Japanese nurses, since no distinction is made in Japan between nurses and nursing assistants. The Japanese nurses stated that their relational role *("talking to patients")* should be recognized as being part of their overall role (along with dispensing care and mastering technical gestures)[2].

Nurses in the younger group: Lack of real contacts with patients and doctors

Half of the young nurses with less than 6 years' seniority seemed to be particularly concerned about the lack of contacts with patients. Seven of them mentioned team-work, 4 in negative terms and 3 in positive terms. Two young nurses said it was difficult to be closer to the patients and presented arguments in favour of nurses' relational role without denying the importance of dispensing care.

During her interview, nurse B.L., who had been working for one year at Saint Luke's Hospital, spoke about the lack of contacts with patients. In response to the question about how she would like to work ideally, this respondent mentioned the importance of nurses' relational role *("talking to patients")*, although she admitted that nursing care was the main priority:

> "On daytime duty, when accompanying patients to have tests carried out for instance, one can talk to them. On afternoon and night duty, I can only talk to them when I'm taking their temperature. And I also talk to patients if they call me. But you have to respect the priorities. For example, you can speak to patients for twenty minutes while washing them and handling technical details. But if you talk to them for twenty minutes while doing nothing else, you are branded as a lay-about. There are patients such as those with diabetes and liver disease who need to have their disease explained to them. But we don't give them any explanations. Rather than talking to these patients, we are expected to go on cleaning up other patients. That's not a good thing."

Likewise, nurse A.I., who had been working for 2 years at Ikashika University Hospital, spoke about the lack of real contacts with patients. In response to the question about how she would like to work ideally, this respondent immediately referred to her utopic quest for closer contacts with patients. *"If I had more time"*, she felt that the relational role should be included along with nurses' other roles (dispensing care and performing technical gestures). However, like her colleagues, she deplored the fact that she was unable to have any real contacts with patients for lack of time:

---

2. French nursing assistants are also demanding to have their relational role recognized, without denying the importance of basic care. (Arborio, 2001, p. 108-109).

"If I had more time, I would talk to the patients. Here we only attend to the treatment because we are short of time. So it's hard to tell how the patients are doing. Some of them are reluctant to call us. For example, there are some patients who don't like to ask us for anything special when we are cleaning or feeding them. Here at the hospital, everything is so standardized. Patients' quality of life should be improved while they are in hospital. Actually I never tell my superiors what I think about the patients' quality of life."

D.L., who had 4 years' seniority, was working at Saint Luke's Hospital. Like the two previous nurses in the younger group, she wished to have closer contacts with patients in order to be able to contribute to *"informing patients"*. She felt this relational role should be part of her overall role as a nurse. She regretted that shortage of time detracted from her relationships with patients and prevented her from providing them with emotional support:

"If I had more time, ideally, I would inform the patients - about their diabetes, for example, and their families too. We don't have enough time to do that. Patients' families have their work and we too are too busy. So we only explain things to them very briefly. I would like to be able to inform them more fully, by showing them posters about diet which I would put together myself and present like a video show.

I would like to spend time with patients. If the hospital gardens were larger, I would like to take patients for walks. I would say *'Isn't this a pretty garden? Can you hear the birds singing?'* Patients in hospital are reduced to the role of patients. And I just play the role of nurse, in the strict sense of the term.

Patients are approached by their families like human beings. But the visiting hours are short, and sometimes the family doesn't even come. If a patient is needing affection, I can't replace the family, but I would like to do something to compensate for the family's absence."

In the latter discourse, we can note the way nurses' professional role often tends to be assimilated with women's family role. This respondent even admitted to having difficulty in separating her professional activity from gender-related issues, especially when young female nurses have to attend to young male patients:

"Young nurses are full of energy, that's a good thing. On the other hand, young nurses have difficulty in coping with patients. If a patient who has undergone surgery is a young man, he will be shy about some things. We don't know how to cope with him."

D.C. had 6 years' seniority and was working as a nurse at Chiba University Hospital. She also deplored the lack of contacts with patients as well as with doctors, due to the heavy workload. In her opinion, it was difficult to achieve the desirable level of cooperation between patients, nurses and doctors:

"The daytime shift is from 8:00. to 16:00. But you must realize that from 11:30 to 13:30, the nurses stop for lunch. So during that time, we usually can't look after the patients. Then there are the doctors' morning and afternoon rounds. In the morning, we get ready for the doctors, accompany them on their rounds and then tidy everything up: that keeps us busy from 8:30 to 10:00. In the afternoon, the doctors do their rounds again from 15:00 to 15:40. So that leaves us with only an hour and a half to attend to the patients in the morning and an hour and a half in the afternoon. It's a really busy day. We are always on the run. If a patient is in pain, we don't have time to discuss the cause of the pain with the doctor, so we call him immediately to come and give the patient an injection. Listening to what's wrong and trying out various ways of alleviating the pain is just not possible. We can only talk to the patients in the afternoons. It's difficult to help them psychologically."

The only male Japanese nurse interviewed, I.I., who had just one year's seniority, responded negatively to the question about cooperation. In his opinion, it was difficult to achieve cooperation between patients, nurses and doctors. To improve this situation, he would have liked to be able to negotiate with the doctors:

> "People can have different opinions about the most appropriate treatment. We should try out various ideas, because in order to apply good nursing practices, each patient's specificities of should be taken into account. If we could have meetings about that, it would be a good thing. But in fact it's difficult. A nurse should be able to say to a doctor 'the patient doesn't want to be given that treatment'. The procedures should be made to evolve on those lines. For one thing, nurses could work more closely together. I talk to the anaesthetists, but they don't want to take the patients' psychology into account. The main thing for them is keeping the patients alive. It's sad to see that nursing is developing on the basis of purely medical considerations. There is a lot of discussion about how the liver and the heart are functioning and about the side-effects of chemotherapy. But we ought to discuss more often what the patients are thinking."

The lack of contact with patients and the difficulty of cooperating with the doctors were obviously due to these nurses' shortage of time. However, this situation had led to a lack of professional commitment rather than inducing them to make to social demands. The fact that nurses tended to choose the "exit strategy" rather than voicing the problem was clearly expressed in the responses of I.I. As this nurse explained, the time-related problems also included the question of the unpaid overtime often imposed on nurses. Instead of inciting them to put forward social demands to have the numbers of staff increased and the working hours decreased, the nurses' heavy workload was tending to weaken their professional commitment:

> "At some hospitals, such as the municipal hospitals in Tokyo, there are many very senior nurses, whereas there is a much faster turnover here. In Tokyo, there is generally a shortage of nursing staff, which is not the case in the provinces. So the workload is too heavy here because of the shortage of staff. One really has to work hard for one's wages. Some people are not too keen on being busy all the time. So they decide to leave. Since many people are leaving, they have to keep on recruiting staff. It's not a good thing."

Another nurse called I.T. suggested that the efforts made by the hospital union seemed to be restricted to negotiating the bonuses paid to the hospital staff:

> "The wages paid at this hospital are almost the same as at the public hospitals. I receive a slightly larger bonus than one of my friends, who is working at a public hospital. The nursing staff is slightly larger here too than at the public hospital. Here we have the hospital union. The negotiations focus only on the bonuses. But I am not particularly interested in that. I never join the demonstrations."

In this respondent's opinion, nurses' status is closely linked to their level of qualification. She said she would like to see the initial vocational training levels required to obtain the State nursing diploma become more homogeneous and to have the nursing assistants' diploma abolished (see Chapter 2 on Japanese nurses' training):

> "Nurses still have a low status because they have always been regarded as doctors' assistants throughout the history of Japan. But nurses with State nursing qualifications are not the same thing as nursing assistants. Some people think they both belong to the same category, but it's not true. Nursing assistants work mostly at small clinics. They are not responsible for real nursing practices."

Nurses in the more senior group: Differences of opinion about the feasibility of cooperation, and the question of nurses' working hours

The statements made by the nurses in the more senior group focused more frequently on cooperation than on the lack of contact with patients. It is worth noting, however, that one nurse stated that contacts with patients could be made while attending to patients' physical needs. Seven of the 22 nurses with more than 7 years' seniority said they were responsible for coordination between patients, nurses and doctors, whereas 8 others said cooperation between nurses and doctors was difficult to achieve. The opinions of these respondents, who were matrons, therefore diverged. How can these positive and negative opinions about making cooperation part of nurses' work be explained?

One nurse with 15 years' seniority, H.C., who was working at Chiba University Hospital, expressed the wish for closer contacts with patients, rather than having to do all the small jobs performed by nurses at the doctors' request. In her opinion, nurses' relational role is bound up with their nursing role. We have already seen how Japanese nurses, unlike their French counterparts, do not make any distinction between nursing and "bodily care". On the other hand, the many tasks carried out by nurses at the doctors' request, such as preparing patients for tests, are not always purely technical tasks. These unspecified little *"doctors' assistants' tasks"* prevent the occurrence of physical contacts such as those involved in washing patients, and set nurses at a distance from their patients:

> "We are called upon to perform many tasks of all kinds, including paperwork and answering the telephone. That weighs heavily on nurses. That is why we don't have more time to spend with the patients. Tasks which are not urgent get put off – including even attending to patients. If they had staff to do the office-work, we could spend enough time at the patients' bedsides.
>
> Sometimes when I take over in the morning, I think about something I must do for a patient, but then I forget because there is so much to do, all the routine work. But when I am not flooded with work, when I have time, I no longer forget to go and see a particular patient.
>
> This is a lung surgery unit. I would like to have more time to help patients who have just come out of surgery to help them clear their lungs. I do it when I have time. That's what I have been doing with a cancer patient at the moment. What I try to do is to make contact with patients while attending to their physical needs - in other words, while washing them or shampooing their hair. At those times, patients open up and speak more frankly.
>
> We are here to look after the patients. But the physicians think of us as people who are there just to be ordered about. We are supposed to dispense the care corresponding to our position as nurses. We are not doctors' assistants. Doctors will have to change their picture of what relations between doctors and nurses are all about. We are being misused by the doctors, and we don't have any time left to spend with the patients. The doctors drop in at all times of day for this and that. They ask us to call other doctors. And it's we who have to prepare everything when there are tests to be carried out, and we who tidy up the instruments afterwards, whereas at some other units, that's the doctors' job."

H.L. was a matron with 11 years' seniority working at Saint Luke's Hospital. When talking about the work relationships in her team, she placed the accent on linking up *"the work of doctors and nurses"*. She said it was up to the matrons to make sure that patients, nurses and doctors meet up together. It is worth noting here that meetings of this kind might provide an organizational solution to the problem of contacts with patients. On the other hand, this respondent was trying to develop the primary nursing approach to care, which she thought was a better way of treating patients than the team approach:

> "Cooperation is worthwhile. It's up to the matrons to harmonise the doctors' and nurses' work. A good therapeutic approach and good nursing practices are complementary. For example, when choosing the date on which a child will be discharged, I check the staff rota to make sure that the nurse who has been dealing with that child will be there that day, so that she will be able to explain to the family what they should do from then on.
>
> And I also arrange meetings at which the doctor, the nurse and the child's mother discuss the case. I feel that is very worthwhile.
>
> We are in the process of introducing the comprehensive *primary nursing* approach. At this children's unit, when a nurse gets on particularly well with a child, she will want to apply the primary nursing approach. I therefore try to encourage each nurse to use this approach. Children behave much more nicely than adult patients. It is therefore natural for nurses to become fond of them. They are able to behave like their parents. The nurse is like the mother, and the doctor is like the father, and it's easy for the two of them to work as a team."

On the other hand, N.T., a matron who had acquired 10 years' seniority, stated that cooperation was difficult to achieve, either between patients, nurses and matrons (*"the nurses don't tell me whether the patients have understood what the treatment involves"*), or between patients, nurses and physicians:

> "I get whatever information the nurses give me, but I am not informed directly whether the patients have understood what the treatment involves. For example, I know that such and such a seriously ill patient needs a great deal of attention. But I don't know whether such and such other patient has understood how this or that medicine works. The nurses don't tell me about these things. There are many surgical cases here, and in the case of each operation, I have to spend time in the office making phone calls, etc. Personally, I would rather be with the patients, but that's just not possible.
>
> At the Internal Medicine department where I used to work, the patients were in need of psychological help. But here in surgery, it's different. Patients ask us and not the surgeons for explanations about their treatment; the surgeons don't realize when the patients haven't understood what the treatment means. At the Internal Medicine department, the nurses have meetings with the doctors, but they don't do that here."

The question of teamwork was a central issue in the eyes of the more senior nurses, many of whom were matrons. In response to the question about nurses' social demands, the respondents in the more senior group said they were interested in improving the conditions of work in order to be able to integrate the younger nurses into the team.

G.I., a matron who had been working at Ikashika University Hospital for 10 years, said nurses' working hours should be reduced and overtime abolished, in particular:

> "Young nurses give up their jobs very quickly here. But the matrons play an important role by motivating nurses to stay. They leave the hospital because of the conditions of work. They often have to do night duty. And they do a lot of unpaid overtime. The daytime shift goes on until 19:00. It's not fair."

H.I., a matron with 12 years' experience working at Ikashika University Hospital, also objected to the overtime often imposed on nurses, as well as to nurses' low wages and short holidays:

"Nurses are leaving the hospital because of the conditions of work as well as the low wages; in addition, we are not allowed to take holidays when we want. We get a lot of overtime. Yesterday I worked until 8 p.m., four and a half hours longer than I was supposed to, because of emergencies."

In order to reduce nurses' working hours, the numbers of nursing staff will have to be increased in proportion to the number of hospital beds. However, this demand has always been submitted to the hospital management and not to the country's health policy makers. In other words, the negotiations carried out between matrons and the hospital management have led only to the staff being re-distributed among the various wards, as mentioned for example by L.I., a matron with 13 years' seniority working at Ikashaika University Hospital, and K.L., a matron with 29 years' seniority working at Saint Luke's Hospital:

"The nursing staff is not large enough because of the limitations imposed by the hospital management" (L.I.).
"What bothers me most is that the nurses are asking to have the staff increased and to have better-quality equipment purchased. We the matrons are aware of these problems and we are trying to negotiate with the hospital management. But we cannot always go on telling the nurses that their demands will not be met immediately" (K.L.).

Since these negotiations take place within the hospital, some nurses have a negative attitude towards social demands, as in the case of O.T., a matron with 17 years' seniority working at Toranomon Hospital:

"In my opinion, the number of employees and the conditions of work are fairly satisfactory at Toranomon Hospital in comparison with other hospitals. Since we have assistants and office employees, we are able to devote ourselves to caring for the patients."

The need for greater social recognition of nurses' field of specialization sometimes came to the fore, as in the discourse of J.L., a matron with 13 years' seniority specialized in stomato-therapy working at Saint Luke's hospital, who planned to developed continuing vocational training courses via the Japan Nursing Association:

"In 1984, I underwent continuing vocational training for nurses in stomatotherapy in the United States. When I was working at a surgical ward, I realized how useful this training was, so I created a continuing vocational training course for nurses in stomatotherapy here at this hospital. In the United States, there are many specialized courses for nurses, in anaesthetist nursing, health education, etc. The Japanese Nursing Association is making efforts to develop specialized continuing vocational training courses of this kind."

Summary of the findings made in the first Japanese survey

As the results presented in *table 4.9* show, the younger nurses deplored the lack of contacts with patients more than their elders, whereas most of the latter group spoke more frequently about the problem of cooperation within the hospital team. The one young male nurse included in the survey also mentioned that cooperation was difficult. This difference between the two age-groups' perception of work relationships was not observed among the nurses surveyed in France. In Japan, those who were most strongly involved in ensuring cooperation between the members of their team were the matrons. In other words, matrons contributed importantly to adapting their teams to the latest modes of work organization, whereas the nurses tended to challenge this approach and to demand more time to be able to form real contacts with their patients.

Work relationships in Japan during the 1980 can be summed up in the term *"team nursing"*, which meant "a split between two hierarchical levels: basic care and complex care; the former are operative tasks, whereas the latter involve responsibility and supervision" (Petitat, 1989, p. 157). This pattern of organization has resulted in a gulf between the younger nurses and the more experienced ones: the former perform simple tasks, whereas the latter deal with organizing the chain of tasks.

As we can see from *table 4.10*, half of the respondents mentioned social demands. Nine of the responses to the question about social demands given by the 24 nurses with less than 6 years' seniority were coded. It is worth noting that 5 of these respondents' discourse was about their conditions of work, especially the need to reduce their working hours and/or increase the numbers of nurses on the hospital payroll. Fifteen of the responses to this question given by the older nurses were coded. Nine of them demanded better conditions of work in order to be able to integrate young nurses into the hospital teams.

During the 1980s, the Japanese company trade unions were fighting to protect the status of regular employees, most of whom were men. Women working in the intermediate professions rarely belonged to the company unions and had little scope to express their social demands. On the other hand, very few nurses belonged to the paramedicals' union *(Iryo-ren)*, which was organized separately from the company unions with a view to improving the conditions of work of those it represented.

Table 4.9. *Work relationships (1989).*

Seniority	Holistic nursing care	Contacts with patients		Cooperation		Organizational constraints	Other	Total
		Possible	Difficult	Possible	Difficult			
Less than 6 years	4	1	13	3	7	2	0	30
More than 7 years	9	3	7	8	8	3	2	40
Total	13	4	20	11	15	5	2	70

Table 4.10. *Nurses' social demands (1989).*

Seniority	Shorter working hours and more staff recruitment	Better wages	Better status	Continuing vocational training	Negative attitude to social demands	Total
Less than 6 years	5	1	1	1	1	9
More than 7 years	9	3	1	1	1	15
Total	14	4	2	2	2	24

Decentralisation of responsibilities and scope for social action in 2007-2008

In the 2007-2008 survey on Japanese nurses, the contrast observed in the 1989 between the younger nurses' insistence on lack of contacts with patients and the older nurses' dual picture of cooperation within the team was no longer observed.

Nurses in the less senior group: Responsibility and the need for better conditions of work

Almost half of the nurses with less than 6 years' seniority expressed the wish to take a comprehensive *"primary nursing"* approach to patients, since they spoke about the patients' evolution. Likewise, almost half of these respondents said that contacts with patients, which it was possible to achieve, were their main motivation for carrying out their work. Unlike the younger nurses interviewed in 1989, the 2007-2008 respondents in this age-group said they felt responsible for promoting the *"primary nursing"* approach as well as for making contacts with patients possible.

In response to the question "On what occasions do you feel particularly motivated to carry out your work?", they answered *"when patients are regaining their autonomy"*, *"when the patients' condition has improved"*, *"when helping patients to recover their autonomy"* and *"when patients have recovered and are discharged from hospital"*.

On the other hand, they felt their work was particularly difficult *"when you are face to face with dying patients and their families"*, when *"the treatment has not succeeded in alleviating the patients' pain"* and when *"one is caring for many patients with serious diseases."*

The younger nurses showed little motivation to perform technical tasks: 4 of them said they found their work difficult *"when treating patients in a critical state"* and when they themselves *"did not understand the disease or the treatment."*

As far as their relationships with patients were concerned, half of the younger nurses said they were motivated to carry out their work when *"we are communicating effectively with the patients"*, when *"patients thank me for what I have done for them"*, when *"the patients are pleased with what I am doing"* and *"when I have gained a patient's trust"*.

However, other nurses referred to difficult contacts with patients. They said they work was difficult when *"we are not in touch with patients and their families"*, when *"the patients are making too many demands"*, when *"we are unable to meet patients' specific demands"*, and when they had to solve *"ethical problems, such as obtaining patients' informed consent"*. They also mentioned *"increasing numbers of unmanageable* patients" and *"being bullied by patients"*.

On the topic of relationships within the team, some respondents said that cooperation was possible to achieve. They felt motivated to carry out their work when *"we work together at treating the patient"* and when *"everyone in the team speaks openly about how to manage the treatment"*. However, some of the younger nurses mentioned having problems in their relationships with doctors, not having *"good contacts with doctors"* and not understanding *"the doctor's approach to the treatment"*.

The working hours were what these respondents complained about most; some of the responses coded focused on the conditions of work: *"tasks which it's impossible to perform in the time available"*; *"too many jobs to do, given the time constraints"*; and *"a lot of unpaid overtime"*.

These young nurses suffered from the fact that the primary nursing approach and contacts with patients were not compatible with the constraints in terms of the conditions of work, *i.e.*, the long working hours and the shortage of staff.

In response to the question "What do you think about the hospital reforms?", 2 nurses stated that it was necessary to *"increase the rates charged for medical interventions, including nursing care"*, and 2 others mentioned improving the quality of healthcare by *"setting up healthcare networks"*, *"and equal healthcare opportunities for all."*

Based on these nurses' responses, the health insurance system would therefore be well advised to increase the rates charged for medical activities in order to be able to increase the numbers of hospital employees.

One third of the younger nurses said they wanted the conditions of work to be improved in order to be able to deal with patients more individually and have closer contacts with them: *"increasing the staff to relieve nurses of their heavy load"*, thus making it possible to *"reduce the time spent at work"*, which amounted to reducing the overtime, in fact.

They also felt the need to have their wages upgraded: *"our pay is not in proportion to our working hours, because there is an enormous amount of unpaid overtime, even with the system where each nurse deals with 7 patients"*; *"our wages should be aligned with our work and our responsibilities: that would solve the problem of understaffing"*.

Two nurses stated the need to *"promote the status of nurses"*, which meant improving the conditions of work and the wages.

In response to the question "To what extent does the Japan Nursing Association defend the interests of your profession?", the less senior nurses focused on the conditions of work more than on other demands. Nine of them said that this Association is capable of conducting *"collective efforts to make the Government improve our conditions of work"*; they thought the Association would make it possible to *"increase the numbers of nurses on the payroll"*; *"improve the conditions of work so that nurses can go on working when they have children."*

Four nurses spoke about the collective efforts which could be made by the Association to *"promote the status of nurses"*; and 5 of them expressed an interest in *"continuing vocational training courses which would improve nurses' skills."*

It should be mentioned, however, that one third of the younger nurses questioned expressed negative opinions in connection with nurses' social demands, as in the case of the following response: *"I pay a subscription to the Japan Nursing Association, but I never see anything about what action this Association is taking."*

Nurses in the more senior group: Challenging the validity of cooperation and the development of a corporation

The younger nurses' efforts to introduce the primary nursing approach to care and closer contacts with patients was not leading to closer cooperation between the members of the team. The more senior nurses questioned in 2007-2008 said team-working was difficult. On the other hand, they wanted to participate in the continuing vocational training courses set up by the Japan Nursing Association, a new space for obtaining qualifications which had opened up outside the hospital.

The nurses with more than 7 years' seniority, like their younger colleagues, expressed interest in following their patients' evolution. Almost half of this group said they were motivated by the primary nursing approach to care. They were also motivated when *"patients recover from a serious disease"*, when *"the patients' condition improves"*, when *"patients are cured and dischar-ged from hospital"*, as well as *"when they provide dying patients with palliative care"*. They also felt their work was difficult *"when faced with a patient in distress who is about to die"*, and when dispensing *"palliative care"*.

None of the nurses in this group were in favour of performing technical therapeutic tasks. However, 2 of them said it was difficult for them to perform these tasks *"to save the lives of patients in a critical state"*.

As regards their relationships with patients, half of the more senior nurses said they were motivated to carry out their work: *"when we are communicating successfully with patients and their families"*; when *"the patients are pleased with what I am doing"*; when *"patients appreciate what I am doing"*; *"when patients and their families thank us"*; and *"when I have gained a patient's trust."*

However, these nurses drew a less positive picture of their relationships with patients when they had not succeeded in *"establishing good contacts with patients"*; when *"patients are not pleased"*; when *"patients have a poor opinion of the care they are receiving, although I try to take each patient's needs into account"*; when *"we cannot satisfy all the patient's demands"*; and when having to deal with *"impatient"* or *"aggressive patients"*.

The more senior nurses also mentioned the relationships among the members of their team. Some of them expressed positive opinions on this topic, saying that cooperation was possible: *"solidarity in the team"*; *"good teamwork to help the patients"*; *"I have gained the trust of my colleagues"*; *"we draw up the nursing care plan together in the team"*; *"good teamwork when drawing up the nursing care plan"*; and *"when the nurses enjoy being trained."*

However, half of these more senior nurses regarded cooperation in a more negative light. First of all, they had problems in their relationships with the doctors when *"we do not com-municate satisfactorily with the doctors"*; when *"we cannot cooperate with the doctor"*; when *"the doctor takes the final decision about everything although the nurse is trying to apply the nursing care plan"*. They also mentioned having problems with other nurses *"when I don't make the right decision with respect to my colleagues"*; and when *"I don't know how to cooperate with other units."*

They were aware that their problems focused on performing nurses' specific role: *"it is difficult to motivate young nurses to undergo training"*; *"the nurses are too young to be able to perform highly technical nursing tasks without making mistakes."*

On the topic of the conditions of work, some of these nurses complained about the long working hours: *"we have to do a lot of unpaid overtime"*; *"I often do 2 hours of overtime caring for patients, and another 2 hours of overtime doing office work"*; *"because of the understaffing, it is difficult to meet the patients' needs."*

In response to the question about the hospital reforms, the more senior nurses, like their younger colleagues, mentioned *"the nursing care networks being set up between hospitals"*, *"the increasing rates being charged for medical care"*, and *"also paying for the medical interventions performed when nurses are educating their patients."* Some criticisms and comments were also put forward about the healthcare reforms: *"extending healthcare beyond the health insurance scheme is not right"*; *"providing public funds for caring for old people in particular."*

Almost half of these more senior nurses spoke of the need *"to improve the conditions of work"*, and especially to increase the numbers of staff and reduce nurses' overtime. Some of them referred to *"upgrading our wages"* and *"introducing night duty bonuses."* They said they wanted the conditions of work to be improved and the wages to be upgraded in order to *"improve the status of healthcare workers."*

The more senior nurses expressed interest in the Japan Nursing Association, since *"exerting collective pressure on the Government is an effective means of improving the conditions of work."* They spoke about *"increasing the numbers of nurses on the staff"* and *"reducing the time spent at work, so as to be able to work only 3 or 4 days per week, for example."*

The skills acquired by nurses throughout their careers are essential to instilling a spirit of cooperation into the healthcare team. The respondents felt that if nurses' demands for better conditions of work were met, they would be more able to advance their careers and develop their skills.

On these lines, eleven respondents expressed their opinions about the various vocational training courses which ought to be provided by the Association: *"continuing vocational training courses for recently qualified nurses"*; *"continuing vocational training courses for acquiring advanced skills"*; *"training courses for clinical nurses and administrative nurses"*; *"courses for training nurses for research in nursing science."*

These respondents realized the importance of the nursing corporation which was developing via the Association: *"to promote the status of nurses, larger numbers of healthcare professionals should be elected to the Parliament or the Senate"*.

Summary of the findings made in the second Japanese survey

By the 2000s, the Japanese healthcare system had adopted industrial logics, since the length of patients' hospital stay had been shortened and nurses' workload had therefore become much heavier. The use of the industrial yardstick had led to a shift from *"team nursing"* to the comprehensive *"primary nursing"* approach to care. This change undergone by the Japanese healthcare system during the 1990s was similar to that which occurred in France during the 1970s. In the *"primary nursing"* approach to hospital work, the former split between the two hierarchical levels (those entrusted with menial tasks versus higher responsibilities) disappeared. From that point on, each nurse "was responsible for the nursing care plan and had to make the day-to-day decisions herself" (Petitat, 1989, p. 169). Contrary to what occurred in France, however, this devolution of responsibility to the nurses was not accompanied by the attribution of the more domestic duties to assistant nurses.

As can be seen from *Table 4.11*, which shows how nurses' statements about their work relationships were distributed, the main difference observed in the 1989 survey between the younger and older nurses was no longer apparent in the 2007-2008 survey.

The Japanese nurses' social movement has been on the go for the past twenty years independently of the company unions *(Rengo)*, which are highly active at the large Japanese firms. As we have seen, the company unions mainly defend the interests of regular male employees, *i.e.*, their right to keep their jobs all their lives. The main mouthpiece for Japanese nurses' social demands is the paramedical union *(Iryo-ren)*, followed by the Japan Nursing Association, which presents the political interests of its members to the Japan Nursing Federation.

As the result of the social movement led by the Association, a move to create a real corporation of nurses has been initiated. In 1990, the Japanese nurses arranged to have "Nurses' Day" declared an annual public holiday on 12th May (Florence Nightingale's birthday) in order to promote the public and symbolic image of the nursing profession.

As shown in *tables 4.12 and 4.13*, the younger and older nurses' demands in connection with their conditions of work and the rates charged by hospitals for medical acts were similar. However, the more senior nurses were more interested than their younger colleagues in the continuing vocational training courses run by the Japan Nursing Association.

Table 4.11. *Work relationships (2007-2008).*

Seniority	Holistic nursing care	Therapeutic care	Contacts with patients		Teamwork		Heavy work organization constraints	Total
			Possible	Difficult	Possible	Difficult		
Less than 6 years	18	2	19	11	4	13	6	73
More than 7 years	14	2	17	9	8	16	8	74
Total	32	4	36	20	12	29	14	147

Table 4.12. *Nurses' opinions about the hospital reforms (2007-2008).*

Seniority	Rates charged by hospitals for medical acts	Reducing nurses' working hours	Better wages	Better status	Continuing vocational training courses	Negative opinions about social demands	Total
Less than 12 years	5	14	5	2	0	4	30
More than 13 years	8	15	4	3	1	5	36
Total	13	29	9	5	1	9	66

Table 4.13. *Nurses' expectations of the Japan Nursing Association (2007-2008).*

Seniority	Rates charged by hospitals for medical acts	Reducing nurses' working hours	Better wages	Better status	Continuing vocation-al training	Negative opinions about social demands	Total
Less than 12 years	0	9	1	4	5	11	30
More than 13 years	2	7	1	5	11	4	30
Total	2	16	2	9	16	15	60

CONCLUSION

The results of the first survey conducted in Tokyo in 1989 show that the social world of the Japanese nurses interviewed was characterized by a strong split between those who had become integrated into the hospital system and those who were not yet integrated or did not intend to cross the borderline. The less senior nurses regarded their commitment to the nursing profession as a short-term affair and complained about the lack of personal contacts with patients; whereas the more senior nurses, most of whom had been promoted to the rank of matrons, were much more attached to the institution and were proud of the spirit of cooperation they had managed to instil into the members of their teams. However, the strong segmentation observed between those who were integrated into the hospital system and the others had not incited Japanese nurses to voice their social demands very strongly. The more integrated nurses (matrons) focused on improving the conditions of work in order to be able to promote teamwork, whereas the less integrated ones had opted for an "exit strategy" rather than voicing their social demands.

Based on the results of the second survey conducted in Tokyo in 2007-2008 using open questionnaires, the segmentation observed in the previous survey in terms of nurses' inte-gration no longer existed. Regardless of their seniority, these nurses stated that they intended to pursue their nursing careers either inside or outside the hospital system. Both the less senior and more senior Japanese nurses who took part in the second survey placed the emphasis on providing patients with comprehensive "primary nursing" care and on their relationships with patients.

The interest in "primary nursing" care shown by Japanese nurses has led them to demand better conditions of work in order to be able to promote/devote themselves/ to this approach. However, they have not voiced their demands via the powerful Japanese company unions: since the 1990s, they have adopted the paramedical union and the Japan Nursing Association as their spokesmen.

REFERENCES

• Arborio AM. *Un personnel invisible. Les aides-soignantes à l'hôpital.* Paris: Anthoropos, 2001.

• Petitat A. *Les Infirmières. De la vocation à la profession.* Montréal: Boréal, 1989.

Part III
Paths to modernization

For historical reasons, the Japanese hospital system is characterized by an apparent lack of differentiation, hierarchical or otherwise, between the various establishments and modes of treatment. As we have seen, this smoothing process also applies to both the medical and paramedical teams, and nurses are having difficulty in imposing a more "industrial" approach to their work. This can be said of the whole Japanese healthcare system. However, this traditionally undifferentiated pattern cannot possibly last for long because it will not be able to meet the increasing demand for technical skills and efficiency. Japanese reformers are therefore focusing on introducing greater specialization. This can be seen from the functional distinctions between hospitals made in the recent law on medical services.

The French hospital system, on the contrary, is pervaded by a strong tendency to specialize, which favours monopolistic competition between hospitals which give them freedom of action and legitimacy. This tendency is now being curtailed, however, because it is wasteful instead of contributing to cost containment. For this reason, many reforms have focused since the 1980s on how to remove the barriers within the health care system. It is worth noting that the recent reform passed in July 2009 concerning Hospitals, Patients, Health and Territories *(loi Hôpital, Patients, Santé et Territoires)* has made breaking down the French healthcare system's internal barriers its main priority.

If we compare the trends at work, it can be said that both countries' hospitals are moving at the same time towards a compromise which is mid-way between a highly expensive set of juxtaposed monopolies and an overall pattern of fuzzy generalization. However, as we will see in this part, the apparent similarities and points of convergence are actually optical illusions. In fact, each of the two perfectly coherent situations reflects the specific way in which hospitals and healthcare professionals are embedded in the surrounding social environment.

5. Regulating hospitals and developing occupational competences

The strength of the French medical profession has been enhanced by the prestige and the high standards of hospital medicine, especially since 1958, when the University teaching hospitals were created. Like the whole French healthcare system, the French hospital system has a pyramidal structure and is regulated on the basis of this structure. The occupational and economic stakes resulting from the segmentation of the medical profession due to the process of technical specialization contribute crucially to the success of this system.

Up to quite recently, the medical power in Japan lay mainly in the hands of the Japan Medical Association, and the Japanese medical profession itself seemed to have a rather non-hierarchical structure. On the other hand, specialists do not enjoy greater prestige than general practitioners (GPs) in Japan. This is due to the close match existing (all over the country between the healthcare supply and the demands, and to the fact that physicians have been able to exercise their profession in many possible ways and enjoy great mobility in terms of their status, their place of work, and even their field of specialization.

Although the weak coordination characteristic of both countries resulted from different causes and took different forms, the outcome in both cases was that this weakness has become one of the main points targeted by the ongoing reforms.

French and Japanese hospitals will be presented here as embedded institutions subjected to a whole set of increasingly complex regulations with which they are attempting to juggle in order to keep some measure of autonomy.

As we will see in the following chapters, the privileged tools used in both countries to relieve the tension between the wish for autonomy and the increasing need for control involve the use of contracts.

In both Japan and France, however, the changes undergone by hospitals cannot be described simply in terms of transferring or appropriating practices, especially at hospital management level. These changes generated, formented and revealed conflicts and friction between various spheres of action, and hence between various conceptions of the performances and competences required. From this point of view, the example of the United Kingdom is particularly interesting, since the forms of regulation introduced in this country could serve as a shining example to reformers all over the world. On the other hand, the British hospital system has undergone considerable changes which are specific to this country and show how deeply embedded in society this system is.

Before embarking on a detailed analysis of the processes and mechanisms underlying modernization in France and Japan, it is proposed for the sake of comparison to briefly outline the process of reform undergone by the British National Health Service (NHS). These comparisons are particularly instructive in view of the fact that from the late 1940s to the 1980s, the NHS was held up as a model by both its admirers and its detractors worldwide.

French hospitals are gradually becoming contractors within the system, whereas Japanese hospitals are evolving towards a form of rationalization which is mainly based on the new taste for differentiation and the will to make this strongly aggregated sector more heterogeneous.

THE UK MODEL: TRUST, CONTRACTS, AND THE INTERNAL MARKET

The British NHS hospital system was established in 1948, when the two previously coexisting systems, one in the voluntary sector and the other run by local authorities, were brought together under public ownership to form a centralised, comprehensive healthcare system (Harrison, 1997). Not until 1962 however was a national hospital development plan introduced, in order to organise the provision of hospital services around local districts (District Health Authorities, DHAs), with a view to ensuring that every district had a general hospital capable of servicing the overall needs of the local population, which at the time could vary in size from 100,000 to 150,000. At the same time, central control was an essential element in the system, with heavy emphasis on the need for government supervision, in order to ensure the implementation of ministerial objectives. Periodic restructuring therefore occurred, particularly in the 1970s, with the introduction of a national planning system and specific definitions of roles and functions to be carried out by practitioners, managers and government officials. As such, although measures seeking to modernise the system were undertaken at different points during the first four decades of its existence, the NHS remained a model of the "command-and-control" approach, corresponding closely to the Weberian ideal-type of the bureaucratic organisation (Ham, 1999). It represented an exemplary case of a comprehensive, universalistic service, provided out of general taxation, which was free at the point of delivery and with relatively low administrative costs. Even as late as the early 1990s, the running costs of the NHS represented approximately 6% of UK gross domestic product (GDP), in contrast with those of the system in the USA, which were twice that figure (OECD, 2009). Criticisms, often emanating from American sources, whilst recognising that for many years following its creation the NHS enjoyed a widespread reputation for usually high quality care once it had been received, also alluded to the fact that this care was rationed, by means of waiting lists and procedural delays prior to treatment, as well as waiting times on arrival for treatment.

Improving efficiency, escaping from "socialised medicine"

From this perspective, the NHS was increasingly seen during the 1980s as under-capitalised and dominated by providers, who defined the healthcare needs of patients, rather than responding to pressures such as the implications of increasing budgetary constraints, especially following the economic crisis of the 1970s, as well as rising expectations on the part of the consumer. According to numerous American observers, the cause of such ills as provider paternalism and unacceptable waiting times for treatment was "socialised medicine", which to this day apparently remains anathema to many commentators and a large section of the public in that country. More specifically, Conservative commentators in the UK highlighted the perverse incentives which were built in to the system, since the rigid budgetary allocation procedures for hospital funding took little account of changes in levels of activity, thereby penalising those seeking to achieve improvements in productivity (Ham, 1999). In response to such thinking, Conservative governments in the 1990s, under Prime Ministers Thatcher and Major, launched a process of reform in which the NHS once more became a model, this time in the sense that their attempts at modernization were so ambitious in their objectives and so apparently audacious in their scale of application that they came to be regarded as a "laboratory" for other countries (Ham, 1993). The NHS thereby became a test case of the extent to which new practices, inspired partly by principles imported from abroad, could be introduced into deeply embedded institutional patterns, structures and values which, according to much neo-institutionalist thinking, would prove capable of inflecting initial policy goals in the direction of a more acceptable "fit".

Among the key aspects of the 1991 reforms, outlined in Prime Minister Thatcher's White Paper of 1989, the most fundamental was the creation of the internal market, involving the separation between purchasers and providers of health care, whereby the Health Authorities (previously DHAs), which had hitherto been responsible for running health services (apart from general practice) for the population within the geographical areas under their jurisdiction, based on budgets allocated by the central state, became purchasers. Providers, the hospitals and community services, became self-governing public sector Trusts, whose capacity to attract purchasers was henceforth to depend on their performance in ensuring efficient, cost-effective delivery of care. In their role as purchasers, the health authorities were responsible for assessing the health needs of their populations and, on this basis, for the selection of appropriate providers. In addition, GPs, who had always had the function of "gatekeepers", deciding whether or not to refer their patients for specialised hospital care, were now authorised to become fund holders, allowing them to manage budgets out of which they could purchase a limited set of services for these patients, particularly in the sphere of elective (non-urgent) surgery. In one of the key phrases in vogue at the time, "money would follow patients" (Klein, 1998).

The rationale for these reforms, underpinned in part by American-inspired ideas emanating from Alain Enthoven, involved imitating the dynamics of the market, generating mechanisms through which providers would be compelled to improve efficiency and responsiveness to the expectations of health care users. Failure to do so could result in loss of income, as contracts would not be renewed by the purchasers, thereby introducing a new drive towards incentivisation into the NHS. In this way, competing policy objectives could be reconciled, meeting rising demands through increased efficiency, whilst satisfying the rising expectations of consumers. Arguably however, despite the general commitment of the Conservatives to a neo-liberal paradigm, such measures did not amount to an explicit paradigm change within the NHS itself, since the policy goals of universality and equity were declared by government to have remained intact, or as Prime Minister Thatcher famously put it, "The NHS is safe in our hands". The focus of the reforms was on what Hall (1993) would describe as second-order change, through the introduction, not of radically different objectives, but of important new policy instruments, most notably that of mechanisms to generate competition.

The outcomes of these reforms fell short of policy makers' expectations, for reasons partly relating to policy design. The NHS internal market was a hybrid, an attempt at generating market dynamics in a publicly financed service. It has thus been variously described as a quasi-market, or a "managed market" which, as Ham has observed, is something of an "oxymoron" (Ham, 1999). The premises of the experiment were therefore somewhat fragile from the outset and in reality; it proved extremely difficult to stimulate the competition upon which the logic of the reforms depended. It is true that many of the features normally associated with competition did begin to emerge, particularly the development of a "contract culture", in which health authorities and GP fund holders negotiated with providers for supply of services. Furthermore, a certain degree of competition did develop with regard to elective surgery through the role of GP fund holding. It has also been suggested (Klein, 1998) that the threat of competition, the possibility that a contract might not be renewed if the performance of providers was deemed inadequate, could prove sufficient to become an important bargaining counter for purchasers. Nonetheless, it became clear that in a large number of localities, especially out with the networks of major urban conurbations; there was very little choice of providers available to purchasers. Indeed, by the mid-1990s, the term "purchasing" had largely fallen into disuse, to be replaced by that of "commissioning", thereby denoting a shift away from attempts to introduce authentically market-driven practices, where purchase involves a genuine choice between the range of goods available, towards negotiating long-term contracts with providers, where the process of purchasing actually served as a mechanism for the purpose of planning service provision.

A further reason for the failure to bring competition fully to bear upon the management and regulation of the system lay in the high level of politicisation characterising all matters pertaining to the NHS, as illustrated by the high profile invariably accorded to NHS-related themes at UK general elections. Prior to the general election of 1992, the cutting of patient waiting times, as promised in the Patient's Charter previously introduced by the Conservatives as part of their attempt to develop a more patient-centred NHS, became an important issue. Government supporters highlighted the recent 35% reduction in waiting lists as evidence that demands for greater responsiveness, combined with measures such as the creation of 100 additional consultant posts, were taking effect. However, research findings suggest that at least part of this reduction was attributable to practices tantamount to "cutting corners" rather than cutting waiting lists, such as the simple abolition of waiting lists for certain forms of elective surgery (Pope, 1992). Strategic reform thus fell victim to the "political football" syndrome, becoming overshadowed by "massaging of statistics", in the pursuit of short-term, electoral advantage. Fundamentally, the twin traditions of centralism and the funding of the system out of general taxation restricted the scope for realignment on the part of the central state, upon which the success of the reforms depended. The constraints associated with government accountability, both to Parliament and to the public, were summed up many years before by Aneurin Bevan, under whose ministerial responsibility the NHS was initially created, according to whom, "When a bedpan is dropped on a hospital floor, its noise should resound in the Palace of Westminster." In a context of embedded ministerial accountability and responsibility, a shift towards decisions driven by market forces inevitably encountered obstacles reflecting the "stickiness" of institutional traditions rooted in a public-service culture. Indeed, the NHS has frequently been likened to a secular religion and its practitioners, along with governments, have long been regarded as custodians of principles which only heretics would call into question. As a result, while the underlying logic of competition is decentralisation, the Tory reforms led to increased centralisation. If the viability of major hospitals appeared to be placed in jeopardy by competition, central government was compelled to intervene, in order to find other, planning-inspired means of ensuring service provision. In addition, the full implementation of the Tory measures was hampered by spiralling transaction costs, as unexpectedly high levels of funding had to be devoted to satisfying the need for increased administrative resources, in order to manage the changes entailed by the reforms. The logic of competition and the long-standing policy logic of the NHS tended to lead in different directions, resulting in a reinforcement of central regulation and control. One of the most significant manifestations of this trend, towards the mid-1990s, was the down-playing of market-oriented measures, in favour of an intensifying emphasis on the introduction of government-generated "best practices" and guidelines, which evolved into benchmarking and performance targets, particularly with regard to mortality rates for coronary heart disease and different types of cancer. It was in such circumstances that the New Labour government under Tony Blair came into office in 1997, seeking to embark upon a "Third Way" beyond both the traditional command-and-control form of regulation and the market-related approach preferred by the Conservatives. Nonetheless, the tensions illustrated above have remained at work under both the Blair and Brown administrations, with significant consequences for the ways in which conceptualisation of NHS regulation now takes place. Institutional stickiness notwithstanding, religious convictions, both secular and theological, are not impervious to erosion.

On coming to power in 1997, Blair's famous declaration to the effect that "the NHS is not a supermarket, but a public service" encapsulated the rhetorical rejection of the internal market by the New Labour administration. And in terms of public investment, New Labour certainly reversed the long-standing trend towards under-capitalisation through a massive injection of funding. Indeed, it has been estimated that from 2000 until 2007/08, government funding of the NHS increased annually by approximately 7.5%, effectively doubling its budget in real terms by the end of this period. By the latter part of the 2000s, such investment had produced clear signs of overall improvement in healthcare services. Hospital waiting times had been reduced to 13 weeks for outpatient treatment and six months for surgery, while Accident and Emergency departments were also attending to patients more quickly after their arrival. Other evidence of progress in overall performance could also be observed in earlier screening and treatment for breast cancer, leading to increased chances of survival. However, an arresting discrepancy was also to be discerned between these improvements and public perceptions of the modernising policies adopted by Labour. According to an attitudinal survey published in 2006, while a significant majority of respondents considered that the service provided by NHS hospitals in general remained high and an overwhelming majority expressed satisfaction with the treatment which they as individuals had received on their last visit to hospital, the level of approval with regard to government policy was below 30% and public confidence in the continuing improvement of the NHS in the future reached an all-time low (Klein, 2007). It is certainly true that such negative attitudes are fuelled by media coverage of the NHS, which tends to focus selectively on specific instances of inadequate care and poor management, rather than less spectacular indicators of overall quality. Nonetheless, the credibility gap which has clearly emerged cannot be dissociated from the nature of recent reforms and it is to their impact that attention must therefore be devoted.

Despite the repudiation in government discourse of the path followed by the Conservatives, many features of the previous administration's reforms were perpetuated, and indeed intensified, but in a new climate. Instead of the Conservatives' overtly proclaimed belief in the virtues of the market, Labour strategy consisted in an attempt to "de-ideologise" NHS reform, insisting on the value of pragmatism (Rowland *et al.*, 2001). Policy was to be driven, not by ideology, but "what will work". This pragmatic approach was to be encapsulated in the principles of devolved responsibility, performance-linked funding, increased provider diversification and enhanced patient choice. In order to achieve this, in return for the budget increases, more work was also demanded of all actors in the system, not only in terms of productivity and efficiency, but also in terms of their cooperation and willingness to adapt to modernization measures. Despite the anti-market discourse, the separation between providers and purchasers (now known systematically as commissioners), was maintained, but many of the labels were changed and certain functions were substantially extended. Hospitals have retained their status as NHS provider Trusts, responsible to the NHS Executive and the Department of Health, the territorial administration of which is organised in England on a regional basis, consisting of ten Strategic Health Authorities. The major commissioning function is now the responsibility of Primary Care Trusts (PCTs), run by Executive Boards, which contract with hospitals for the provision healthcare services. The "gatekeeping" role remains the responsibility of GPs, most of whom are paid by PCTs, through a "mixed-economy" combination of salary, capitation and fee-for-service (Boyle, 2008). On the basis of referrals by GPs, PCTs purchase the appropriate health care on behalf of their patients, serving therefore as proxy consumers, and now control over 80% of the NHS budget, which is allocated to them essentially on a capitation basis.

In search of "efficiency", introducing New Public Management principles

Within this overall framework, significant changes have been introduced, particularly since 2002, which reinforce market-related mechanisms, in pursuit of the government's modernising agenda, inspired by New Public Management (NPM) principles. However, the implementation of these measures has been beset by problems comparable to those encountered by previous Conservative governments, as different strands of policy appear to lead in divergent directions. On the one hand therefore, while GP fundholding was officially abolished when Labour came to power, in reality it has mutated into a different manifestation, taking the form of practice-based commissioning. This system allows for PCTs, which are now legally required to delegate responsibility for certain services to general practices, to allocate a proportion of their budget to GPs who wish to avail themselves of this possibility, for the purpose of purchasing hospital care for their patients. Any financial savings made by GPs in this way may be used for the purchase of further services. A certain decentralising tendency has thus emerged, which has met with a favourable response from numerous general practices. At the same time, contrary to the principle of patient choice, PCTs have been subject to considerable government pressure to reinforce scrutiny of GP hospital referrals, with a view to deciding whether to approve or reject them, or indeed to re-direct patients towards alternative treatment centres, deemed to be more cost-effective. A renewed emphasis has also been placed on the setting of national standards and targets, which serve as assessment criteria through which the performance of trusts can be evaluated. In this way, moves towards greater local autonomy have been undermined by other measures.

Further instances of tension between different policy strands are to be observed in the combination of New Labour's drive towards diversification in service provision and the introduction from 2002 of Payment by Results (PbR), a version of the American Diagnosis Related Groups (DRG)[1] system, which is the NHS equivalent of the *Tarification à l'Activité* (T2A) (see below) implemented in France, to be discussed at greater length below. Under PbR, in contrast with the traditional block grant approach, providers are paid for the activity which they carry out, according to standard tariffs for each activity, applied in both the private and public sectors. According to the official rationale, providers are thereby given incentives to improve their performance, since PCTs will direct patients towards high-performing hospitals. However, in implementing its diversification policy, the government has promoted the development of private sector providers, known as Independent Sector Treatment Centres (ISTCs), and has exerted considerable pressure on PCTs to pay for procedures at ISTCs (Delamothe, 2008), even when their prices have exceeded NHS rates and irrespective of the level of demand (Klein, 2007). In view of such evidence, it appears difficult to sustain the claim that ideology has been replaced by pragmatism and cost-effectiveness, or indeed patient choice. Similarly, the quest for new sources of funding through the involvement of the private sector in hospital-building projects, under the system known as the Private Finance Initiative (PFI), has

---

1. DRGs: Diagnosis related Groups. These were initially developed in the USA for funding hospitals in the framework of public insurance schemes. The concept was subsequently applied in practically all the industrialised countries.

led to unintended consequences which hinder the attainment of other objectives. Trusts have thus found themselves committed to costly PFI projects, involving substantial, long-term repayments to private financiers, precisely at a time when the introduction of PbR entailed ever-increasing uncertainty as to the level of their own income and therefore their capacity to meet such financial obligations. Factors of this kind have led to a paradoxical situation, where PCTs have run up financial deficits, despite the huge increase in funding injected into the system under successive Labour administrations, resulting in what Klein (2007) has described as "famine among plenty". From this perspective, it becomes possible to understand the hostile reception from healthcare professionals to government claims in the mid-2000s, to the effect that the NHS "had never had it so good", as occurred in April 2006 when the Secretary of State for Health was attending a conference of nurses and was subjected to such vociferous protests that she was unable to complete her speech.

Beneath this apparent lack of coherence, a certain change in underlying policy logic seems to be emerging, in which responsibility for balancing clinical decisions against budgetary constraints has begun to move downwards. Rationing due to financial pressures has of course always influenced clinical decisions in the NHS, but the difference in the current climate is that the onus of responsibility for turning budgetary decisions into clinical decisions is shifting away from government, towards doctors and local managers. It seems that the trend towards attempts at state control from a distance, involving delegation and "blame avoidance" by government, which has been observed in relation to the French hospital system (Pierru, 2009), may also be discernible within the NHS. However, seeking to shift the locus of accountability is not without its pitfalls, as illustrated in the practice of ministerial target-setting in the spheres of both healthcare quality and cost-efficiency, followed by the publication of league tables reflecting the performance of individual hospitals in terms of the criteria established, thereby resulting in the "naming and shaming" of hospitals deemed to be under-performing. This rebounded on government on a number of occasions when causal connections during post-league table enquiries began to be made between poor quality and government pressure to meet cost-cutting targets, and the publication of official league tables was discontinued in 2006.

This "boomerang effect" is also to be discerned in the implementation of other measures, such as the introduction of Foundation Hospital Trusts from the mid-2000s. In application of the concept of "earned autonomy", this scheme involves rewarding selected hospitals, deemed to be performing at the highest levels according to official targets and assessment criteria, by granting them new, more prestigious status as Foundation Trusts, with greater budgetary freedom and devolved managerial responsibility (Robinson, 2002). A recent illustration of the problems which may be associated with this emphasis on incentivisation has been provided by the case of the Mid Staffordshire NHS Foundation Trust, into which an investigation was undertaken by the national regulatory body responsible for the monitoring and assessment of providers, the Healthcare Commission, following widespread public disquiet and official complaints from patients as well as relatives, regarding the quality of care at that institution. There is no suggestion here that this case necessarily typifies the performance of all Foundation Trusts, but it nonetheless highlights the dynamics which can be generated through recourse by government to incentivisation mechanisms. Following its investigation, the Healthcare

Commission submitted a report which found that, while the consequences of these dynamics may not become immediately visible, they begin to take effect well in advance of the attainment of Foundation Trust status. The root causes of the problems in this case are starkly summarised in the following way: "In the Trust's drive to become a Foundation Trust, it appears to have lost sight of its real priorities. The Trust was galvanised into radical action by the imperative to save money and did not properly consider the effect of reductions in staff on the quality of care" (Commission for Healthcare Audit and Inspection, Investigation into Mid Staffordshire NHS Foundation Trust, March 2009, p.11) Among its more detailed findings, the report cites evidence of poor hygiene and general standards of cleanliness, a lack of regard for the dignity of patients and "unacceptable" levels of patient care, as well as inordinately high mortality rates among patients admitted as emergencies. In addition, a certain "lock-in effect" came into operation when the Foundation Trust was alerted to the problem of high mortality rates, since its response was to look for an explanation in the coding of statistical data, rather than in qualitative information regarding the quality of care. A dangerous confusion thus seemed to have emerged between means and ends, leading to the absence of an open, learning culture and a reluctance to engage in self-critical review of assumptions and practices when they are challenged by the apparent emergence of negative outcomes. Even in cases like this, where the responsibility of local managers and practitioners for severe failings in the duty of care appears to have been established, there remains an undeniable relationship between bureaucratic, centrally-driven incentivisation and local reliance on statistical data, rather than qualitative information on actual standards of care.

The devolution issue

There is considerable truth in the assertion that central government responsibility for all that takes place in so complex an organisation as the NHS is a "managerial nonsense" (Walshe, 2003), but it is an apparently inescapable one, as efforts to develop alternatives have resulted in vicious circles of accountability leading back to the centre. Modernising reforms have been adapted to fit with pre-existing elements, but the "goodness of fit" between embedded principles or practices and the modernising measures introduced remains far from perfect, thereby generating a need for further rectification, which has spiralled into a process of perpetual reform. The detrimental effect of the combined processes of diversification and continual reorganisation has led some commentators to describe the regulation of the NHS as "resembling an organisational shantytown, in which structures and procedures are thrown together" (Walshe, 2003), creating a situation where morale is undermined and instability has often come to be regarded as the norm. The ensuing fragmentation, coupled with intensifying pressures on professionals in the "blame culture" which has developed, generates an impression at local level of increased responsibility without genuine empowerment and produces cynicism with regard to further reform among both practitioners and the public, despite objective evidence of overall improvements in the quality of the services provided, in terms of waiting times, early diagnosis of cancers and accelerated treatment of patients suffering from heart disease. In this sense, the once so powerful, quasi-religious faith in the values and principles of the NHS has been eroded, but not destroyed.

The foregoing overview, particularly as far as the period since 1997 is concerned, is focused primarily on developments within the NHS in England, where decentralist trends have been reflected in ever-changing forms of localised administrative or managerial delegation. In contrast, recent trajectories with regard to regulation and policy logic have been significantly different in Scotland, Wales and, in less clear-cut fashion, Northern Ireland, following the introduction since 1997 of more wide-reaching, political forms of decentralisation, or devolution, manifested in the creation of the Scottish Parliament and Executive, eventually recognised as the Scottish Government, the Welsh National Assembly and moves towards a degree of self-government through the Northern Ireland Assembly. Despite the considerable freedom enjoyed by these elected bodies to develop distinctive policies in health and a range of other devolved spheres, healthcare is still delivered within the overall framework of the UK NHS and financed out of general taxation, over which Westminster retains control, continuing to allocate healthcare funding to devolved governments through the Barnett formula, block grant system. Numerous constraints and tensions therefore remain, since these devolved governments do not have powers of state over taxation and other economic levers which affect health policy (Maslin-Prothero *et al.*, 2008).

Numerous commentators have observed that it has become highly problematic since devolution to collect comparable data across the four UK countries with regard to detailed policy outcomes, especially on matters such as expenditure and waiting times. (Alvarez-Rosete *et al.*, 2005). However, recent econometric research seeking to assess the impact of the presence or absence of Payment by Results, using complex proxy techniques and taking Scotland as a control, has found evidence of an association between the introduction of PbR in England and an increase in the volume of surgical activity, combined with a faster reduction in the length of stay, as compared with Scotland, with no identifiable decline in quality of care, although the proxy variables available for the measurement of quality of care were limited. Equally therefore, no evidence is presented of a correlation between increased efficiency, as represented by this reduction in unit costs of care, and improvements in quality of care (Farrar *et al.*, 2009). Nonetheless, increased autonomy has led Scotland, Wales and Northern Ireland to take different paths from that followed in England and one of the most immediately identifiable areas of divergence is that none of the other constituent countries of the UK has adopted the Payment by Results system of funding, introduced in England from the mid-2000s. However, it is important to note that these divergent trends have not developed *ex nihilo*, but have been largely shaped by pre-existing traditions, structures and patterns of power in the different countries of the UK, forming the basis for varying levels of capacity to enact policy change.

In Scotland, one of the most significant elements of this political capacity is represented by the long-standing existence of a healthcare policy community in which an important component is constituted by élite medical professionals, based in prestigious institutions such as the Medical Schools in leading Scottish Universities, which are closely associated with the major Teaching Hospitals. These élites play a significant role, both in agenda setting and in health policy making, which is thus more heavily influenced by the input of expertise from within the medical profession than has been the case in England, where market-oriented managerialism has been predominant. This institutionalised recognition of professional expertise in the policy-making process is doubtless an important contributory factor to the greater degree of stability and coherence which can be observed in Scotland, as compared with England, and policy developments have remained largely consistent with the direction initially set out in 1998 by the first Scottish Health Minister Dr. Sam Galbraith, himself a surgeon (Greer, 2004). The priority accorded to professionalism over markets and managerialism has been reflected in the removal of the separation between purchasers and providers, upon which much of the dynamics of pre-devolution regulation depended. In similar vein, the system of Trusts with managerial quasi-autonomy which was at the heart of the contractualisation mechanisms previously in operation has also been abolished, giving way to 14 Regional Health Boards (Greer, 2009). The fragmented, multi-tiered structures established prior to 1997 have thus been replaced by a flatter, more integrated system of regulation, based on the Health Boards. Significant moves have also taken place towards decompartmentalisation and an organisational focus on quality of care, through the development of new forms of service configuration, particularly Managed Clinical Networks (MCNs). In order to concentrate on the provision of treatment for patients during their entire trajectory through the system and facilitate the forging of links between professionals working in hospitals and all other sub-sectors of NHS Scotland, specific funding for improvements in particular kinds of care is allocated to different MCNs, the most advanced of which specialise in cancer care.

The relative weakness of established medical institutions and élites with the capacity to exert strong influence over policy making has been a significant factor in the impact of devolution in Wales. In the absence of an embedded tradition of concentrated professional expertise within several prestigious institutions, serving as the basis for a cohesive, high-status policy community to drive forward a policy agenda emanating from within the medical profession itself, developments in Wales have been marked by the influence of other traditions, rooted in local government. The direction taken by policy initiatives has thus reflected significant input from this source, seeking to bring about more effective integration between local government and the social services, with an emphasis on addressing wider public health issues linked to life-style and behaviour, such as binge-drinking (Greer, 2004). Although there appears to have been little more enthusiasm in Wales for market-driven dynamics than in Scotland, as suggested by the non-implementation of PbR in hospitals by the Welsh National Assembly, the purchaser-provider separation was not dismantled. Instead, in line with the localist tradition, commissioning has not been carried out by PCTs, but entrusted to 22 local Health Boards, whose boundaries correspond almost exactly with those of the 22 Welsh units of local government, with a view to harmonising the role of these bodies at local level. However, hospital Trusts themselves have not been abolished, resulting in an uneasy co-existence between localism and market-related pressures and leading to problems of coordination between fragmented local Health Boards and local government, on the one hand, and hospital Trusts on the other. Recent proposals to address such difficulties of policy capacity have involved the amalgamation of local health bodies into regional boards, along the lines of the Scottish model (Greer, 2009).

Devolution in Northern Ireland has been intermittent, since reversion to direct rule from Westminster has periodically been required, depending on the progress of the peace process. Even when it has been in operation, the need to avoid re-igniting or exacerbating long-standing sectarian divisions has overshadowed all other policy issues and acted as a constraint on the capacity of the Assembly to take a leading role in hospital regulation and health policy generally. Northern Ireland also lacks the kind of medical élite policy community which exists in Scotland and a prominent role has therefore been played by health service managers, but in the form of what Greer has dubbed "permissive managerialism" (Greer, 2004), whereby radical change of any kind would be regarded as undesirable. Indeed, such has been the inertia in the field of hospital reform that it was a Minister in the New Labour government under Blair who had to insist upon the implementation by one Northern Ireland Health Board of the internal market established under Thatcher. The shift towards Trusts and market dynamics nonetheless took place, but in incremental fashion and it was not until 2003 that the GP fundholding introduced under the Conservatives was eventually removed (Greer, 2009). The NHS in the UK, once regarded as a monolithic, Weberian edifice of archetypal proportions, has not therefore responded in uniform manner to the influences exerted by modernization, cost effectiveness and New Public Management, but has evolved in the direction of diversity, reflecting the different historical legacies of its constituent parts.

FRENCH HOSPITALS:
FROM "STRATEGY-MAKING" TO "CONTRACTING"

The various contributions published in a collective work entitled *L'hôpital stratège (The hospital as strategist)* (Contandriopoulos & Souteyrand, 1996) showed that despite the existence of regulatory and financial constraints, French hospitals continued for a long time to be fairly self-sufficient. By obtaining increasingly large resources via the institutionalized bargaining processes which were often carried out directly with the Ministry of Health, both public and private hospitals enjoyed much greater scope for action than what might be expected in view of the tools (such as *healthcare maps* and budgets) applied at that time.

The break with the previous regime occurred in 1991, when individual hospitals were encouraged to develop their own strategic plans, and then in 1996, when the Regional Hospital Agencies (ARH for *Agences Régionales de l'Hospitalisation*) were created. These successive reforms, which seemed to endorse contracts as the chief mode of regulation, imposed increasingly heavy constraints on French hospitals. Although these constraints were more of a qualitative than directly quantitative or financial kind, they nevertheless weighed quite strongly. With the advent of contractualization, a new, paradoxical requirement was made of hospitals: they were henceforth obliged to engage in contracts, the aim of which was explicitly described as meeting healthcare requirements while rationalizing the allocation of resources. These changes in the modes of funding formed the main framework for the new compulsory contractual approach.

State-supervised contracts: Is a one-sided contracting process possible?

Since the reforms introduced in 1991 and the endorsing orders passed in 1996, the self-assigned role of the French State as far as defining and developing proper hospital policies became clearly visible. The idea was to carry out legitimate restructuring, *i.e.*, to contrive to make the strict control of funding compatible with meeting the increasing healthcare demands. The introduction of contracts and increasing recourse to experts and Regional Health Agencies have contributed to making the hospital system a privileged locus for what several successive governments have called "modernizing the State". The latest hospital policy developments cannot be fully understood without referring to a wider movement (the advent of New Public Management and the reform of public action) which was sweeping across all the European countries. Leaving aside national specificities and the differences in market practices, it was attempted in all these countries to encourage public agencies to rationalize their methods painlessly. This resulted in the proliferation of efficiency indexes and guidelines to practices drawn up by bodies which often did not depend on the central authorities.

However, as far as hospital matters were concerned, the solution adopted in France was quite original. Contrary to what happened in other sectors after the advent of decentralization, regional devolution processes in the hospital sector did not rely on the pre-existing actors (such as the Regional and General Councils, the Regional Directorates for Health and Social Affairs [DRASS[2]], etc.), but on a new player, the Regional Hospital Agency (ARH).

This trend has been accelerated since the Regional Health Agencies (ARS, for *Agences Régionales de Santé*) were created in April 2010 in order to replace the ARHs, the Departmental Directorates for Health and Social Affairs (DDASS[3]), the DRASS and the regional healthcare insurance funds, or rather to encompass these institutions in a single body. At the time when the ARHs were created, there was some conjecture as to whether this new institution was of the Jacobine or Girondist obedience (*i.e.*, whether it was intended to serve centralising or decentralising purposes). It was obvious to all the protagonists, however, that the main mission of the ARHs was to set up suitable conditions for carrying out the restructuring that the previous orchestrators (The National Health Insurance Fund and local State authorities) had been unable to achieve.

Some people felt that the creation of the ARHs was an attempt by the French State to regain control of hospital affairs, which had become bogged down by compartmenting processes and local rivalry; whereas others suspected rather that it was an attempt to divest the de-concentrated State of its prerogatives by decentralizing the country's healthcare system, which was bound to increase inequality and arbitrariness.

With hindsight, although this heated debate has subsided, a state of ambivalence can be seen to have persisted, and the controversy has been sparked off again because the fact that the Regional Prefects are entitled to keep an eye on the ARS has not sufficed to solve the problem.

---

2. The *Directions Régionales des Affaires Sanitaires et Sociales* are the regional departments of French Ministry of health and social affairs.
3. The *Directions Départementales des Affaires Sanitaires et Sociales* operate at the level of the country (*Département*).

Two contradictory conceptions of the role of the State are therefore now firmly embodied in the procedures and the representations of those involved in regulating the French hospital system.

On the one hand, the contract process is incontestably based on a spirit of mutual commitment between each establishment and the Agency on which it depends. The Contract on objectives and means (COM or CPOM, where the P stands for "pluri-annual") drawn up first via internal negotiations (on the establishment's strategic plan: see below), followed by external negotiations (with the Regional Scheme of Healthcare Organization [SROS[4]]), is an innovative form of State intervention. At the same time, it is in keeping with hospitals' long-standing aspirations to autonomy and recognition.

On the other hand, the State continues to play an authoritative rather than facilitating role by imposing a forward-planning technical approach. The field of application of this approach, which initially included only financial affairs, is being gradually enlarged. Apart from standards and certification procedures, which naturally have to be defined at national level, most decisions about the main aspects of hospital budgets are still being made at central level. In the days of overall budgets, the French Regions were awarded lump sums by the Ministry of Health in Paris. Contrary to what occurs in European countries with a traditionally federal or regional structure (such as Germany and Italy, respectively), the French Regions were not willing or able to raise additional funds. Since the introduction of activity-based rates *(tarification à l'activité, or T2A)*, prices have been set for the specific medical interventions and hospital stays involved in treating each type of pathology, based on a national average. In addition, COMs are compulsory between hospitals which have adopted the contractual approach and their ARH (or an ARS) Agency, which is bound to go on acting like a de-concentrated rather than a decentralized player. All attempts to bring actors such as the Regional Councils onto the scene have had disappointing results so far: very few regional Councils have managed or even wanted to seize this opportunity of entering the arena. The process of decentralization of hospital regulation is therefore beginning to look rather like a mixture between a game of "hot potato" and a gift horse.

In order to instil new life into the process of decentralization, the Ministry of Health therefore decided in 2003 to launch a plan called the "2007 Hospital Plan", which has been replaced by the "2012 Hospital Plan", which was drawn up in a fairly similar spirit (Guerrero, Mossé & Rogers, 2009). One of the objectives which was not achieved in the first of these plans was precisely to bring the Regions and their political counterparts, the Regional Councils, into the arena with a view to renovating the hospitals, which were under-equipped and in a very poor state of repair.

In France, two opposite patterns (a top-down pattern in the case of resources, and a bottom-up pattern in that of projects) have persisted because of the apparent segregation existing between their respective fields. This situation follows in the footsteps of hospital policies where

---

4. The SROS, for *Schéma Régional d'Organisation Sanitaire*, is drawn up through a negotiation process under the responsibility of the ARH (henceforth the ARS). Its main goal is to organise the dynamic of the health care delivery system at the regional level.

the match between the main objective (restructuring) and the procedures (contracts) promulgated was achieved thanks to the efforts of the actors responsible for implementing the central authorities' directives more than to the directives themselves.

In the days of overall budgets, these arrangements were perfectly visible at the national level because the lump sums calculated using technical algorithms were put to the vote democratically by the French Parliament; and in these matters, the Parliament always used to ask many pertinent questions. The so-called "equalization process" was therefore introduced to smooth out inequalities between Regions by promoting voluntaristic national policies. These policies subsequently had visible effects at regional level, since the distribution of funds between establishments was partly based on the previous budgets and partly on the extent to which establishments participated in contract schemes.

When the T2A activity-based system of payment was introduced, one might have expected the dual pattern described above to be replaced by a single approach, whereby hospitals are regarded as enterprises capable of increasing their own resources by increasing their activities unilaterally. One should not forget, however, that 1) each establishment's level of activity is limited by contract, mainly depending on the needs estimated by the SROS, 2) identical fees are charged throughout the country, and 3) the whole process therefore revolves around the conflicting demands of autonomy and dependence.

The situation was quite different in the 1960s and 1970s, when hospitals were allowed to adjust their *per diem* price quite freely to increase their resources. It also differs from what occurred during the first few years of the overall budget, when the only path open to hospitals to laboriously contain their increasing costs was to adopt the same budgets from one year to the next.

The overall budget, which was applied only at non-profit making public and private establishments, consisted in giving each hospital an annual sum (paid out in monthly instalments) which corresponded to the maximum level of expenditure allowed. This sum was calculated on the basis of the previous year's expenditure. The first disadvantage of this system was obviously that hospitals which were "heavy spenders" were advantaged to the detriment of the "careful spenders". In addition, it did not encourage hospitals to develop new activities meeting the needs of the local population. Accountancy held sway over all other considerations, or so it seemed. Paradoxically, however, at the same time, hospitals were not being obliged to report as closely as before on their activities. And since hospitals which were running at a loss could not be left to struggle on indefinitely, extra funds were often allocated, and hospitals in difficulty sought to obtain complementary resources of other kinds. The fact that hospitals in the public and private sectors were not funded in the same way favoured strategic manœuvres, whereby customers were shared out between the two and the inequalities between different parts of the country were therefore maintained if not increased.

It is therefore not surprising that hospitals' overspending continued despite the adoption in 1995 of the *Objectif National des Dépenses de l'Assurance Maladie* (ONDAM – the National Sickness Insurance Expenditure Objective), which is voted every year by the French Parliament, based on experts' reports. Together with the National Audit Office, these experts draw up the maximum rate of healthcare expenditure increase covered by the health insurance fund (therefore not including the items for which patients have to pay). This rate of increase and the report on which it is based are debated and voted by the French Parliament. It is up to the social partners to make sure that this democratically set rate is complied with. In actual fact, however, despite the existence of some adjusting mechanisms, expenditure is very difficult to contain. The ONDAM gradually became a simple indicator rather than a political objective. It has rarely been met because of the pressure exerted by the high demand for hospital services, and even more by the supply. In 2010, it was decided to issue the ONDAM only every few years and to make sure that it would increase slowly - but surely, by 3% in 2010 and 2.9% in 2012. However modest this objective may seem, it seems rather likely that it may not be met.

In view of the specificities of local situations, it is hardly surprising that despite these attempts at national regulation, the combinations of resources and constraints described above have resulted in a highly diversified picture. The move towards contractual modes of operation actually had difficulty in materializing, for example. In June 2000, almost 10 years after COMs were launched, only about 8% of French hospital establishments had signed a COM. Worse still, this percentage varied greatly from one region to another (it ranged between 3 and 75% among the ten largest regions). And yet these contracts were attractive, since they were supposed to promote the renovation of hospital buildings and equipment as well as favouring a more equal distribution of the hospital supply between the various administrative Regions. These disparities and the priority given to operating costs to the detriment of capital investment contributed greatly to keeping the hospitals in a state of disrepair. It is worth noting, however, that at the beginning of this century, the regions in which the largest numbers of COMs had been signed were not always the most dynamic ones in terms of their investments or their restructuring efforts. The validity of the model initially adopted was therefore not confirmed: the hospitals and ARHs which adopted the contractual mode most whole-heartedly did not turn out to be more highly rewarded than the others.

Even more strikingly, whatever the mode used to fund the most powerful hospitals (the University teaching hospitals and establishments having political affinities with national decision-makers), they are still able to draw on direct or indirect resources in addition to those acquired via the formal procedures prescribed. The crux of the matter was the question of incentives. Hospitals naturally did not stand to gain by declaring their strategies to the French healthcare authorities, and the latter therefore could not obtain the information required to be able to distribute resources optimally among hospitals.

The ARHs will therefore no doubt have to extend their field of action; from this point of view, this is thought to be an opportune moment for reactivating the project to transform ARHs into ARSs in the framework of the HPST Act (on Hospitals, Patients, Health and local Territories). The scope of the ARHs will be extended to include private practices and ambulatory care and the medico-social sector, which is expected to facilitate modernization, restructuring, economies of scale, etc. But since the protagonists have expressed the wish to test cooperative solutions (local hospital communities, public/private partnerships, etc.), the Republican rule of procedural equality has had to be broken in some places all over the country. The ARSs will therefore not acquire full legitimacy unless they manage to distance themselves from the central State which brought them into being. As history has shown, this is by no means a small task.

Harmonisation via funding and standardisation

Public and private establishments long shared the same mode of funding, based on the *per diem* price. Despite the criticisms often voiced these days, one must admit that the *per diem* price contributed to the spectacular development of the French hospital system and enabled it to acquire considerable income. In addition, it contributed to the successful accomplishment of the technological and occupational changes occurring at French hospitals.

However, since this method of allocating resources was regarded as inflationary and conducive to inequalities between hospitals, and since it did not even meet the objectives of quality and efficiency, it became the reformers' scapegoat during the early 80s. After the introduction in the mid 70s of a flat rate designed to slow down the increase in expenditure and the failure of the *healthcare map* as a planning tool, it was decided that it was time to abolish this approach, which was being used too opportunistically by hospital directors.

The main reason, however, for introducing overall budgets at public hospitals instead of the *per diem* price was that they provided an opportunity of shifting from the previous *a posteriori* mode of funding (which seemed to be impossible to control) to an *a priori* mode (which seemed to be more controllable). Unfortunately, as the figures show all too clearly, this did not turn out to be the case, and the overall budget did not prevent the mishandling of funds or the persistence of inequalities, at least up to the 1990s.

Meanwhile, the private profit-making hospitals continued to apply *per diem* price rates, which facilitated their development and their use of specialization strategies. However, the PMSI (the Project, and subsequently the Programme of Medicalisation of the Information System; *programme de médicalisation du système d'information*) had been set up in parallel to monitor hospital activities, although it was initially designed to improve the highly inefficient current system of information and not for calculating hospital budgets. It took more than 15 years for the information thus collected to be integrated into the procedures used to allocate hospital resources, thanks to the introduction of the French system of DRGs. In order to adapt the amount of the overall budget allotted to each hospital's activities, each homogeneous group of patients (*Groupe Homogène de Malades*, GHM) was allotted a value expressed in ISA (for *Indice Synthétique d'Activité*, an overall activity index) points. This index was used to classify similar establishments. Here again, these calculations were based on the median national value.

This method was soon abandoned, however, in favour of one which came to be used at all public and private establishments, the activity-based (*tarification à l'activité* or *T2A*) method of payment, which was gradually implemented as from 2004 in both the public and private sectors. The aim in this case was to harmonize modes of public and private hospital funding, based on a common nomenclature of medical interventions. Apart from harmonizing accountancy practices, this reform was intended to promote closer relations between establishments and thus to prevent unfair privileges. In the long run, the aim of the rationalisation involved in this mode of funding was to modernise the whole French hospital system.

The restructuring process for which the ARHs were responsible was very slow, especially in the public sector. The delay was partly due to the lack of response on the part of the public hospitals and the obstacles, which prevented hospitals in the two sectors from merging, or at least from developing closer relations and setting up local contracts on their own. In this context, introducing a single rate of payment was expected to reduce or at least channel the amount of specialized care dispensed.

However, to attenuate the undesirable effects of the *T2A* method of payment, and especially to reduce competition, some activities have continued to be subject to a single flat rate of payment. These activities, namely emergencies, networking, prevention, medical research work, etc., which could not be described in terms of a nomenclature of interventions, have been called MIGACS *(Missions d'intérêt général)* and their funding is defined in special contracts with the ARH and ARS Agencies.

To prevent the untoward effects of reforms which might lead to each establishment playing the game its own way, the HPST Act was designed to put regulation back into the centre of the scheme by placing the emphasis on plans, maps and contracts.

Some of the differences between these two paradigms are therefore quite obvious: on the one hand, we have the "hospital enterprise" which cares very little about public welfare and deploys its activities to the detriment of local equilibrium – the model nobody wants; and on the other hand, we have a comprehensive system designed on the basis of some rather questionable indicators – the model everybody fears. From now on, each of the protagonists will be obliged to take up a position on this spectrum.

JAPANESE HOSPITALS: THEIR ENVIRONMENT AND THEIR ACTORS

Although the numbers of hospitals and the numbers of beds per inhabitant[5] are much larger in Japan than in France, hospitals do not play the same central role in the Japanese healthcare system as they do in France. This rather paradoxical situation has arisen for historical reasons, which it is proposed to describe in this section. As we will see, this paradox partly explains the situation of Japanese nurses today. It has also resulted in a lack of transparency as far as

---

5. Although these data should be handled with care, it has been claimed that there are approximately 7 hospital establishments per 100,000 inhabitants in Japan, *versus* 5 in France and 1.2 in the United Kingdom.
It was established in a survey published in 1996 that 45% of Japanese patients spend more than one hour in hospital waiting-rooms at each visit and that the numbers of hospital patients is constantly on the increase (1995 MHLW Report on Health and Welfare).

hospitals' performances are concerned. The information systematically collected about hospital equipment and activities (diagnoses, beds, the length of hospital stays, etc.) is certainly reliable, but the hospital system cannot be run on a qualitative basis, since this information cannot be collated with the quality of care, and hospitals have not been properly classified. It is therefore not surprising that the ongoing reforms tend to focus mainly on classifying, differentiating, counting, and generally tidying up the whole agglomerated mass of indistinguishable components.

The actors involved in rationalisation

In Japan as in France, patients are free to choose their own physicians. In Japan, however, this freedom is traditionally accompanied by very one-sided relationships between doctors and patients. Patients play a rather passive role in a paternalistic scheme of affairs which has never been fundamentally challenged. They are given little information about their diagnosis, their GPs' decisions and the possible consequences thereof, and people have to put up with consulting their doctors frequently and regularly to have their prescriptions renewed and delivered.

In line with the Chinese tradition, physicians do not only prescribe medicines, but they have also been dispensing many drugs themselves at their consultancies up to quite recently. Although this practice is gradually disappearing, pills and phials are still being delivered in quantities corresponding to the entire expected length of the treatment: the whole treatment is often handed over in a bag without the patients even being given the names of the products they are about to take. Hospital patients therefore have to attend the outpatients' department regularly and wait for anything up to a whole day to obtain their prescriptions and medicines[6]. These practices have resulted in a rather unusually familiar relationship between patients and hospitals, based on dependence and familiarity, which is probably to be found nowhere else among the industrialized countries. This relationship may explain why Japanese patients file very few legal complaints against their physicians.

Some observers have expressed the fear that the 15% increase in the rates of co-payment recently applied to 30% of light medical interventions may affect this paternalistic relationship and increase the number of legal claims (Feldman, 2008). Docile patients might thus be transformed into demanding customers. In line with this hypothesis, it can be noted that the number of claims increased two-fold between 1990 and 2007. But the actual figures were only 500 and 1000, which is nothing compared to the USA (OECD, 2008).

The following surprisingly high figure, which set a world record in 2007, illustrates the relationship we have just described between the Japanese and their physicians: on average, every Japanese citizen consulted a doctor 14 times that year; whereas in France, the annual number of visits *per capita* amounted to only about 6. The difference is all the more noteworthy in

---

6. It was established in a survey published in 1996 that 45% of Japanese patients spend more than one hour in hospital waiting rooms at each visit and that the number of out-patients is constantly on the increase (MHLW, 1995).

view of the fact that the number of doctors per inhabitant is approximately twice as high in France (3.4 per 1,000 inhabitants) as in Japan (1.8) The number of annual consultations therefore worked out at approximately 7,000 per physician (as against 2,000 in France) (OECD, 2008).

Another original feature of the Japanese healthcare system focuses on the supply, since there exist an unusually large number of *clinics* in this country.

General practitioners and specialists

There are three forms of medical practice in Japan[7]. First of all, independent GPs' medical practices account for approximately 26.1%. In the private sector, physicians are not obliged by the Ministry of Health to undergo any occupational training and they are allowed to go on practising indefinitely. The certification process is much simpler than in France: diplomas are not subject to any national authorities' approval. Specialists are mainly certified and authorized to work in specific fields by professional medical associations (or learned societies), which co-opt colleagues on the basis of criteria which tend to vary from one group to another.

Secondly, specialist care is mostly dispensed at hospitals as in many other developed countries, often under the control of local or national bodies (the Municipality or the Region and its Prefecture). Approximately 60% of Japanese physicians work at hospitals, and most of them have the status of salaried employees (MHLW, 2006). The number of establishments at which they work has decreased slightly since 1999, from 9,286 to 8,943. But the fact that the number of hospitals with more than 300 beds remained stable (about 1,600 hospitals) during the same period has slightly increased the mean number of beds per hospital (from 177 in 1999 to182 in 2006). In 2007, there were 1 626 000 hospital beds in all.

Thirdly, in between independent practices and hospital work, an extensive network of *clinics* covers practically the whole country. These establishments tend to attract physicians who have acquired solid experience at hospitals and want to capitalize on their reputations. The mean age of the physicians working at *clinics* is 58 years, as compared with 48 years, which is that of all Japanese medical practitioners combined *(ibid.)*.

The *clinics* have less than ten beds on average. Their number increased from 78,000 to 98,000 between 1984 and 20047, whereas their overall capacity decreased during this period from 283,000 to 196,000 beds. Although *clinics* account for 85% of Japanese in-patient establishments, they therefore provide only 10.7% of the hospital beds *(ibid.)*, and this percentage is gradually decreasing as ambulatory care is on the increase. The number of cataract operations performed at *clinics* has increased ten-fold during the last ten years, for example.

---

7. The density of medical provision is relatively low in Japan (there were 2.0 doctors per 1,000 inhabitants in 2004), but it has been on the increase (there were only 1.1 doctors per 1,000 inhabitants in 1970). In France, for instance, there were 3.4 doctors per 1,000 inhabits in 2004: this figure has increased even more sharply than in Japan, since there were only 1.2 doctors per 1,000 inhabitants in 1970 (OECD Health data, 2008).

The policies traditionally adopted in Japan, which gave the physicians owning *clinics* consi-derable autonomy, have made it difficult to differentiate between the various sectors respon-sible for the country's healthcare supply, namely the public and private sectors, the hospital sector, *clinics* and the ambulatory care sector. This situation is largely due to the existence of a single tariff. The same flat rate is charged for a given medical intervention, whether it is performed under ambulatory conditions or at an in-patient establishment, by a specialist or a GP, in Tokyo or in a rural setting. There therefore exist few incitements for doctors to set up as specialists. This apparent equality[8] has greatly favoured the development of ambulatory practices throughout the country's healthcare system. This no doubt explains why less than 30% of Japanese doctors are specialists, as compared with 50% in France, although it is rela-tively easy for Japanese doctors to acquire specialist status (Kondo, 2008).

This situation helps, however, to explain the special role played by hospitals in the Japanese healthcare system, which contrasts with what occurs in other industrialized countries.

Although the mean hospital stay has been on the decrease during the last 20 years in Japan, it is still 2.7 times longer than the mean hospital stay in the OECD member countries. This difference can be accounted for in the first place by the fact that the system used to classify general hospitals in Japan makes no distinction between establishments where the patients' stays are of medium length and those where they are short. This anomaly is beginning to disappear, however slowly. The mean duration of hospitals stays in France and Japan are given in *table 5.1.*

Twenty years ago, the mean duration of patients' hospital stays was around 18 days in France, as compared with 50 days in Japan. This difference was mainly due to the method used to classify establishments and the fact that no distinction was made even between patients themselves, depending on whether they were treated at short-stay or medium-stay establish-ments. At a more fundamental level, however, this distinction corresponds to different prac-tices in each of the two countries. Once again, continuity and declared equality are the de-clared ideals in Japan, whereas the hierarchy existing among establishments France also corresponds to a hierarchy among hospital practitioners.

This explains the considerable difference observed in the latest data between the overall length of hospital stays in France and the length of patients' stays at general hospitals and *clinics* alone in Japan (excluding the medium-stay establishments). In 2000, the average length of stay in Japan was 40 days. At short-stay establishments alone, the mean duration of hospital stays in 2005 was around 20 days in Japan and 6 days in France. In the United Kingdom, since the length of acute care hospital stays decreased from 9.5days in 1990 to 7.8 days in 2005, the situation was similar to that in France. Despite this similarity, while the underlying UK trend is downwards, the pattern is markedly less consistent than in both France and Japan. Figures for overall UK stays display a sharp decline from 1990 to 1995, but subsequent evolution is more erratic, suggesting an absence of stability in this domain. However, the

---

8. This similarity is only apparent, since additional fees sometimes have to be paid in Japan (as in France) "under the counter" (a practice which is referred to in Japanese as "into the sleeve").

figures are quite sensitive to the way hospitals are listed. This difference shows that patients and the members of the medical profession in France and Japan have a completely different picture of what hospitalisation involves.

This difference is due in particular to the fact that hospitals are much more comprehensive and less compartmented into specialities in Japan than in France.

Far from resulting simply from healthcare procedures and programmes, the duration of hospital stays results in Japan from interactions between many other complex factors and ideas, including the medical profession's representation of patients' expectations, various ideas about efficiency, and various levels of compliance with economic constraints. In Japan, all these imbricated aspects make the overall structure less responsive and less sensitive to economic and organizational changes, however real they may be. This inertia explains why the mean length of hospital stays decreased slightly more slowly between 1980 and 2002 in Japan than in France (– 36% in Japan, *versus* – 38% in France).

Table 5.1. *Mean hospital stays in France and Japan (acute care dispensed at all hospitals combined).*

Year		1980	1985	1990	1995	2000	2005
France	Overall	21.2	18.1	15.1	14.1	13.2	13.4
	Acute Care	10.2	8.6	7.0	6.2	5.6	5.4
Japan	Overall	55.9	54.2	50.5	44.2	39.1	35.7
	Acute Care	–	–	–	33.2	24.8	19.8
UK	Overall	–	–	17.9	10.3	9.9	9.0
	Acute Care	–	–	9.5	7.1	8.2	7.8

Source: Adapted from OECD, 2008.

This pattern has mainly resulted from economic and medical decisions. By keeping the *per diem* price fairly low, regulators have prevented the intensification of care and stopped the density of paramedical hospital staff from increasing (there were 2.5 times fewer of these employees per hospital bed than the mean number published by the OECD: MHLW, 2004); all these factors have led to hospital stays being extremely long in Japan.

Length of stay is not in itself an index to performance, however. At most, it may reflect the level of technicality involved in the care dispensed, or the fact that many patients' trajectories include several periods of hospitalization, etc. Now as we have seen in the previous chapters, the technical aspects are being combined, as they should be, with the relational aspects in Japan, giving an approach to patients' care which might be perceived as being of a high standard. Japanese nurses have in fact adapted all the more readily to this situation as it justifies their claim for more multi-task work. The opposite side of the coin is that the overall picture which consistently emerges (in terms of the length of hospital stays, the domestic care model and the role of women) is perfectly in line with the way gender issues are handled in Japan, which is far from being egalitarian.

Nurses marching towards emancipation

As Y. Oryu (2007) has put it quite clearly:

> "It looks rather as if Japanese women have for a long time integrated or chosen a philosophy of life whereby women are destined to leave the world of work after their marriage, or at least at the birth of their first child."

As the latter author has explained, however, this penchant or philosophy is not in fact either culturally rooted or natural: it actually results from a set of measures, such as the Japanese income tax regulations in particular. Women actually keep their working hours to a minimum so that their husbands will not be liable for extra tax and social contributions. Up to a given income level, married couples benefit from the same tax relief as households earning a single income. Similar conditions apply to people's contributions to the sickness insurance and old-age pension funds.

The data on the age-distribution of nurses in France and Japan[9] illustrate this situation both objectively and highly significantly. At the national level, the two countries show very different patterns in this respect. In Japan, the 25-34 age-group was that which included the largest numbers of nurses in 2004, whereas in France, it was the 45-49 age-group which showed the largest numbers in 2005. It is worth noting in particular that more than 44% of French nurses are over 45 years of age, as compared with only 26% in Japan (Cash & Ulmann, 2008; MHLW, 2007).

French nurses manage to develop proper careers by acquiring the ability to organize their time both at work and at home[10]. They make use of whatever family and collective resources (nurseries, etc.) are available, and usually manage to juggle fairly successfully with the various demands made on their time (Bouffartigue & Bouteiller, 2003; Maisonneuve, 2005). As described in a previous chapter, this is not easy because keeping one's job often means accepting changes of timetable and moving from one hospital ward to another.

The above statistics therefore confirm the findings made in our 1988 and 2008 surveys, which have been presented earlier in this book. It emerges that one large wave of Japanese nurses tend to give up their jobs, especially when they are hospital jobs, upon reaching the age of thirty; and a second wave of departures occurs around the age of 45. Since there is a high proportion of very young nurses in Japan (where this proportion is 2.5 times greater than in France), the outcome is extremely problematic: on the one hand, very few Japanese nurses stay long in the profession, and on the other hand, many of them are inexperienced and they tend to have very short careers.

There has been a move towards female emancipation in Japan, however. Women are now entitled to take their employers to court if the latter have not obeyed the Act passed in April 2007, whereby it is illegal for firms to oblige female employees to give up their jobs when they are pregnant (Oryu, 2007, p. 24).

---

9. These figures include both male and female nurses, but since there are very few male nurses in Japan, it is legitimate to analyse the data in terms of gender-related issues.

10. In the survey conducted in France by the APHP in 2008, one third of the participants who responded to the question about their partner's profession declared that he or she worked in the medical or medico-social sector.

The Japanese female labour market is highly sensitive to the economic situation, since female employment has always served as an adjusting variable. However, comparisons made between 1975 and 2006 by the Japanese Occupational Institute for employment policy and vocational training (JILPT, 2007-2008) show the existence of some perfectly clear-cut trends *(Figure 1)*.

In both 1975 and 2006, the rate of female employment in the 25 to 30 age-group was around 66%. But in 1975, this figure depended strongly on age, as it dropped to 42% in the 25 to 35 age-group, which confirms that many women gave up their jobs when they became of marriageable age. It increased again to 61% at the age of 45, reflecting a tendency to return to work, before dropping off gradually again after the age of 50.

In 2006, Japanese women's age-dependent activity curve showed a quite different pattern: the minimum occurred slightly later than in 1975 (between the age of 30 and 34); and despite this slight decrease, the rate of activity was still relatively high (62.8%) at this age. It continued to increase up to the age of 45-49 (74%), and the drop which occurred around the age of 50 was less conspicuous than in 1975.

This means that the difference between the age-groups showing the lowest and highest rates of employment, which amounted to 50% in 1975, had fallen to 15% by 2006. It is true that in the case of men, this difference was consistently very small (about 5%) throughout the period under investigation, and the mean rate of activity was much higher in the case of men (97% between the age of 25 and 60) than women. This remarkably high level of stability was responsible for the life-long employment model par excellence, the "Japanese model" as it is known, which actually applies only to Japanese men (Nohara, 1999).

As these labour market changes show, the road to equality between Japanese men and women is bound to be long. The chances are, however, that if the trends pointed out here persist, it will become easier than previously for nurses to stay on the labour market and pursue more consistent and continuous career paths. The wage data published suggest that the problem is not a question of pay rates. Based on the data published by the Japanese Nursing Association in 1986 and 2003, the mean monthly wage earned by Japanese nurses in 2001 was around 360,000 yens, which amounts to around 1,860 euros after making purchasing power adjustments (it was 243000 yens in 1985). The mean wage earned by French nurses in 2001 was 1 700 euros per month. It is difficult of course to draw conclusions from comparisons of this kind, since nurses' income includes various bonuses, but it can be said on the basis of these rough comparisons that nurses' wages are similar in both countries. In both cases, considerable pay rises have occurred since the strikes which took place in both countries in the late 1980s.

Japanese hospitals have therefore evolved concomitantly with the nursing profession; this is no coincidence, of course. Both processes have been driven by the development of nurses' skills, corresponding to a shift towards more specialized practices.

The present picture seems to suggest that the Japanese nursing profession has been one of the first to benefit from the general trend towards greater emancipation, although this trend has not yet been translated into policy. At the occupational level, this trend has taken the form of recognition for nurses' technical skills. Nurses and their associations are aware that their skills are more likely to be put to good use in a more highly compartmented system.

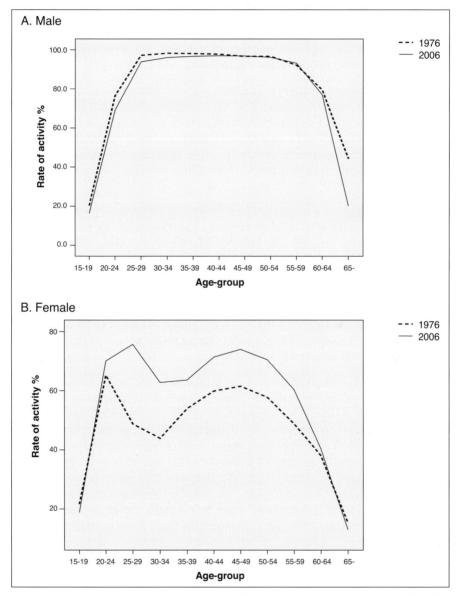

Figure 1. *Rates of activity of Japanese males (A) and females (B), depending on their age-group (1975-2006).*
Source: CM and MM, adapted from JILPT, 2007-2008.

Improving transparency and providing incentives

In the context we have described, the recent reforms have mainly been designed to "organize" the hospital system. The need has been felt to sort things out between hospitals and to reorganize the links between each establishment and the authority on which it depends (the Prefecture or the State). The key point common to both of these goals is the importance of the quality of information, especially that relating to hospitals' activities and their clientele, on which negotiations between protagonists are based.

In a healthcare system giving patients the freedom of choice between hospital establishments, the division of labour between hospitals and *clinics* cannot be easily defined. Although the principle of freedom of choice still exists, some efforts have been made to distinguish between establishments' respective roles. To encourage patients to choose *clinics* for primary care (and thus reduce the hospital attendance rates), for example, patients are therefore being made to pay an additional cost for their first hospital stay if they have not been referred by a *clinic* (Akiyama, 2001).

The classification of Japanese hospitals was explicitly placed on the agenda as part of the move towards institutional specialization. Hospitals have been subdivided into three categories (University teaching hospitals and other specific types of hospital, *clinics*, and "social hospitals", which are nursing homes for the elderly), in line with the 1985 Act on Medical and Hospital Care. This led to the creation around 1986 of "geriatric hospitals" (which are long-stay establishments) and "convalescence" homes of a medico-social kind, which are medical retirement homes. The criterion officially adopted to distinguish between the various establishments was the maximum length of stay allowed, which is equal to 6 months at geriatric hospitals, for example. In fact, patients spend longer periods than this at geriatric nursing homes, and they often make repeated stays.

It was indeed partly to prevent care for the elderly from weighing too heavily on the sickness insurance funds' budgets and to make the Japanese government rather than the family responsible for care for the elderly that a compulsory insurance scheme was launched in April 2000 and revised in 2006 to cover the cost of long-term care for people over the age of 70. These programmes, which depend on the patients' level of dependence, cover both care dispensed at institutions and home care. All Japanese citizens over 40 years of age contribute to this fund. In the framework of this programme, hospitals were given the possibility of improving the quality of their accommodation (by providing more spacious rooms, for example), but not the number of hospital beds, which means that a non-negligible proportion of long-term care is still being reimbursed as previously by the sickness insurance fund (Campbell & Ikegami, 2000).

Whether they focus on long or short stays, the reforms applied since the creation of the regional schemes in 1985 were designed to contain the supply, *i.e.*, the number of hospital beds, while constantly accentuating the differences between the various places at which medical care is dispensed. With these aims in mind, special attention has been paid to hospital funding. The DRGs, which are now called DPCs *(diagnosis procedure combinations)*, started to be used in 2003 at Japanese University teaching hospitals. In comparison with what has happened in France, it is surprising to see how suddenly this intrusion occurred. It was set up less than one year after it first began to be seriously discussed.

Since these reforms were taking place so fast, the 2000 version of the World Health Organization's classification of diseases was adopted in Japan. Unfortunately, this system of classification is not suitable for use with hospital patients, which is the reason why it has not been adopted in other industrialized countries, most of which have developed their own *ad hoc* systems of classification.

The advent of DPCs did not do away with the *per diem* fee: this includes nursing care and varies, depending on the size of the nursing staff, which is usually large at University teaching hospitals and smaller at the little hospitals. The price decreases with the length of stay, starting at the point where the patient's hospital stay is longer than average; it therefore does not correspond to a set rate as in France, but was designed to strongly promote shorter hospital stays and improve the quality and intensity of care.

At a more general level, several changes have occurred or are about to be introduced with a view to improving transparency and aligning hospitals' revenue with their medical activities. The DRGs arrived rather suddenly in Japan, in a context where there was a long tradition of fees for services. These practices therefore have to be changed in order to contain medical healthcare expenditure by adapting them to the hospital system, which has already been transformed into a plural entity. The stakes involve more than just the fair distribution of resources, since practices have to be changed and it will be necessary to join the move towards greater specialization, which is recognized as being indispensable. The system based on a single flat rate of payment, which was long held to be fair, is becoming less widely practised due to the development of increasingly sophisticated methods, the increase in the rates of chronic disease and the increasing demand for long-term care.

The new regulations took effect on 1st. April 1997, when a new *fee schedule* was introduced, in which one of the main aspects of Japanese hospital funding was abolished: the *per diem* price was henceforth made to depend on the length of patients' hospital stays. Eight *per diem* price levels were set, the highest of which applied to stays shorter than 15 days. The daily rate then decreased step-wise as the length of stay increased. This innovation paved the way for the DPCs which were introduced a few years later, and helped to make them more readily acceptable.

The measures described above resulted in more clear-cut distinctions between hospitals with specific functions (such as University teaching hospitals) and other establishments, especially *clinics*. To stress even more strongly the existence of this newly founded hierarchy, it was decreed that patients wanting to attend "specific function" hospitals must be referred by a *clinic* or a GP, otherwise they will have to pay an extra fee corresponding to the first consultation.

The changes made on all these lines were not intended so much to ensure equality of access for all as to promote a mode of regulation whereby negotiations between actors are based on mutual recognition of the other partners' legitimacy. The latest reforms have been accepted because they have been deliberately and explicitly introduced incrementally, which has made them both credible and effective: the teething phase has triggered a "virtuous circle" based on trust and mutual commitment. At the operational level, the reforms have been accepted because they have been officially legitimized by the democratic procedure whereby the new nomenclature of medical interventions and the corresponding *fee schedule* were introduced.

The nomenclature of medical interventions and fees was published in an extremely large book consisting of more than 2000 pages, which lists an enormous number of interventions and practices, each of which is given a score destined to be subsequently translated into financial terms. This nomenclature is central to the regulation of the Japanese healthcare system. Since it is methodical, objective and efficacious, it epitomizes the strengths and limitations of the consensus-seeking approach (Mossé & Takeuchi, 2003; Campbell & Ikegami, 1998).

The Council responsible for drawing up the *fee schedule book* consists of twenty members: 8 representing sickness insurance funds, 8 representing healthcare professionals (the majority of whom are members of the Japan Medical Association) and 4 representing the hospital world. There are also six so-called "public interest" delegates, who are in fact appointed from academic spheres.

The *fee schedule* book is revised every 2 years. This very regularity confirms the efficiency of the process, which involves two main steps. First, the central decision-makers set the rate of increase of the "point" *(tensu)* in the total healthcare expenditure for the forthcoming 2-year period.

This approach is rather similar to that adopted in France with the National Sickness Insurance Expenditure Objective (ONDAM), where the Parliament votes a legal objective based on information provided by experts. In France, it has been decided that the ONDAM rate would be set for a period of three years and that it would be gradually decreased. In Japan, however, predictive measures of this kind would be thought to detract from the fairness of the bargaining process. The decision to gradually reduce the increase in hospitals' expenditure was taken unilaterally by the administration because of the lack of confidence in the protagonists' ability to reach a consensus. Since professionals are not consulted, the outcome is bound to be of little consequence, and the rates set are unlikely to eventually become negative. The French Government is expecting the ONDAM rate to be +3% in 2010, + 2.9 in 2011 and + 2.8 in 2012. Although this hypothetical containment mechanism is also accompanied by an alarm system, it has been completely ineffectual up to now. Since it is not associated with any efficient regulatory instrument worth mentioning, the present system is of purely symbolic value: as Shakespeare might have said, it amounts to much ado about nothing, in fact.

In Japan, the value of the "fee schedule rate" is a much more effective regulatory tool. Since it results from real negotiations, it can show significant variations. It amounted to +9.6%, for example, in 1998, and dropped to -3.16% in 2006. Sometimes its value remains negative for several years running, as occurred from 2006 to 2009. The fee schedule rate is used to calculate the fees of all the medical practitioners in Japan. It was set at +0.19% in 2010. Contrary to what occurs in the UK, where hospital funding is included in the quasi market budget, the regulation is exerted *a posteriori* rather than by setting amounts *a priori*. Several persons are appointed by Japanese public insurance agencies to check the relevance of specific medical tests and prescriptions. If any errors or "fraudulent practices" are detected, the doctors in question may have to reimburse all or part of their fees.

In Japan, it is the Ministry of Health's Cabinet members who make the decisions, after weighing up the opinions of conflicting pressure-groups. It is hardly surprising that the Japan Medical Association traditionally insists on increasing medical expenditure, whereas the Ministry of Finance advocates containment. The second stage is more complex, as the fee is not applied consistently to all interventions (of which there exist several hundred kinds) by upgrading the values of all the scores. On the contrary, discussions about the forthcoming rates lead to defining which interventions are to be encouraged by increasing the corresponding fees, and which are to be discouraged by reducing the scores. This debating procedure makes it possible to finely control medical practices while neatly preventing conflicts. On the one hand, these regulations are not irrevocable, since they can potentially be challenged anything up to 24 months later; and on the other hand, all those involved are given an opportunity of expressing their opinion. The physicians' objective is to steer prescription practices, while that of the patients is to control the modes of drug consumption (Ikegami & Campbell, 2008). As the result of this bargaining process, expenditure is contained on the whole and since the changes introduced are fairly unsubstantial, they are usually accepted. The heavy technical and political artillery required to define and control the ONDAM in France certainly looks extremely unwieldy and inefficient by comparison.

It is worth mentioning, however, that pressure groups sometimes grasp these discussions as an opportunity for delaying decisions which may seem reasonable at first sight, but are likely to be strongly criticized when it comes to putting them into practice. The resulting ping-pong battle can sometimes look like a lack of determination and end up with the *status quo*.

Despite these pitfalls (or possibly because of them), this institutional bargaining procedure serves to drive the whole system without laying a finger directly on physicians' freedom of practice or the "medical power" they enjoy. The rationale underlying the bargaining process is as follows: first, it sets up favourable conditions for inciting physicians to carry out socially necessary and economically sound interventions; and secondly, these negotiations serve a basic political purpose: the round-table discussions between the healthcare system's protagonists promote cooperation and at the same time result in a consensus on matters extending beyond the schedule itself.

The principles on which these negotiations are based make it possible for actors who are not closely involved *a priori* to take part in the process. For instance, the way the Council responsible for nomenclatures and fees functions has directly influenced decisions about hospitals' medical imaging equipment. This reflects the fact that the Japanese healthcare system and its regulation have been successfully integrated into the economy as a whole. For many years, the fees paid by patients undergoing medical imaging were consistently high. Although the manufacturers decreased their prices considerably, the sickness insurance schemes and the Japanese Government deliberately attributed high scores in the *fee schedule book* to the use of scanners and nuclear magnetic resonance imaging methods. This incited hospitals to use non-invasive procedures more extensively (Ikegami, 2007). The reasons for this policy were industrial as much as medical: the idea was to boost the growth of this industrial sector in Japan by actually making the sickness insurance funds bear the cost of this growth. In 2007, the number of MRI apparatuses available in Japan per million inhabitants was 40.1, as compared with 5.7 in France, 8.2 in the UK and approximately 11 on average in all the OECD member countries combined (OECD, 2010).

However, in 2002, this situation was reversed since it had become more urgent to master healthcare expenditure than to support industrial objectives. The main change made that year consisted in reducing the fees paid for MRI interventions by about 30%. Meanwhile, between 1980 and 2002, the main Japanese manufacturer of medical imaging equipment became one of the four world leaders in the field, thanks to the supporting policies from which this company had benefited.

CONCLUSION

The modes of hospital funding and regulation which have undergone several fundamental changes in France during a relatively short period have failed so far to yield a simple, stable, motivating mechanism.

The present mechanisms certainly cannot be stable because of the feelings of mistrust (in the vertical direction, *i.e.*, between establishments and the authorities) and the unfair competition (in the horizontal direction, *i.e.*, among establishments) which still prevail. The trouble is that reforms tend to be presented in France as a set of long-term changes which do away completely with the previous mode of regulation. This pattern, whereby a reformer acquires the status of a veritable hero, may be partly due to the fear of consensuses (which tend to raise the suspicion that they may result from a guilty compromise) and belief in the principle of alternance which has always characterized French political life. However, if this course of action fails, it will set up a spontaneously negative reaction (the "duck's back" reflex) among protagonists. Strategies based on reticence or opposition have nothing to do with the "resistance to change" of which French reformers so frequently complain. They actually provide the impetus required for handling change successfully.

Japanese reformers are not faced with this dichotomy between success and failure (Jullien, 1996). Each new measure is explicitly presented in Japan as part of a collective mechanism, which both generates and nourishes a relatively stable political situation and a consensus culture. However, in this incremental process which is openly recognized as such, efficiency tends to be sacrificed in favour of social harmony.

The integration of healthcare policies in Japan has depended on the idea that regulation should be driven voluntaristically and not left to the laws of the market. At the same time, however, if the regulation is to be effective, the tools used for this purpose have to be used cooperatively. During the late 1990s, the relevance of introducing *managed care* methods based on the American model was discussed (Mayer & Tanaka, 1999). Introducing a whole battery of controls handled by the fee-payers themselves would no doubt have led Japanese hospitals to completely abolish the original model. The present-day domestic model based on relationships of proximity would have had to be replaced by a market model, which Japanese society finds objectionable for all kinds of reasons. In actual fact, the relevance of the *managed care* approach has never been debated or envisaged very seriously in Japan, and this option is no longer on the agenda.

Two highly reputed specialists in the field of Japanese healthcare (Ikegami & Campbell, 2008) have claimed that Japan was "lucky", in matters of healthcare policy, to have had no pro-market proponents, "which made it possible for the actors to take the decisions dictated by their intuition and courage". However, according to these authors, the pro-market partisans now have an opportunity of launching a new offensive with a view to reforming the system.

Although the proponents of individual hospital plans and the planning of the healthcare supply are in the majority, various forms of compromise are developing and an edulcorated version of the market approach is beginning to emerge.

REFERENCES

• Akiyama H. Health care reform in Japan. *World Hospitals and Health Services* 2001; 37 (2): 3-6.

• Arturo Alvarez-Rosete A, Bevan G, Mays N, Jennifer Dixon J. Information in practice, effect of diverging policy across the NHS. *BMJ* 2005; 331.

• Bouffartigue P, Bouteiller J. Jongleuses en blouse blanche. La mobilisation des compétences temporelles chez les infirmières hospitalières. Communication aux IXᵉ journées de sociologie du travail, Paris, November 2003.

• Boyle S. The Health system in England. *Eurohealth* 2008; 14 (1): 1-2.

• Campbell J, Ikegami N. *The Art of balance in health policy.* Cambridge: Cambridge University Press, 1998.

• Campbell J, Ikegami N. Long-term care insurance comes to Japan. *Health Aff* 2000; 19 (3): 26-39.

• Cash R, Ulmann P. La migration des professionnels de santé : le cas de la France. *OECD Health Working Papers* 2008.

• Contandriopoulos AP, Souteyrand Y. (ed). *L'Hôpital stratège : dynamiques locales et offre de soins.* Montrouge : Éditions John Libbey Eurotext, 1996.

• Eymard-Duvernay F, Favereau O, Salais R, Dupuy JP, Thévenot L. Économie des conventions. *Revue Économique* 1989; 40 (2): 141-6.

• Farrar S, Yi D, Sutton M, Chalkley M, Sussex J, Scott A. Has payment by results affected the way that English hospitals provide care? Difference-in-differences analysis. *BMJ* 2009; 339: b3047.

• Greer S. Devolution and divergence in UK health policies. In: Dawson S (ed). *Future Public Health.* Basingstoke: Palgrave Macmillan, 2009: 15-38.

• Greer S. *Four way bet: How devolution has led to four different models for the NHS.* London: University College London Constitution Unit, 2004.

• Guerrero I, Mossé P, Rogers V. Hospitals investment policy in France. *Health Policy* 2009; 93: 35-40.

• Ham C. Improving NHS performance: Human behaviour and health policy. *BMJ* 1999; 319: 1490-2.

• Ham C. How go the NHS Reforms? *BMJ* 1993; 306 (6870): 77-8.

• Healthcare Commission. Investigation into Mid Staffordshire NHS Foundation Trust. Commission for Healthcare Audit and Inspection, March 2009.

• Harrison AJ. Hospitals in England. *Medical Care* 1997; 35 (10): 55-61.

• Japan Institute for labour Policy and Training (JILPT). *Japanese working life profile 2007-2008*. JILPT, 2008.

• Klein R. Why Britain is reorganising its National Health Service - yet again. *Health Aff* (Millwood) 1998; 17 (4): 111-25.

• Klein R. The new model NHS: Performance, perceptions and expectations. *Br Med Bull* 2007; 81-82: 39-50.

• Kober-Smith A, Feroni I. Nursing careers in France and Britain: Age-related policy matters. *Equal Opportunities International* 2008; 27 (1): 34-48.

• Maisonneuve C. Les Jongleuses en blouse blanche, vingt ans après. *Soins* 2005; 10: 5-7.

• Maslin-Prothero SE, Masterton A, Jones K. Four parts or one whole: The NHS post-devolution. *J Nurs Manag* 2008; 16: 662-72.

• Ministry of Health, Labour and Welfare (MHLW). *Statistical report on Public Health Services 2004*. Tokyo: MHLW, by Statistics and Information Department, 2007.

• Ministry of Health, Labour and Welfare (MHLW). *Hospital report 1980-2005*. Tokyo: MHLW, by Statistics and Information Department, 1982-2007.

• Ministry of Health, Labour and Welfare (MHLW). *Report on survey of physician, dentists and pharmacists 2004*. Tokyo: MHLW, by Statistics and Information Department, 2006.

• Mossé P, Takeuchi M. Le système de soins japonais ; l'impossible et permanente réforme. *Med Sci* 2003; 19 (2): 223-30.

• Nohara H. L'analyse sociétale des rapports entre activités féminine et masculine. Comparaison France-Japon. *Revue Française de Sociologie* 1999; 40, 3: 531-58.

• OECD. *Health Data*. OECD, 2005-2010.

• Oryu Y. Les femmes japonaises. *Après-demain* 2007; 2: 23-28.

• Pierru F. Hospital Inc. *Enfances & Psy* 2009; 43: 99-105.

• Pope C. Cutting queues or cutting corners: Waiting lists and the 1990 NHS reforms. *BMJ* 1992; 305: 577-9.

• Primomo J. Nursing around the world: Japan - preparing for the century of the elderly. *Online J Issues Nurs* 2000; 5 (2): 2.

• Rowland D, Pollock AM, Vickers N. The British Labour Government's Reform of the National Health Service. *J Public Health Policy* 2001; 22 (4): 403-14.

• Robinson R. NHS foundation trusts: greater autonomy may prove illusory. *BMJ* 2002; 325: 506-7.

• Walshe K. Foundation hospitals: A new direction for NHS reform? *J R Soc Med* 2003; 96 (3): 106-10.

6. What projects for what teams?

As we have seen in the previous chapters, questions relating to economic and financial regulation cannot be dissociated from questions of hospital management, which in turn are closely linked to professional logics. The efficiency of a hospital system therefore depends on the ability of its healthcare teams to find a trade-off between the requirements of rationalization and the public health objectives. This is exactly the purpose for which the "strategic plan" was designed. Since it is supposed to balance the internal need to mobilize funds with the external need to allocate resources sensibly, this instrument has met with unanimous approval in both France and Japan. However, there exist some important differences between the two countries due to the professional practices resulting from nurses' strategies, expectations and problems. Comparisons with the situation in the UK shed some light on the social specificities which the purportedly universal concept of "modernization" may tend to mask.

To explain the impact of the "strategic plan" and the way it has been put to use, it is necessary first to describe how it developed. This will lead us to discuss questions about leadership, governance and the nature and role of healthcare teams. Lastly, our analysis of these practices will yield another explanation for the societal differences between France and Japan, which focuses on the regulatory space in which hospitals and their decision-makers operate.

THE KEY ROLE OF THE STRATEGIC PLAN, A DELICATE TOOL

Strategic plans have been compulsory at all French public hospitals since 1991. They are in fact an absolute prerequisite for hospitals to be able to sign contracts on objectives and means (COMs).

Strategic plans have been introduced in several stages in this country. Starting with hospitals' medical projects, which normally determine the nature of their future activities, those which will have to be abandoned and those which will be based on contracts with external partners, they have gradually been completed by nursing plans and social plans, and the latest addition has been the financial and accountancy plan. Hospital managers are responsible for coordinating these various plans and making them compatible with each other, but the medical plan is naturally given priority. Up to the 1980s, medical decision-making took place in the framework of each establishment's Medical Commission, consisting of the heads of all the hospital departments. Since the members of this Commission were not all equally well-informed, hospital directors often found it hard to judge how relevant their proposals were. With the latest methods of governance, the procedure has become much more complex but hospital directors, who often serve as adjudicators, have acquired greater legitimacy.

Once a hospital's strategic plan has been duly drawn up, discussed and approved by the various internal instances involved in concerted decision-making activities, it is eventually submitted to the ARH Agency. These plans can be rejected if they are not judged to be in keeping with the regional scheme or the Agency's own objectives, in which case the whole procedure has to be repeated. It sometimes happens that hospitals fail to submit the strategic plans required for the ARH to be able to decide how the funds should be distributed among the various regional establishments. In the days of the global budgeting system, the ARHs could decide that the funds allocated to non-compliant hospitals would be increased at a lower rate than the mean rate applied in the region as a whole. With activity-based payments *(T2A)* and MIGAC missions, the procedure has become even more complex[1]. Although the conditions imposed in contracts and other means of exerting pressure on recalcitrant establishments still weigh very heavily, these pressures are now being exerted more indirectly.

The procedure used to draw up and apply establishments' strategic plans provides a good example of how difficult it is in the French hospital system as a whole to achieve the delicate balance between constraints and contracts.

In Japan, on the contrary, strategic plans are part of the negotiation process. They are not legally compulsory, but they are indispensable for negotiating with the Prefecture, which can issue recommendations (about the activities on which hospitals should focus, in particular).

It has therefore become all the easier in Japan to integrate strategic plans into regional planning, since the principle of strategic plans existed before the negotiating process was launched. It was decreed in the 1985 Act (known as the "Medical Care Act") that each Prefecture would henceforth be responsible for planning the regional healthcare supply. The right to increase the number of beds available was made in this legislation to depend on the existence of functional distinctions between establishments.

The non-question of leadership and the benefits of competition

The healthcare supply is monitored and reorganized in Japan by a special Commission set up by the Prefect. This widely representative Commission includes spokesmen from the medical profession, the pharmacists' association and other professional associations. Elected members of the Communes and local territorial authorities concerned all sit on this Commission.

Since 2007, each Prefecture has had to draw up its own regional plan rather than simply applying a national plan (Kondo, 2008). Since the same dichotomy has arisen in this country as in France (the regions are being given more autonomy and power than they actually want), Japan has opted for a broadly representative method of negotiation in which elected public figures (and hence, in democratic countries, the citizens) are directly involved.

---

1. Some commentators even predicted (quite mistakenly) that the *T2A* heralded the death of hospital plans and contracts.

It might in fact be argued that in France, hospital Boards of Administration are presided by the City Mayors[2]. This arrangement might arguably be said to protect public interests in the event of hospitals being closed down, inaugurated or restructured. At closer sight, however, it turns out that the power is not exercised in this way. On the contrary, the Mayors are often obliged to take up arms on behalf of their electorate to defend their local establishments at all costs, sometimes to the detriment of the quality of the care dispensed. This is the main reason why the issue of keeping or abolishing this privilege has been so heatedly debated for many years. The point is that instead of helping hospitals to become less isolated and enter the political and social arena, this leadership which is openly proclaimed, and even demanded in times of crisis, serves to protect hospitals and contributes to their being referred to as bastions.

In Japan, hospital governance is more widely distributed both internally and externally. As a result, methods of hospital administration are generally accepted - but at the expense of greater inertia.

On the other hand, the whole Japanese system benefits from the fact that the directors of most establishments are doctors themselves. Hospitals are therefore probably less well managed, technically speaking, in Japan than in France, but their role and their right to intervene in neighbouring spheres (such as prevention, ambulatory care, etc.) are strengthened because their competitors are colleagues.

Recent reforms have led to changes in this respect, since hospital directors are now sometimes being recruited from economic and industrial spheres, in line with the move towards greater compartmentalization.

The funding procedure is about to be made more complex by introducing "establishment coefficients" based on the quality of the services provided by each hospital. These coefficients are attributed by the Ministry of Health, Work and Social Affairs, although the negotiation process has not been completely abandoned. In the first stage, this coefficient will differ very little between establishments. In the second stage, it will be used, however, to distribute resources unequally but equitably among duly classified hospitals.

In the future, the main criterion will tend to be the quality of nursing care, which is bound to give rise to competition between hospitals. On the other hand, once specialization has been recognized, it may serve to justify a new method of allocating resources.

In addition, the coefficients allotted will be closely linked to the strategic plan negotiated by public and private hospitals with the Prefecture on which they depend. These negotiations will be carried out in the framework of a scheme which is rather similar to the French SROS,

---

2. After a first attempt made in 1996, the legislators are planning in the HPST Act to take up this question again as to whether Mayors should be automatically appointed to hospital boards of administration. The forthcoming move to reinforce rationalization will mean a change of context, although the French Minister of Health confirmed in October 2008 that none of the country's hospitals would be closed down. This time, however, the mayors themselves, instead of demanding this privilege as they used to do in the name of local democracy, may be prepared to relinquish it much more willingly.

which will be implemented by the Prefecture. A new spirit of rivalry is therefore beginning to develop between establishments about the value of this coefficient. It will therefore serve as an index as well as promoting competition.

In 2004, the Japanese Ministry of Health, Labour and Welfare, which has been given greater power since 2000, and the Government headed by J. Koizumi joined forces with the Ministry of Education to define the conditions under which the hospitals, especially the University teaching hospitals, were to be reformed. Some of the main changes made at that time were favourable to market strategies. Since 2004, for example, University teaching hospitals are being managed increasingly autonomously and hospital practitioners no longer have the status of civil servants (as the result of the country's public sector reforms). The strategic plan therefore became the instrument mediating this move towards autonomy, which has already boosted hospitals' use of external services and private operators.

The way local hospitals have been reformed in Japan strongly reflects the orientation of public policy. Small hospitals managed by local authorities account for approximately 15% of the country's hospital beds, and two thirds of them have been running at a loss although the local authorities can raise special funds and loans. In December 2007, the Japanese Government set up a scheme of modernization for these hospitals, based on strategic plans. Those in charge of launching and implementing this scheme planned to transform these establishments into ideal management models. For this purpose, each of these establishments (and the local authorities on which they depend) will be expected to draw up a 3-year strategic plan consistent with a list of general overall objectives. These include the creation of a network of satellite *clinics*, incitements to externalize some activities, and setting up a database for monitoring hospitals' performances. The hospitals' book-keeping data and medical results will be disclosed to patients for the explicit purpose of promoting competition between the small public hospitals and the *clinics*.

In order to ensure that this scheme will be independent and effective, its implementation has been entrusted to the Japanese Ministry of the Interior and Communications rather than the Ministry of Health, Labour and Welfare, which will be responsible for chairing the *ad hoc* Commission. The latter Ministry has decided to adopt three main criteria for restructuring this sector of the hospital supply: balanced budgets, the ratio between medical expenditure and the number of nurses, and the rate of hospital occupation. Hospitals where the latter rate drops to less than 70% for 3 years will be closed down and their wards will be transferred to other *clinics* in the district.

This reform, which began to be implemented in 2009, confirms that strategic plans are already being widely used to modernize the hospital system in Japan, more so than in France.

In France, strategic plans serve rather as a vector for discussions between the actors and hospitals themselves. It is therefore not surprising that the process of internal contract-making has evolved faster in France than elsewhere. Although relatively few hospitals were involved in this process in 2000, the latest reforms will probably cause it to accelerate. After the abortive attempts made in the days of overall budgets to transform hospital wards into "departments", the focus is now going to be on specialized sectors or clusters *(pôles)*.

At the beginning, the idea was to create accounting centres *(centres de responsabilité)* in order to promote the internal autonomy of some hospital departments via contract agreements. However, this formula, which runs contrary to the principles of creating separate hospital units and giving doctors and managers completely distinct roles, was implemented at less than 10% of French hospitals. Despite this lack of success, the "2007 Hospital Plan" has again advocated a kind of delegated method of accountancy, which has not met with the approval of many heads of hospital departments. The new approach based on *pôles* (sectors or clusters), which is still in the early stages, is causing both staff nurses and executive nurses some concern, as we will see below: a sort of real-life test is being conducted to find out whether hospital managements, including matrons, will be able to comply with these new rules of governance.

It is true that in Japan, negotiations are being carried out at some hospitals between various specialized sectors. However, the policies designed to reduce the length of hospital stays via the introduction of *per diem* price rates and DRGs do not seem to be promoting the development of a hierarchy of specialized sectors.

This will not affect Japanese physicians' occupational training in any way. Since specialized physicians' associations constitute powerful pressure-groups, it is impossible for the State to have any real say in the field of medical training; whereas the numbers of nurses are gradually increasing and specialized nurses are beginning to appear on the scene.

The density of hospital staff and matrons: What is the role of healthcare teams?

The tendency for nurses to specialize will certainly be accelerated in Japan by the introduction of coefficients. By promoting higher quality standards, this system should quickly lead hospitals (especially those in the large cities) to compete with each other in hiring well-trained specialized staff. This is all the more predictable as the numbers of nurses began to increase even before these incitements were launched.

Some occupational developments have occurred, however, which run contrary to those described above. They focus on the role of healthcare teams. As we have seen, Japanese nurses still have a rather familiar, domestic relationship with their patients and depend strongly on the physicians with whom they work. The have to perform many tasks which are carried out in France by hospital nursing assistants. Japanese nurses are therefore not very highly trained, whereas French nurses often become highly specialized. In addition, after three years of negotiations, French nurses have also succeeded in having their diplomas recognized at the same level as a bachelor's degree, since they require three years of study after obtaining the *baccalauréat*. The first nurses to benefit from this situation will be those who qualify in 2012.

Nurses' quest for recognition has therefore involved taking several simultaneous paths. Some of them have made the nursing profession more homogeneous, while others have banked on its increasing diversity.

In this context, the Japanese Ministry of Health's proposal to create a new category of nurses is particularly noteworthy. It is also particularly noteworthy that the Ministry is having great difficulty in bringing this project into fruition. An article about this reform published in the "Japan Times" was headed "Nurses operating in a gray zone". The idea on which this project was based is to appoint "special nurses", who are able to provide a wider range of medical services than ordinary nurses - services which have been provided up to now by doctors. These "special nurses" will be able, for instance, to prescribe chest X-rays and perform ultrasound tests. The Ministry of Health has stated that if these activities are supervised by doctors, they will constitute "assistance with medical treatment" under the Public Health, Midwifery and Nursing Law. However, as the Ministry has not specified exactly what activities are involved, nurses are working in a gray zone, legally speaking. "Now that a Ministry project is encouraging the expansion of nurses' duties, a legal definition is essential" (Japan Times, April 2010).

This idea of qualified nurses replacing doctors is nothing new in the United States. In France, it has been tested experimentally "on an exceptional basis" at some pilot hospitals which volunteered for the job. Since the HPST Act was voted in July 2009, these practices have become widely recognized and may be adopted on a much larger scale in the future. For this purpose, projects focusing on the right to transfer duties will have to be authorized *a priori* by the ARS and assessed *a posteriori* by the HAS *(Haute Autorité de Santé)*.

In both countries, these ongoing changes are bound to completely transform the relationships between healthcare professionals working at hospitals.

Taking a look at the hospital staff density data in France and Japan should help to set this question of the new division of work in its demographic and professional context. In the early 1980s, the hospital staff density was 17 per 1,000 inhabitants in France, as compared with less than 10 in Japan. As *table 6.1* shows, this difference is still quite large although it has decreased during the last 20 years[3].

These changes are boosting the trend towards short, intensive hospital stays in France (as in the UK, since 1995) and long, technically simple stays in Japan. The position of the UK, as in *table 5.1*, exhibits greater volatility than in France or Japan. While both these countries show a steady, incremental increase, the upward trend in the UK is punctured in 1990 with a slight decrease, followed by a sharper increase from 1990 to 1995, which continues at a slightly slower rate from 1995 to 2005. Although it may be irrelevant to attempt to distinguish between the causes and the effects, it can be said that a large nursing staff will no doubt reduce the length of hospital stays. And the shorter the stay, the more intense the care will be. The decrease in the mean hospital stay observed in both countries is therefore being accompanied by an increase in the nursing staff density". One might be tempted to take this farther by increasing the staff density in order to reduce the length of hospital stays, but this

---

3. In view of the contribution of wages to the hospital costs, these differences also explain why, from the macro-economic point of view, hospital expenditure accounts for 30% of the healthcare expenditure in Japan, versus almost 50% in France.

Table 6.1. *Total hospital employment (density per 1,000 inhabitants).*

Year	1980	1985	1990	1995	2000	2005
France	–	17.3	18.0	18.5	–	19.8
Japan	8.4	9.8	10.7	12.2	12.9	13.1
UK	17.1	17.9	17.4	21.3	22.2	24.1

Sources: OECD, 2008, and MHLW Hospital Report.

would not suffice because the quality of the division of work between physicians and nurses is probably a more decisive factor. This is no doubt why the density of hospital staff per 1,000 inhabitants does not reflect the same facts and does not have the same significance in both countries.

The fact that the staff density has been consistently high in France results from endogenous specificities relating to how hospitals function, they tendency to develop, etc. – despite the authorities' desire to contain the supply. The high staff density has been accompanied of late by a highly popular irreversible move to transfer the doctors' tasks and responsibilities to the paramedical staff.

This process has been driven in Japan by the Government's explicit incitement policies designed to modernize the country's hospitals and improve the technical quality of the care dispensed.

Although the numbers of all Japanese hospital employees other than nurses decreased from 2003 to 2007, the numbers of nurses increased very slightly from 121,188 to 121,760, whereas the numbers of doctors decreased by 4%, the administrative staff by 7%, and the nursing assistants by 30% (OECD). The numbers of Japanese nursing assistants decreased because they were not taken into account in the flat *per diem* rate or the establishment coefficients. The Japan Nursing Association has managed to introduce this distinction in order to keep a sort of monopoly over the work in which "care" is combined with "cure".

Since nurses' professional identity is defined in France in terms of the differences with respect to nursing assistants, nurses are demanding wage increases for all categories of nursing staff. In order to define the specificities of their own role, other clearly defined categories have to exist. However, independent nurses show a similar "corporatist" spirit to that of Japanese nurses. Nursing assistants are not allowed to be self-employed in Japan, although they are demanding to obtain this right via their professional associations. However, they are meeting with strong opposition on the part of the nurses' lobby.

In view of the ambivalent relationships (based on both competition and cooperation) existing between the groups of which healthcare teams are composed, it seemed to be worth comparing the density of nursing staff with the rates of supervision. Now according to the results of the surveys mentioned in Part II, there are twice as many matrons at the Japanese hospitals studied as at French hospitals (they amount to 14.3% and 6.6% of the nursing staff, respectively). Although it is difficult to make comparisons because of the different ways in which categories of staff are defined, these proportions can be said to apply at national level, at least at the large hospitals.

The large numbers of executive staff employed in Japan are actually compatible with the idea that matrons serve to hold their teams together as well as performing several tasks directly at the patients' bedside - more so than their French equivalents. This links up with the Japanese tradition of multi-tasking and the relative absence of hierarchical distinctions observed at Japanese hospital wards. This difference, which was previously observed in the surveys conducted in Tokyo and Paris therefore turns out to also apply at national level. The ratio between nurses and nursing assistants at all public and private hospitals combined works out at about 1:1 in France and 1:4 in Japan.

There is naturally a greater need for close supervision at Japanese hospitals because the nurses are younger, and relatively inexperienced, and they have shorter careers.

This finding confirms those obtained by Ivan Sainsaulieu in the case of France about nurses' "culture":

> "Despite the managerial constraints, various forms of collective work are being developed by hospital teams [...]. Strong involvement does not necessarily mean self-sacrifice, but it does make the collective organization of work easier." (Sainsaulieu, 2006, p. 76)

When speaking about the opposition between relational and technical work, Ivan Sainsaulieu is even more categorical:

> "The choice open to nurses is obviously between technical work on the on hand (surgery, intensive care), and relational work on the other (paediatrics, geriatrics, psychology, emergencies)." (*ibid.*, p. 78)

The results of the surveys carried out in both countries in 2008 show, however, that in France, feelings of commitment can actually be reinforced by managerial constraints: but because of the *pôles*, they will no longer focus on the ward but on the whole hospital institution, which is regarded as a kind of home. On the other hand, as we have seen, the tension between relational and technical work is not so much a question of having to make a choice in Japan, but simply a source of ambivalence. Japanese nurses are therefore taking up the challenge of specialization and obtaining social recognition, which continuing to hold a kind of monopoly on nursing care, consisting of both *curing* and providing basic *care*.

The Japan Nursing Association, which has more than 400,000 members, has been militating for a long time to have the nursing profession recognized. For this purpose, the Association has developed many nursing research activities, for example. It has also created links with other health professionals to reduce the power of the physicians, especially those with whom nurses come into contact every day in the course of their duties. The Association is also making equally strong efforts to impose a sharper distinction between nurses who have achieved a high level of education (4 years' study after obtaining the *baccalauréat*) and their less qualified workmates. In this way, the Association is defending not only the profession itself but also the quasi-monopoly enjoyed by its members.

The Japan Nursing Association, which is not a trade union, is responsible for accrediting mental health nurses and community health nurses. Since 1999, it has also been delivering certificates corresponding to the vocational training courses it runs in emergency care, handling pain, etc. (Primomo, 2000).

It is therefore not surprising that the latest strategy adopted by the Association is to go along with the move to improve the quality of nursing care and its assessment.

CHANGES IN NURSING MANAGEMENT AND THE MANAGEMENT OF NURSES

In order to extend these comparisons between empowerment and modernization processes in the nursing profession, relevant developments of two kinds in the UK will be discussed here, starting with the extent to which reform has inflected the traditional British model of gender-related career pathways in British nursing, and going on to look at the impact of changes in hospital management structures.

Balancing work and family life

The relative empowerment and professional identity of UK nurses must also be assessed from the perspective of equal opportunities, raising the question of the compatibility between professional and family life. This issue is particularly acute in a predominantly (90%) female work force (*cf.* Nursing & Midwifery Council), for whom unsociable working hours are "part of the job". Until recently, the UK had little in the way of an explicit policy in this regard, adopting a position consistent with the principle of non-intervention in the private life of the individual. In reality, for much of the 20th century, the underlying model in force remained underpinned by traditional assumptions about the complementary social roles of men and women, whereby most women's work would become superseded by domestic responsibilities after the birth of their children, in contrast with the French Republican model which, at least in principle, has been based for a long time on notions of equal rights and opportunities. In this sense, gendered nursing career patterns in the UK arguably displayed greater commonalities with those of Japan than with those of one of its closest European neighbours.

This perspective is supported by the contrast between the paucity of public child-care provision in Britain and the much more extensive availability of nursery and crèche facilities in France. In consequence, a very high proportion of UK nurses adopted part-time working as a mode of adjustment to the conflicting pressures of domestic and professional responsibilities. Thus, in 2002, over 42% of nurses in the English NHS aged over 30 worked part-time, as opposed to 15% of those up to 29 years of age (Kober-Smith & Feroni, 2008). In comparison, although a correlation between child-rearing responsibilities and part-time work can also be discerned in France, the proportion of part-time nurses has always been very significantly lower and there is less evidence of a sharp increase at any particular age, with 22% of nurses under 40 adopting this mode of adjustment in 1998, whereas the figure for those of 40 and above was 26%. Analysis by Kober-Smith and Feroni further develops this comparison with particular reference to career breaks, demonstrating that the consequences for nurses who temporarily interrupt their professional activity for domestic reasons have differed markedly between these two countries, due to the embeddedness of their respective national gendered models, with particularly detrimental effects in the UK. Thus, while French nurses have for many decades enjoyed a certain security of employment through their status as public service employees, allowing them to take a career break and return to work at the same level and often in the same place as before, due to the relatively weaker level of statutory job protection in the UK and more limited opportunities to transfer to different hospitals, British nurses taking this option have often found themselves downgraded on their return to work, or indeed have lost their jobs altogether (*ibid.*).

Significant changes have taken place in the UK since the late 1990s, bringing about a certain degree of convergence with a "European Social Model" with regard to the reconciliation of professional and family life. Under pressure from the EU, through regulations such as the Working Time Directive, government initiatives have encouraged hospitals to establish child care strategies and by the early 2000s, 56% of NHS hospitals provided nursery care for the children of staff, some of which, but not all, was subsidised. Other improvements in the rights of all mothers have been particularly important for nurses, given the nature of their profession, such as successive extensions between 2003 and 2007 to maternity leave entitlement, increasing the possibility for female staff to return to work. At the same time, such measures should also be seen as a response by government to problems emanating from within the national nursing labour market, such as the growing recruitment shortage with regard to young nurses and the problem of staff retention, particularly of nurses with young families (*ibid.*).

As a result, the main thrust of UK policy measures to improve the position of nurses has displayed an emphasis on the need to recruit young, newly qualified nurses, who represent an attractive workforce in terms of salary costs, time availability and physical fitness, whereas much lower priority has been given to the needs of older nurses, whose obligations as carers for elderly or infirm relatives may represent no less a burden than that of nurses with young children. Recent reforms have therefore produced some degree of convergence towards the position obtaining elsewhere in Europe, but within a framework which continues to owe a great deal to pre-established trends and policy legacies.

From "matrons" to "modern matrons"

The role of the nursing profession in UK hospital governance has evolved through a series of identifiable stages, each of which has been driven by the imperatives of modernization and improved efficiency. However, when considered from a longitudinal perspective, the process displays a certain circularity, rather than representing a linear progression towards ever-greater effectiveness. As suggested above, the management structures established within the nursing profession from the end of the 19th century until the 1940s consolidated the position of the matron at the apex of the nursing hierarchy. However, during the period from the advent of the NHS until the mid-1960s, the always idealised image of the omnipotent, omniscient matron became more and more unsustainable. In the interests of administrative efficiency, many hospitals were grouped together and matrons were increasingly required to work in partnership with senior administrative officers and representatives of medical staff. Senior management groups were established, with responsibility for several hospitals collectively and important policy measures were decided between members of this management team. Matrons of individual hospitals were excluded from this administrative élite, although they were expected to attend meeting called by such governing bodies when issues affecting their particular hospital were to be addressed (Wildman & Hewison, 2009).

The marginalisation of matrons in local policy making was exacerbated by the acceleration of other, pre-existing trends, including the professionalization of activities such as physiotherapy, or dietetics, for which separate departments were established, independently of the matrons' control. The amalgamation of individual hospitals into larger units, especially in urban areas, combined with the continuing existence of establishments with more limited capacity (cottage hospitals) in smaller towns, resulted in major occupational and administrative inconsistencies, whereby the matron of a hospital with 30 beds would have equal status with the matron of a hospital with up to 1,000 beds, despite the huge discrepancy in their work loads and responsibilities. The definition of roles and functions became increasingly problematic, between nursing and administrative staff, as well as within the nursing profession itself, with the boundaries between the responsibilities of matrons and sisters with responsibility for several wards grouped together in larger units becoming more difficult to define.

The Salmon Report of 1966 sought to address this need for clarification and the implementation of its recommendations represented a move towards a more industrial mode of nursing management. This entailed the creation of line management structures, whereby the ward sister was the first-line manager, responsible for nursing care and implementing new policy directions in her own ward. Above this level, middle managers, or nursing officers were placed in charge of coordinating the work of groups of wards, or units, which involved staff management and fulfilling a role of "consultant" to sisters and their immediate subordinates (charge nurses), on clinical issues. The top level of nursing management was represented by chief nursing officers, with responsibilities covering an entire hospital, or even groups of hospitals, participating in policy formulation and advising governing bodies of hospitals on matters relating to nursing. The rationale adopted here was that efficiency measures and rationalisation were to be brought about through "consensus management" (Bolton, 2004), where the chief nursing officer enjoyed equal status with senior doctors and financial administrators, as far as the organisational hierarchy was concerned. This kind of professionalised management owed a great deal to the Taylorist perspectives adopted in other major bureaucracies.

The traditional role of the matron, as overall coordinator of other services, was coming to an end and by the mid-1970s the position of matron had given way to that of nurse managers with responsibility only for nursing matters. During 1970s and early 1980s, such changes enhanced the status of the nursing profession, through the recognition of the value of investment in nurse training and development, as well as the importance of a wider involvement of staff with clinical expertise in the management of nursing services. However, despite their clinical experience and expertise, senior nursing officers were increasingly required to devote the majority of their time to administrative matters, and the clinical focus of their activities was reduced.

From the mid-1980s, the advent of New Public Management, with its emphasis on the primacy of markets, contractualisation and financial efficiency, led to the dismantling of this system whereby professionals could take responsibility for managing themselves. Instead, a different direction was taken with the appointment of general managers, some from the private sector, to be responsible for the control of resources. Within these new structures, there was very limited provision for nursing management above the level of the ward manager (formerly sister). Another trend was reinforced by this shift however, the increasing distance being established between senior, experienced nursing staff and nursing management. Such staff invariably had minimal input in terms of the provision of professional advice to general managers with responsibility for units or entire hospitals. Instead, a host of new administrative posts were created, such as directorate managers, service managers, or operations managers, but these positions were not directly related to specific professional expertise. As a result, a significant reduction took place in the scope for nursing staff to seek professional advancement through [internal market] promotion based on the particular expertise which they had developed. The new administrative posts often represented the only route through which nurses could reach senior positions, thereby compelling them to seek promotion out of their particular sphere of competence (Wildman & Hewison, 2009).

At the beginning of the 21st century, attempts have been made to put an end to this divorce between management and clinical expertise, with the advent of the so-called "modern matron", a senior nursing staff appointment. Such change should not be seen as a "counter-revolution" however, since this function has been grafted on to existing structures and differs markedly from that of the traditional matron. The Ministerial Circular setting out the details of the new post was careful to avoid an excessively prescriptive stipulation of precise structures and competencies, allowing individual Trusts to exercise considerable latitude in the implementation of the reform, according to their particular needs. However, certain clear priorities have emerged and reflect an attempt to respond to public concern with regard to problems such as MRSA and, more generally, the apparent absence of clear lines of authority and clinical accountability at the point of contact between nursing staff and patients or their relatives. Thus, the "modern matron" should provide leadership for nursing staff and represent an accessible figure of authority, from whom advice and support can be sought by health care consumers. Their sphere of accountability is restricted to a group of wards, rather than the entire hospital as was traditionally the case, with particular responsibility for cleanliness and the quality of food. By mid-2008, 5,538 modern matron posts had been created within NHS hospitals and available evidence points to a reduction in patient complaints since their introduction. While it is too early to reach definitive conclusions as to their overall impact, the findings of current research suggest a continuing tendency for the provision of clinical leadership to become overshadowed by administrative responsibilities, since the position no-netheless entails the fulfilment of a middle-management function by women who happen to be highly experienced nurses. The picture of the modern matron which is beginning to emerge is that of a hybrid, situated at a point determined by local conditions on a continuum between a "super ward manager" and an administrator (Savage and Scott, 2004).

REGULATING THE QUALITY AND CONTINUITY OF CARE BOTH INSIDE AND OUTSIDE HOSPITALS

Under the impetus of the move to promote professional and institutional interests, the question of the quality and the continuity of care has gradually come to the fore in all the industrialized countries. As we have seen in the case of the United Kingdom, however, this question has been addressed on specific lines in each country. There are two processes at work in this context. First there has been the advent of quality assurance procedures. In France, these procedures based on industrial models were intended to improve the technical quality of hospital care: the quality in question here is that of the care dispensed. In Japan, where patients have to make choices in a system presented as evolving towards the laws of competition, the accent is being placed on the quality perceived. In both cases, however, the non explicitly stated goal is to avoid quality assessments bearing on medical acts themselves.

The second process at work is the development of networks. These entities, which are mid-way between markets (which are open and freely accessible) and organizations (which are closed and constrained), lend themselves potentially to all kinds of coordination. They are therefore regarded in both France and Japan as the best possible remedy to all ailments. But some networks are better than others.

Measuring quality as an incentive for making improvements

The accreditation process provides a good example of the optical illusion which tends to occur when identical concepts are used in different contexts. One might be tempted to assume that since Japan and France have both adopted energetic policies on the assessment and monitoring of the quality of care, accompanied by appropriate "accreditation" procedures, both countries are simultaneously embarking on similar paths inspired by industrial logics, but this is not at all the case.

In France, after an early phase when it was announced that the *Agence Nationale d'Accréditation and d'Évaluation en Santé* (ANAES) was responsible for standardization procedures on ISO (International Organization for Standardization) lines, some considerable changes occurred. It was no longer simply a question of applying exogenous standards or assessing the gap between standards and practices. What is now being measured is the cohesion between the procedures adopted by establishments themselves and their own priorities. Therefore, before contracting with the supervisory authorities *(tutelle)*, their partners and even their patients,

French hospitals have to first sign a contract with themselves. This procedure was set up in a highly constrained context, since all public and private hospitals have been obliged since 1996 to apply for accreditation. This seemingly heavy constraint has actually not had any very noteworthy effects so far. On the one hand, accreditation took a long time to implement (in 2003, only 400 establishments out of 3,700 had been duly accredited), although by 2007, 98% des recommendations put forward by the HAS inspectors had been carried out. These recommendations did not bear directly on hospitals' medical practices, however. They mostly had to do with risk management, occupational safety, the circulation of information and drug supply circuits. On the other hand, 12 years after this initiative was launched, it is still being heavily criticized. A survey conducted in 2007, the results of which were summarized by the HAS in its activity report, showed that:

> "Health professionals are complaining because they find the procedure unwieldy and inflexible, and that it was necessary to inform hospitals more fully about the purpose of the process and explain the objectives in greater detail." (HAS, 2008)

In addition to this self-criticism, the following comments were made by the organization which carried out the survey:

> "There are many criticisms to be made about the rigidity of the framework [...], about the procedure being too time-consuming, too little attention being paid to medical practices and the whole approach being far too scholastic, stressful and demotivating." (HAS, 2007)

In order to improve the procedure and the way it was applied, accreditation was first replaced by certification, and version 2 (V2), in which medical practices were addressed more closely, was then introduced in 2005, and the HAS subsequently published a third edition of its handbooks and quality standards. The latest version of the procedure, which took effect in 2010, was a simplified version in which professionals and establishments were incited to take their self-assessment processes a step farther.

The assessment of professional practices (EPP[4]) set up for this purpose in 2005 was a tool for analysing medical practices in relation to best practices recommendations endorsed by the HAS. The explicit aim of EPPs was to improve the quality and the continuity of care, and it is therefore applied to all public and private doctors in France. It is on the curriculum of continuing vocational training courses for doctors, which were revised and made compulsory in 2008. Doctors working at hospital establishments undergo EPPs, which are organized and supervised by a *commission médicale d'établissement* (CME). EPPs are now an integral part of the procedure followed by hospitals to obtain accreditation and certification from the HAS. The latter organization has claimed that this was necessary to reduce "the gap between medical knowledge and actual practices". The requirements (especially as far as methodologies are concerned) for passing EPPs successfully are now listed in the certification handbooks published by the HAS, and the certification procedures are gradually working down to the level of individual medical practices.

---

4. The evaluation of professional practices (*Évaluation des Pratiques Professsionnelles*) is both an internal system of self-evaluation and a collection of procedures required for the certification/accreditation of health establishments.

To support this procedure and promote rationalisation in general, the HAS publishes recommendations for good practices to inform and sustain the whole French healthcare system. Since the 2007 Act on the funding of the health insurance system was passed, these recommendations explicitly include criteria for defining medical cost-efficiency. This new turn of events hails the arrival of Evidence Based Medicine (EBM) in France: in this case, the aim was mainly to decrease the variability of medical practices.

In Japan, on the contrary, there is a shortage of specialists and since medical techniques and treatments are becoming increasingly sophisticated, specialists mastering technical skills are required to prevent the quality of care from decreasing. By refusing to incite doctor explicitly to specialize, Japanese legislators risk depriving patients of the "labels" informing them about the quality of the care they receive. Now patients are supposed to be players in the competitive game between the various establishments, especially at local level.

It seemed difficult to fill this gap without departing from egalitarian principles and challenging the privileges enjoyed by the medical specialists' associations. To overcome this problem, an independent agency: the Institute for the assessment of hospital functions, was set up in 1995 under the auspices of the Japan Council for Quality Health Care.

Contrary to what has occurred in France, however, the hospital assessment process managed by this agency is not yet compulsory but strongly recommended. In addition, these quality assessments focus on specific themes obviously corresponding to fields in the present system: number of nursing staff, nurses' competence, preventing nosocomial diseases, etc.

One of the most important themes in which this agency is interested is no doubt the patients' informed consent process and the information in general with which hospital patients are provided. Japanese doctors traditionally give their patients very little information about the treatment they were undergoing or about to undergo. Recent insistence on the relationships between doctors and their patients was not motivated so much by the idea of making medicine more democratic (as in France) or safer from the legal point of view (as in the USA) as by the aim of creating a new lever for controlling hospital practices. Assessments of the information received by patients are explicitly linked in Japan to the quality of the relationships formed by hospitals with their partners (*clinics* and cabinets). What is assessed here is the quality of the commerce waged at hospitals as much as their ability to collect the right information upstream and diffuse it downstream to patients during their stay. In the 1990s physicians and nurses were incited to comply with this injunction by paying them for the time spent informing patients. Nowadays, this practice is systematically paid for and no longer treated as an additional item.

Although the agency's recommendations about improving the transmission of information have no financial consequences, this is not so in the case of the hospital procedures. The authorities attribute a "coefficient" to each establishment based mainly on the quality of the treatment dispensed, and the allocation of funds depends on these "coefficients". Now it has been said that hospitals which have principle of accreditation are given better "coefficients" than the others.

Here again, reforms are being introduced without applying heavy constraints but via incitements, with a view to achieving three goals which French contracts are having difficulty in reaching: compelling hospitals to disclose information about their own performances; allocating resources rationally; and setting hospitals in the right direction as far as quality and respect for patients are concerned.

The healthcare networks existing in France and Japan provide another interesting example of the difference between the methods used in the two countries.

The development of networks: Regulating informal structures

Most of the actors involved strongly believe that the development of healthcare networks contributes to improving the quality of hospital care. In the first place, it meets the demand for continuous, coordinated care. The popularity of networks has also resulted from the need felt by healthcare professionals for wider scope than what traditional internal managerial tools allow them. Networks fulfil all the conditions of occupational acceptability and legitimacy which have to be met by institutional innovations if they are to emerge and survive. In their present configuration, networks also correspond a means of collecting resources which escapes centripetal patterns of management.

In both France and Japan, networks are thought to be capable of achieving several apparently contradictory objectives, namely containing hospital costs, reducing the numbers of hospital stays, and improving the quality of care (by promoting the individual approach to patients and continuing vocational training for healthcare professionals).

In France, what we have called "hospitalocentricity" *(hospitalocentrisme)* has led to a sharp increase in outpatient consultations *(consultations externes)*. After reaching 40 million per year in1998, the numbers have been constantly on the increase for the last 12 years, possibly because there is a strong demand for light treatment. This trend also corresponds to the need felt by hospital workers (doctors and administrative personnel) for hospitals to develop activities liable to attract new types of resources.

The present period is also characterised, however, by a consistently increasing numbers of admissions to emergency services, which are often completely saturated in some places. This increase simply due to a great demand for hospital care: it is mainly due to the lack of regulation and coordination between the hospital sector and the emergency sector. It is also due, although to a lesser extent, to the internal partitioning which occurs at hospitals. This is why, by instituting "medical homes", the recent reforms are attempting to clear the emergency wards and organize "round the clock" services in which the advantages of the private and public services are combined (if possible).

In Japan, where networks are less highly developed than in France, it will also be necessary to make provision for decreasing the length of hospital stays and the numbers of beds, while attempting to train patients to see things differently rather than imagining that all the members of hospital staff with whom they come into contact are interchangeable.

Since they have to reduce the number of beds and decrease the length of patients' stays, "specific function" hospitals are having to negotiate with local partners to set up networks with clinics and private consultancies. At the macro-economic level, the injunction to reduce the number of beds was dictated for reasons having to do with the internal working of the system itself rather than for strictly budgetary reasons, which has made it seem more acceptable. In fact, there are several explanations for this regulation, which contrasts with previous less restrictive habits. On the one hand, it was obviously necessary to contain spending and rationalise the allocation of resources. On the other hand, it was necessary to predict the probable consequences (from the healthcare and economic points of view) of the aging of the population and to modernise coverage practices, giving priority to ambulatory care. In short, Japanese hospitals are opening up to their surroundings in order to be able to deal with aging populations, provide better services and emancipate their patients, etc. rather than simply to achieve greater cost- efficiency.

Whatever the reasons why hospitals are opening up, all of them (at least the University hospitals) have a department responsible for "organising networks". This development seemed indispensable in the mid-1980s, when Japanese hospitals began to be classified. It became necessary, for example to coordinate patient referrals to establishments for the elderly or other downstream establishments. Prior to this reform, patients' whole trajectory was catered for at the same establishment. These negotiations and the corresponding strategy are promoted by a whole set of subtly targeted incitements. The 2000 Annual Report on health and well-being, for example, listed a fairly complex set of incitements designed to guide patients through the healthcare system, while rewarding the members of the healthcare professions who played the game of controlling their trajectories.

However, people in some circles tend to be alarmed by any attempt at differentiation. In 2006, a plan to reduce the length of stay of acute care patients who could be sent to long stay hospitals came to nothing. The Ministry of Health wanted to change the *per diem* and activity-based price rates accordingly. But between the moment when the project was drawn up in May 2006 and the moment when it was to be implemented (in august 2007), the cohabitation government which came into power resulted in all ongoing reforms being blocked (Kondo, 2008). The detractors of the project in question only needed to claim that changing the tariffs would lead to differentiating and therefore discriminating between patients for it to be abandoned, and this incitement to decrease the length of patients' hospital stays at medical wards never took effect.

It was never in fact intended to question the specificities of the various segments, which would have been an offense to the sacrosanct principle of patients' freedom of choice; so there are no contracts (of the kind French patients have with their GPs, for instance) and no constraints (of the *gate keeper* kind as in the UK and the USA, for instance).

Once again the solution adopted has been to introduce an index of doctors' medical acts via a negotiated change of nomenclature. Since the 2000s, the above incitements have to take a new challenge into account: keeping the balance between doctors' private practices (at clinics) and public practices (at hospitals).

It is well known of course that doctors working at public hospitals have to put up with heavier constraints (as regards their work schedules, in particular) than those employed at *clinics*, and are less well paid despite these constraints. According to a 2006 Japan Hospital Association survey, 71.6% of hospital doctors worked on night shifts and said they worked more than 56 hours a week. Although the annual wages are the same at *clinics* and hospitals (14 million yens in 2007), the income of those who own *clinics* are twice as high (25 millions yens). This situation is liable to jeopardise the highly desirable possibility of cooperation between professionals. Mr Akira Nagatsuma, the Japanese Minister of Health, Labour and Welfare in 2010, was therefore given the task of increasing the wages of public hospital doctors with a view to stopping the increase in the number of resignations. The wages paid to doctors performing complex operations was therefore increased by anything up to 30%. The evening out of public and private hospital doctors' wages was also partly intended to prevent doctors from leaving rural areas and to prevent local facilities (such as obstetric services) from being closed down by the Prefectures. According to the Central Social Insurance Medical Council, however, the main effect was to improve the continuity of care. The same fees were to be charged for a follow-up examination in both sectors: and 690 yens (instead of 710 yens in the private sector and 600 yens in the public sector, as previously). At the same time, higher fees were also to be paid in both sectors for telephone consultations outside opening hours.

Japanese hospital doctors are now being paid for all information transmitted from *clinics* to hospitals or *vice-versa*, from doctors to auxiliaries or downstream of the hospital (to chemists, long-stay hospitals, retirement homes, etc.): a letter of referral from a *clinic* to a hospital can be worth up to 10 000 yens, for example).

As in France, Japanese people are allowed to attend hospital consultations directly without being referred by their GP. This practice is all the more common in Japan as there are hardly any waiting-lists in this country. In a 2008 survey conducted by the Japanese Ministry of Health, Labour and Welfare, it was reported that in 88% of cases, the time elapsing between making an appointment and seeing a hospital doctor was less than three hours. However, since the nomenclature and tariffs were adroitly changed by the reformers (this was their main trump-card if not their only one), these practices have been discouraged since 2008. An addition charge of about 35 euros now has to be paid by patients making appointments directly at hospitals with more than 200 beds. By basing this rule on the size of hospital, patients are still allowed some freedom of *manœuvre* and choice, while becoming gradually accustomed to the *gatekeeper approach* thus being silently and stealthily introduced.

The complexity of this situation is due to the fact that the question of patients' referral has been intentionally linked to the transfer of information as well as to the creation of formal networks around hospitals. Patients' mobility is facilitated by that of their doctors: after acquiring a few years of experience, Japanese hospital doctors used to create or purchase their own *clinic*, thus promoting the circulation of the patients constituting their clientele. It used to be fairly easy to enlarge these *clinics*. Since the number of beds is now limited, this substitutive strategy is being gradually replaced by a strategy based on complementarity. The mean age of doctors migrating from hospitals to private practices is on the increase, partly due to the increasingly high cost of the latest equipment required for doctors to be able to conduct their activities at "clinics".

The most rational strategy for Japanese doctors to adopt is therefore to specialize and to develop networks. This change which started to occur in 1985 resulted from the policy of reducing the number of hospital beds. Networks were therefore set up for extremely utilitarian purposes: to prevent the loss of patients, control the flows of patients and tap resources which used to be more randomly distributed.

It can be seen from the above analysis of the changes undergone by the French and Japanese hospital systems that the accent is no longer on freedom of choice but on quality and controlling the hospital supply. We are no longer in the framework of the Bismarckian model but more in line with the corresponding Beveridge model.

Regional quality differences are no longer a matter of debate in Japan since this goal is thought to have been achieved. Each Prefecture has at least one public or private University hospital, for example, and some of them have two or three. Although the density of hospital beds varies from one Prefecture to another, the emphasis is mainly placed on controlling the supply, so that the increase in hospitals' expenditure is being unequally reduced. To make the inequalities acceptable, the decisions about these reductions have been integrated into the bargaining processes and the amounts involved are not in fact very large. The question of freedom of choice arises in France in a completely different context, where the main preoccupation is inequality of access to health care. This preoccupation pervades most current public health debates as well as the criticisms to which activity-based methods of payment have given rise. A process of compromise or give-and-take seems to be occurring, where less freedom of choice is being traded off against better follow-up and mastery of treatment processes.

It is rather paradoxical, however, that the emerging networks are strengthening the role of hospitals in the Japanese healthcare system; whereas these networks are being presented in France as useful weapons for combating the inflationary effects of "hospitalo-centrism". This expression obviously does not have the same meaning in the two contexts under investigation here.

Each to his own form of "hospitalo-centrism"

Hospitals' importance can be measured quite simply in terms of the density of beds. The density of both long-term and short-term hospital beds can be seen from *table 6.2* to be much higher in Japan than in France, due to the increase in the supply which has been occurring in Japan during the last 20 years.

These data reflect the policies adopted in Japan, whereby the supply is regulated indirectly via incitements rather than directly. This has led to the density of beds (12.9 per 1,000 inhabitants in 2005) being 2.5 times greater than the mean figure recorded in the OECD member countries. The density of beds also varies considerably from one region to another and from one Prefecture to another (from 9.6 to 28 per 1,000 inhabitants).

Table 6.2. *Hospital beds per 1,000 inhabitants.*

Years		1980	1985	1990	1995	2000	2005
France	Total	11.1	10.5	9.7	8.9	8.1	7.5
	Acute care	6.2	5.7	5.2	4.6	4.1	3.7
Japan	Total	11.3	12.4	13.6	13.3	13.0	12.9
	Acute care	7.6	8.9	10.2	9.8	10.0	8.5
UK	Total	–	–	–	4.8	4.1	3.7
	Acute care	–	–	–	4.1	2.4	2.3

Source: OECD, 2009 and MHLW Hospital Report.

However, in view of the policies adopted in Japan in 1985, one might have expected the number of hospital beds per 1,000 inhabitants to have decreased. The statistics show that this has not been the case.

Although the number of beds at long-stay establishments has increased in both France and Japan, the density of short-stay beds has remained practically unchanged in Japan, whereas it has increased considerably in France. More specifically, the density of beds increased in Japan from 1981 to 1990 before decreasing slightly at short-stay establishments and increasing concomitantly at long-stay establishments. In France, by contrast, the density of beds has been constantly on the decrease. At short-stay hospitals, this decrease was only possible because of overall changes in the approach to the hospital supply, although the demand for hospital services has not decreased at all. Similar observations may be made regarding the UK, although the rate of reduction in short-stay bed density from 1995 to 2000 is significantly greater than in France.

Apart from these quantitative aspects, there exists another important difference between the situation in France and Japan, in terms of the professional and economic stakes with which hospital orchestrators are confronted. This difference focuses on the regulatory aspects.

The way hospitals function in France and the reforms they have undergone could be described by simply looking at the healthcare system as a whole. In the 2009 "Hospitals, Patients, Health and Territories" Act (HPST), a half-hearted attempt was made to include the medico-social sector. However, the fact that this Act was renamed changed shortly after being passed shows how difficult it is to remove the hospitals from the centre of the picture in France; the new name began with the word "Hospitals" in order to reassure hospital staff, who were afraid of losing their central role because they were being incited to sign contracts with external partners. Although the new contractual procedures between regional healthcare players have been defined by Law, the initiative and the powers of decision are still mainly in the hands of the hospital. The Ministry's central administration and its agencies have therefore reorganized themselves on the basis of Missions for improving hospitals' Performances.

The way in which the concept of "magnet hospitals" has been adopted in the French context shows how this self-centred hospital reflex comes into play. This concept was first developed in the USA in 1990 as a means of informing hospital nurses about the quality of their conditions of work. "Magnet recognition Status" is now delivered by the American Nurses' Credentialing Center, which depends on the American Nurses' Association. The idea was to incite the nursing profession to use its stronghold on the labour market and benefit from the competition between hospitals. The term "magnet" is used to stress the fact that some hospitals are more attractive employers than others and more likely to keep their staff because of the good conditions of work they enjoy and the good salaries they receive. The situation is quite different in France. On the one hand, the concept started to be used only quite recently (Canasse, 2008) and on the other hand, the movement was not initiated by nurses themselves but by hospital managers. Since most French hospitals invest in vocational training, they naturally try to prevent "poaching" by looking for means of keeping their paramedical staff. But since the administrative and medical model described a in previous chapter has such a strong hold in this country, the French promoters of the "magnet" concept deliberately copied the certification procedures used by the HAS. The main criterion which has to be met by French hospitals to be qualified as "attractive" is not based on the nurses' conditions of work and their quality of life, but on whether the quality of nursing practices is in keeping with the national standards.

In Japan, whether or not one approves of the idea of a consensus society, that the role of hospitals and the changes they have undergone during the last few decades obviously cannot be understood unless one takes the background into account. The way healthcare networks are being set up in Japan illustrates this point rather well. Other signs of "total immersion" can be seen at various very different levels, ranging from industrial policy (on medical imagery, as mentioned above) to gender issues (women's emancipation des femmes).

To return to the question of how Japanese hospitals are opening up to their surroundings and integrating public policies, it is worth mentioning that since 2009, the question of "medical tourism" is being taken very seriously and handled not by the Japanese Ministry of Health but by the Ministry of Economy, Trade and Industry, which published guidelines advising hospitals how to go about attracting "medical tourists". This new policy came into being because medical tourism is developing all over the world and the Japanese healthcare system, which is recognized as being one of the best, has not been taking advantage of this trend.

Visitors can now combine sightseeing with their hospital visits, staying at hot spring resorts or playing golf during their week-long stay. The Japan Tourism Agency convened a panel of experts to study medical tourism. The Agency, which aims to boost the number of overseas tourists to 20 million by 2020, interviewed hospital officials in Japan and their foreign patients. One of the Agency's officials stated: "We think of medical tourism as one of the ways to achieve our 20 million target" (Japan Times, July 2009).

At the same time, in the legislation on health insurance for dependency which was recently set up in Japan, hospitals were given a key role to play.

As all these examples show, Japanese hospitals are the focus of considerable attention these days, and are being expected to participate in meeting a wide range of social and economic challenges. Contrary to what is happening in France, where hospitals are at the peak of a pyramidal hospital system, Japanese-style hospitalocentricity has several facets.

It is worth mentioning one of the findings made at Saint Luke's Hospital in Tokyo, which participated in our surveys: there are as many voluntary workers as salaried employees at this hospital. The voluntary workers, who include many retired members of the paramedical professions, actually account for the equivalent of only 15% of the full time work at this hospital and many of them only come to work for a few hours per week. There is so much coming and going at Japanese hospitals that one can easily imagine that they are wide open to the local environment. This was confirmed by visiting some of them. At least in the large cities, hospital waiting-rooms and corridors are meeting-points for patients and those who accompany them, as well as places of transition for pedestrians who use them as a convenient short-cut to wherever they are going. They often contain all kinds of shops and sometimes even a post office. Another sign that healthcare establishments are part of Japanese people's everyday lives is the fact that *clinics* are allowed to advertise their services by extolling the qualities of the doctors who own them: their portraits are even posted up in public transport vehicles and on the walls of buildings.

Japanese hospitals are therefore not placed majestically at the summit of the healthcare system as they are in France, but they are more discreetly omnipresent (politically, socially and economically speaking) in many everyday social settings.

CONCLUSION: CONVENTIONS IN TRANSITION

In the Japanese and French contexts, where hospital regulation is both centralised and based on a compulsory comprehensive healthcare insurance system, a particularly decisive process seems to be occurring, which occasionally gives rise to tensions. It focuses on political and economic decisions about the modes of rationalisation to be adopted. In order to avoid the cost of bureaucracy while not convinced that widespread competition would be entirely beneficial, both countries have taken steps to define and set up highly original forms of regulation. In both cases, the aim is to leave the power in the hands of the central authorities, while giving hospitals the freedom of action they require to be efficient.

Contrary to what this convergence might lead one to expect, however, quite different economic, legislative and professional processes are at work in each country, which it is proposed to summarize here.

Convention theory is rather useful for this purpose. It can be used to look at various situations corresponding to different "worlds", where compromises are reached by actors who have adopted contradictory principles. Conventions are the means whereby these actors reach and legitimize their decisions, which have been described as "mutual expectations" and are either intentionally or explicitly formulated. Like institutions, conventions are involved in a process of coordination (Eymard-Duvernay *et al.*, 1989; Béjean & Peyron, 2002). According to this theory, agents are endowed with limited rational powers, and conventions enable them to make cognitive savings. In this scheme, the world of market transactions (which is regulated on the basis of prices) is one particular case of coordination. Secondly, the industrial world is governed by external bureaucratic rules and standards which their customers have no power to assess. In the third kind of world, the domestic world, the keywords are trust and proximity, which make it unnecessary to assess technical performances and efficiency. Lastly, the civic world is ruled by the idea of promoting general welfare and upholding the principles of solidarity.

If we compare the data and the material presented in this book, these four "worlds" all provide relevant means of explaining the specificities, connections and dynamics at work in the two hospital systems compared. The above analyses have yielded the following empirical conclusions: in the Japanese system, hospital stays are long, nurses are young and not very highly qualified, and there is a high rate of turnover in this profession. In the French system, hospital stays are short, nurses are specialized and experienced, and they pursue long careers. In both cases, "mutual expectations" have been involved.

The fact that French nurses pursue long careers encourages hospitals to invest in human capital. In return, nurses commit themselves to training for their profession, knowing that they will benefit from this commitment, even after their marriage. The vocational training they acquire contributes to increasing the standardization of practices in line with the industrial model. Along with patient turnover, this standardization has led to hospital stays being shortened in line with the principle of tense flows, if not of "Just in Time" *(flux tendus)*. Intense hospital care is therefore expected and implicitly demanded by all those involved (patients, doctors, families, etc.), which naturally promotes increasingly technical work. This explains why there are as many nursing assistants as nurses at French hospitals. This makes the two ends meet between the short term (length of hospital stays) and long term issues (nurses' continuing vocational training).

Japanese hospitals and their medical directors expect nurses to give up their jobs when they get married. Hospitals therefore do not invest in training their nurses. As nurses are well aware of this situation before joining the profession, they know that it will be impossible to find a balance between their work and their family lives. This attitude makes everyone accept the fact that most nurses' careers are bound to be short and they will not have many opportunities of acquiring technical skills. This whole process is also in line with the commonly held idea that nurses' qualities are essentially feminine ones (*caring* and *curing*) involving trust and attentiveness. This is why there are so few nursing assistants at Japanese hospitals, whereas there are many matrons in comparison with the number of nurses. Long hospital stays therefore meet the efficiency and quality criteria which pertain in the "domestic world". In short, it can be said that Japanese hospitals are open to their local social environment and make a compromise between the persistent domestic convention and a combination between the market and industrial models, whereas French hospitals are firmly rooted in the industrial world and do not seem to lend themselves to the market model which some reformers would like to impose on them.

The conclusions we have reached in this book suggest recommendations for future policies and reforms. In the first place, this analysis shows that it is pointless to propose universal recipes and that concepts such as competition and quality which seem *a priori* to be shared by several countries actually have very different practical applications. In Japan, for instance, shortening hospital stays will promote efficiency only if proper vocational training policies are adopted for nurses, which in turn depends on introducing full-scale social policies for emancipating Japanese women. The increasingly sophisticated medical equipment which French hospitals are currently acquiring raises the costs, which can only be contained by transferring some of the doctors' duties to nurses.

REFERENCES

• Béjean S, Peyron C. *Santé, règles et rationalités*. Paris: Economica, 2002.

• Bolton SC. A simple matter of control, NHS hospital nurses and new management. *Journal of Management Studies* 2004; 41 (2): 317-33.

• Delamothe T. The NHS at 60. A fairly happy birthday. *BMJ* 2008; 337: 25-31.

• Eymard-Duvernay F, Favereau O, Salais R, Dupuy JP, Thévenot L. Économie des conventions. *Revue Économique* 1989; 40 (2).

• Hall PA. Policy paradigms, social learning, and the state: The case of economic policymaking in Britain. *Comparative Politics* 1993; 25 (3): 275-96.

• HAS. *Certification des établissements de santé : horizon 2010*, Rencontres HAS, 2007.

• HAS. *Rapport d'activité 2007*. HAS, 2008.

• Ikegami N, Campbell J. Dealing with the medical axis of power: The case of Japan. *Health Economics, Policy and Law* 2008; 3: 107-13.

• *Japan Times*, numerous issues, 2009 and 2010.

• Japan Nursing Association. *Report on Status of Nursing 1985*. Tokyo: Japan Nursing Association Press, 1986.

• Japan Nursing Association. *Report on Status of Nursing 2001*. Tokyo: Japan Nursing Association Press, 2003.

• Jullien F. *Traité de l'efficacité*. Paris: Grasset, 1996.

• Kondo J. Evaluation of the Japanese health system. Conference at the London School of Economics, July 2008.

• Mayer G, Tanaka S. Health care reform system innovations in the Managed Care Era in the US. *Keio Business Forum* 1999; 17 (2): 19-38.

• Ministry of Health, Labour and Welfare (MHLW). *Statistical report on public health services 2004*. Tokyo: MHLW, by Statistics and Information Department, 2007.

• Ministry of Health, Labour and Welfare (MHLW). *Hospital report 1980-2005*. Tokyo: MHLW, by Statistics and Information Department, 1982-2007.

• Ministry of Health, Labour and Welfare (MHLW). *Report on survey of physician, dentists and pharmacists 2004*. Tokyo: MHLW, Statistics and Information Department, 2006.

• OECD, *Health Data*. OECD, 2005-2010.

• Primomo J. Nursing around the world: Japan - preparing for the century of the elderly. *Online J Issues Nurs* 2000; 5 (2): 2.

• Sainsaulieu I. Les appartenances collectives à l'hôpital. *Sociologie du Travail* 2006; 48 (1): 72-87.

• Savage J, Scott C. The modern matron: A hybrid role with implications for continuous quality improvement. *Journal of Nursing Management* 2004; 12: 419-26.

• Wildman S, Hewison A. Rediscovering a history of nursing management: From Nightingale to the modern matron. *Int J Nurs Stud* 2009; 46: 1650-61.

General Conclusion

To end this book, two main points seem to be worth mentioning in particular. The first point focuses on how the modes whereby the paramedical professions were set up in the past have determined the present-day approach to hospital organization. The second point focuses on how individual nursing careers have been collectively shaped by combating gender inequalities. In both cases, real "societal conventions" have been identified (Verdier, 2002). These conventions have been developed and inscribed in each country's national heritage along with their institutional substrates (customs, routines, rules and regulations).

As we have seen in the previous chapters, these conventions have evolved during the last few decades as the result of both sectoral-specific and more general processes. In France, the changes which occurred were due to the emergence of an industrial approach where market logics had to be taken into account at all costs. In Japan, the traditional domestic convention still predominates, although market logics are gaining an increasingly strong hold.

In the light of these international comparisons, the crisis or malaise from which the nursing profession is suffering in both countries can therefore be seen to have a highly specific content in each case.

PROFESSIONS AND INSTITUTIONS

In the long history of the nursing profession, macro-social changes have played a decisive role. In France, for example, the struggle between clericals and Republicans, which was particularly fierce in the fields of education and health, contributed directly to the emancipation of the members of professions which were previously associated with religious spheres. In addition, the victory of the lay contenders was partly attributable to the technical and scientific revolution, which in turn was closely linked to the changes resulting from Pasteur's discoveries. The French nursing profession was born of the doctors' need for assistance. Since doctors were in charge of nurses' training, they could easily keep nurses under their thumb. Doctors acquired their dominance over nurses before they even took the hospital power into their own hands. This was clearly the starting-point on which the evolution of the French nursing profession was based.

During this period, Japan was undergoing a process of modernization, which subtended the development of the nursing profession. Since the Meiji period was characterized by efforts to multiply exchanges with the Western world, foreign influences were beginning to make themselves felt at that time. In the field of healthcare, the influences which had the most long-lasting effects were those which could be combined with pre-existing ways of life, especially those involving clearly defined female roles. Along with the opening effects of the Meiji period, Japanese doctors became the main actors at hospitals, which have always had strong local roots. It is symbolic of the doctors' supremacy that Japanese hospitals have always been directed by people who are doctors themselves, and the existence of a few very recent exceptions to this rule are regarded as a sign of great modernization. The fact that senior hospital doctors can create their own clinics also favours these rather individualistic practices.

Since doctors have been the main actors at Japanese hospitals until very recently, it is difficult for nurses to find a professional space in which to work and fulfil themselves both individually and collectively. They are therefore reduced to performing operative tasks leaving them little scope for initiative, and even less for teamwork. French nurses, who are accustomed to clearly defined frontiers and occupational roles, would no doubt be puzzled by the lack of clear-cut statutory distinctions between Japanese nurses and nursing assistants, which gives these hospital workers an extremely fuzzy status.

In France, on the contrary, the concept of teamwork was further promoted by the 1958 hospital reforms initiated by Professor Robert Debré. By reinforcing the role of hospital doctors, especially at University teaching hospitals, this reform created what amounted to real "hospital organizations" over the whole country; whereas there exist only a few organizations of this kind in Japan, in the large cities.

Giving nurses greater power is still being presented in France as a clever organizational solution to the endless sterile conflict between doctors and managers. It therefore seems quite logical that the newly allocated power should be strongly based on the team approach, which in exchange is gaining increasing recognition.

Nurses' occupational identity owes a great deal to the identity of the hospital institutions at which it was forged. However, the "new governance" system, especially the gradual replacement of wards by *pôles*, is shaking the hospitals where nurses' identity was acquired down to their very foundations. One should not be tempted to jump to the conclusion that previous relationships between hospitals and nurses were perfectly smooth and idyllic: the tensions which occurred simply led to compromises which were quite in line with what was going on at the time in society as a whole.

Vocational training was another central issue. At a fairly early stage, vocational training for French nurses became the means whereby they managed to acquire a strong identity, based on the concept of nurses' own specific role and the primary nursing approach, although the latter approach was hard to apply and may seem in a way to be incompatible with nurses' aspirations. Nurses' voluntaristic, rather militant attitude ended up by yielding concrete results, although they were obtained via somewhat unexpected means: by joining the overall move towards specialization, French nurses mainly achieved emancipation thanks to the advent of medical technology.

The interviews conducted for the purpose of this study with various professionals in both countries were most informative in this respect. They showed that in France, the standards have always been based on specialization and actual nursing practices, as well as being strongly rooted in collective modes of learning. The status of the nursing profession has been further consolidated in France by recent improvements in their working conditions, especially in their wages. It is worth noting that this consolidation has further strengthened the commitment of all nurses to pursuing occupational paths, and possibly a real career.

Nevertheless, although the scope for qualifications and occupational mobility has undeniably been increased, French nurses are experiencing even greater feelings of frustration than in 1987-1988, since their hopes and expectations have also increased since that time.

A completely different process of change has occurred in Japan. Because of the deeply entrenched domestic traditions, patients and even the nurses themselves regard hospital nurses as the heirs of the devoted family attendants who used to cater for patients' every whim.

The question of the time spent with patients is of great importance in this context. All the protagonists in both countries attribute strong symbolic connotations to this aspect of nurses' role and feel that nurses should be able to spend more time than they do by their patients' bedside, in addition to the time spent dispensing the care prescribed by doctors. This lack of time is due to the fact that the physicians have disposed of nurses' time, creating a gap between their picture of their vocational calling and the hard facts of their everyday work. This discrepancy is partly to blame for nurses' claims for more time. The feeling that they are unable to tend to their patients properly is giving rise to considerable discontent among all nurses.

However, this overall picture can be mitigated in the light of the findings made in the present study. Many of the nurses interviewed admitted having time to spare when they really made an effort (as the British say, "where there is a will there is a way"). This does not mean that they did not feel overworked: at some times, they certainly had a very heavy workload. The fact that they referred so frequently to time may also have been due to their being influenced by the rhetoric used by militant union members, who often complain about the problem of mastering time.

Judging from the respondents' statements, however, nurses do not make the same use of time in both of the countries of interest. As one of them put it very prettily, Japanese nurses tend to spend any time gained "listening to the birdsong" with their patients in a garden, wishing it was larger; whereas French nurses would like to spend more time listening to their patients' complaints and assessing the evolution of their disease more closely in order to adapt the treatment more suitably. In other words, Japanese nurses would like to have extra time to enable them and their patients to forget their respective social roles; whereas their French counterparts would use any extra time they were given to perform their own occupational role more efficiently.

THE COLLECTIVE CREATION OF INDIVIDUAL TRAJECTORIES

As we have seen from the above comparisons, most Japanese nurses, contrary to their French counterparts, give up their jobs when they get married. This is in line with what can be observed on the Japanese female labour market as a whole, but in the case of nurses, the trend is particularly marked because of the strong historical links existing between Japanese nurses' occupational characteristics and the domestic world.

Most French nurses manage to juggle between their work and their personal lives, and for this purpose they often resort to part-time work. Paradoxically, this has consolidated their occupational identity, and hence their autonomy. It enables them to envisage embarking on long-term career projects (by specializing, training to become matrons, etc.). French nurses have therefore obtained recognition of a kind that Japanese nurses have little hope of acquiring either individually or collectively.

Matrons play an essential role at French hospitals, partly because they have been there for so long. To be promoted to the status of matron in France, nurses have to obtain special continuing vocational training qualifications.

In Japan, acquiring the status of matron involves a whole change of lifestyle: it requires deep commitment to nursing and often life-long commitment to the institution. Not many young Japanese nurses are prepared to commit themselves to this extent. It means making a frequent change of timetable (rotating between day/night/afternoon shifts) instead of having regular working hours. Various shifts also mean various working practices (the intensity of the work will differ and the technical skills required, etc. are liable to vary from one shift to another). Being obliged to constantly change their working patterns in this way is synonymous with poor conditions of work and a low level of autonomy.

In France, on the contrary, most nurses are free to choose their working hours or to make arrangements with their superiors, and they usually manage to keep the same schedule for several years – by switching to other units if need be. Their choice usually depends on the circumstances of their jobs and their family lives. The dilemma with which French nurses are faced these days shows how closely imbricated nurses' working hours and their personal lives are: being fairly free to choose between day shift and night shift work contributes importantly to the success of most French nurses' efforts to reach a compromise between their work and their family lives.

Japanese nurses do not have to cope with dilemmas of this kind, since neither the system of hospital organization nor the possibility of pursuing a nursing career leave any room whatsoever for choices of this kind. Taking this analysis a step further, one might argue that since the patient turnover is much lower in Japan, the content of the nurses' work is bound to be different. In addition, the diversity of their work is typical of the whole Japanese healthcare system, which is characterized by much less specialization than in France. To solve the issues relating to nurses' autonomy, it would in fact be necessary to revisit all the links between hospitals' modes of internal and external organization.

The identity of Japanese hospitals has always played an important role. Contrary to the highly technological French hospitals, where there is a particularly high rate of patient turnover, Japanese hospitals tend to keep their patients for long stays; not to mention the clinics run by doctor-proprietors, at which the nurses are required to perform many different tasks.

One of reasons for the lack of differentiation between Japanese nurses and nursing assistants is that there exists a ruling which stipulates that there must be one member of staff for every four patients. But as this ruling makes no distinctions in terms of qualifications and functions, employers tend to recruit staff with low qualifications, who do not demand high wages. Although separate training courses were initiated for nurses and nursing assistants in 1951, the official systems of classification do not take this distinction into account. Since this situation differs completely from what occurs in France and other European countries, direct statistical comparisons are simply not valid. The lack of differentiation between nurses and nursing assistants, which parallels the relative lack of differentiation made in Japan between medical specialities, is nevertheless a highly relevant fact which helps to explain the situation of all Japanese medical and paramedical staff.

In France, the distinction between nurses and nursing assistants is part of the strong process of specialization which has occurred in this country. It has helped to reduce gender disparities by giving nursing assistants an opportunity of moving up the hierarchical ladder. However, the above comparisons with the situation in Japan also suggest that by calling nursing assistants' advancement "promotion" because it enables them to abandon the domestic sphere, we are tending to denigrate female qualities. The gender relations which are central to the Japanese mindset have therefore not been entirely evinced from the field of action in France.

The maternal image is not entirely absent from popular representations about French nurses, but these representations include other more professional and technical components. This combination is all the more valid as it was set up collectively and individually over a fairly long period of time. However, despite the strong formal distinctions made in terms of hospital employees' status, the picture at the workplace is much more complex, and the actual tasks performed may not always be so unambiguously defined. Arborio has described (Arborio, 2004) how nursing assistants can adopt individual career strategies which meet the hospital institutions' needs in order to benefit from "horizontal" mobility in a normally rather unrewarding profession. Since administrations and physicians are demanding greater flexibility and willingness to perform multiple tasks and nursing assistants are aspiring to improve their lot, diversity has become the rule of the day. The same label can therefore often cover very different occupational identities, in the case of both nursing assistants and nurses themselves.

As we have seen, less attention is paid in Japan to occupational distinctions of this kind, for historical reasons. The absence of tensions has led to the degradation of the nursing profession, and thus to the persistence of the gender differentials from which French nurses have freed themselves, mainly by acquiring specialized skills. It is true to say that French nurses' fight for equality and emancipation has served as a driving force towards greater professionalization.

Gender relations in Japan have always been strongly marked by the traditional picture of women's social role. However, Japanese women often run their households, where they have acquired greater power than most Frenchwomen are able to enjoy.

Although the nursing profession and nurses' social status have always depended in Japan on the extent to which gender relations and the family institution have evolved, they are changing slowly but surely at their own speed without being propelled by the faster and more spectacular ongoing technical and organizational developments.

This is the fundamental characteristic which has always transformed Japanese hospitals into communities: they are perceived as such by all the protagonists, including the patients, whereas French hospitals are first and foremost productive organizations.

Although we must take care to avoid over-simplification, the various stages on the road to the modernization of Japan, as defined by several authors, started in economic circles, continued via political circles, and gradually reached domestic circles. This pattern of development provides a very rough but nevertheless relevant framework, as some of the actors involved have agreed. The interplay between caricatures and clichés, which is one of the ingredients of most social representations, is having real behavioural effects. Here again, it would be worth looking more closely at the links between private/domestic spheres and public/occupational spheres in order to avoid making hasty judgements about the slow development of some countries and the advanced post-modernism of others.

The description given in 1970 by E. Freidson of the situation of American nurses fits that of present-day Japanese nurses rather well:

> "[...] in spite of Nightingale's efforts in the nineteenth century, the nurse, because she is a female, has not been able to shake off the sexually rather than professional determined mothering role. And the nurse's commitment to her occupation is not consistently and uniformly profound, for marriage is the aspiration of many and turn over is high." (Freidson, 1970, p. 21)

E. Freidson's description of possible American future developments in view of the way hospitals were organized applies very well to what is emerging today in Japan:

> "Identification with a job seems particularly important for those who [...] work isolated from colleague observation and supervision, but is equally important as a device for motivating and controlling work in complex organizations, the most prominent of which is the hospital." (*ibid.*, p. 22)

The comparisons between Japanese and French nurses suggest that the 21st century will herald a new era for Japanese nurses. Emancipation will no doubt ensue from better working conditions (which will make it easier for all Japanese women to reconcile their careers with their family lives), along with the fast process of specialization of medical and paramedical practices and the rationalization of work.

As we have seen throughout this book, the variables at work (gender relations, nurses' professional identity and the scope for career building) are not linked by causal relations. It has emerged on the contrary that the links between these variables and the way they have reinforced each other have resulted in different configurations in each of the two countries in question. In terms of hospital organization, each of the two configurations has created its own pattern of incentives: a centrifugal pattern in Japan and a centripetal pattern in France. Therefore three main actors are present on the stage: the physicians, the nurses and the hospital institutions. These actors cooperate and compete with each other in an alternating series of alliances and conflicts; their diversity often gives rise to tensions which are resolved by other protagonists. But at every turn in history, their relationships have been redefined by the authorities as well as by individuals (militants) acting as spokesmen for the three spheres involved.

The above comparisons have shown how importantly uncertainty, ambiguity, and even irrationality have weighed on the decisions and attitudes of the protagonists. Successive measures have sometimes been adopted for no other apparent reason than the urge to make changes. The same can be said of many unexpected series of collective strategies.

Room for manœuvre has been opened or conquered by individual defenders of a cause, whose efforts coincided providentially with the macro-economic and macro-social events of the day (such as scientific breakthroughs, Keynesian economic crises, the Meiji period, etc.).

The impact made by these individuals has sometimes resulted in creating a bridge from one world to another.

REFERENCES

• Arborio AM. Climbing invisible ladders. *Ethnography* 2004; n° 5, 1: 76-105.

• Freidson E. *Professional dominance*. New York: Atherton Press, 1970.

• Verdier E. Institutions et régulations: pour une analyse en termes de conventions sociétales. Symposium on "Institutionalismes et évolutionnismes", Lyon, 2002.

IMPRIM'VERT®

Achevé d'imprimer par Corlet, Imprimeur, S.A.
14110 Condé-sur-Noireau
N° d'Imprimeur : 133788 - Dépôt légal : décembre 2010
Imprimé en France